MEXICO
LIVING AND TRAVEL

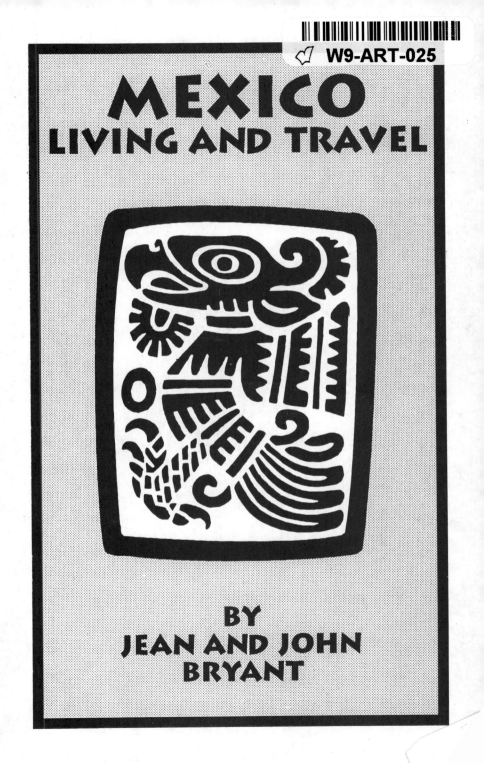

BY
JEAN AND JOHN
BRYANT

MEXICO LIVING AND TRAVEL

by Jean and John Bryant

Published by
Mexico Retirement and Travel Assistance
6301 S. Squaw Valley Road, Suite #23
Pahrump, NV 89048-7949

MEXICO LIVING AND TRAVEL, copyright 2000© John D. Bryant.

Revised Fourth Edition
ISBN 1-878061-01-1

Mexico Retirement and Travel Assistance also publishes a quarterly magazine entitled "M.R.T.A. Mexico Living and Travel Newsletter" and markets a video cassette tape, a package of maps of Mexico and a Spanish Language Guide. For more information see end of book.

"M.R.T.A. has the Lion's Share of Information about Mexico."

*M.R.T.A. Has the Lion's Share
of Information about Mexico*

Mexico -
A Kaleidoscope of Color

The mere word "Mexico" conjures an image of exotic flowers, food, sunsets, beaches, music and yes, the beautiful women and handsome men!

These images reflect our often second-hand knowledge of an exciting country full of history and tradition, however, Mexico is much more than just a kaleidoscope of beauty.

Those of us who have come to Mexico to live or others who are attracted by the wonderful climate for vacationing and travel will find a treasure chest of fascinating 16th and 17th century architecture in the old buildings which are part of every Mexican city, along with the stories behind them.

Mexico has always been thought of as an exciting place to go for vacations. You will never tire of its beauty, fabulous beaches, breathtaking views of the snowcapped mountains, and tropical jungles blazing with colorful plants , not to mention the charming people proud of their country and heritage, who welcome visitors whether they come for a week, month or for years. More and more retirees, young and old, who want an alternative to the usual retirement choices of Florida, Arizona, California or Texas in the United States, are choosing to travel "south of the border," satisfying a need for travel and adventure in a foreign country. Mexico, with its close proximity to the U.S. border, answers that need.

As you read this book, you will learn much about Mexico, where to go, what to see, and also learn of the changes that are rapidly taking place in a country where any change at all has taken centuries to occur.

Mexico Living and Travel offers helpful tips to assist you in your travels as well as many outstanding color photographs showing places of interest in various parts of Mexico.

Read and learn more about a different country, its culture and traditions. It will whet your appetite to see first hand what Mexico has to offer.

Acknowledgments

This book would not be possible without the skilled team of writers, word processors, artists, photographers and printers who assisted us.

Among the writers are E. Wright Sargent, Julie Vargas Muñoz, Ilse Hoffman, Jane Davis, Bruce Allen, June Summers, Melba Bourdeau Wasey, Professor Enrique Moreno, Adele Woodward, Liz Monty, Jack Cathell, Judy Crawford, Florence Gilbert, Jane Brown, Paul Katz, Barbara Thompson, Wendy A. Luft, Susan Kaye, Tony Burton, Mary Fuller, Nancy and Ray Christian and James Bowers.

Many color photographs were furnished by José Hernández Claire, prominent Guadalajara photographer, Susan Kaye, professional photographer and travel writer. Illustrations and sketches are by Gabriela Tello, professional artist in Guadalajara, Grace Godino, noted artist from Santa Monica, California, and Enrique Velazquez, whose studio is in Ajijic, Jalisco.

Special recognition is given to Avril Forsythe for her patience, guidance and skilled word processing and type setting.

Also to Sr. Pedro Barajas for his technical advice and printing.

Thank you, each and everyone

Sincerely

Jean and John Bryant

Foreword

Mexico Living and Travel, published by Mexico Retirement and Travel Assistance, gives practical and basic information which will be useful to those planning a trip to Mexico for vacation or retirement.

Mexico Living and Travel specifically covers Guadalajara and the Lake Chapala area, but also has chapters on many cities and coastal areas where North Americans and Canadians have found excellent retirement locations. The chapters point out historical places of interest about each city and have information on where to look for recreation and entertainment. This book contains suggestions to help in adjusting to a new and different country where customs may seem strange. There are articles on fun and relaxing day trips to take, dates of Mexican holidays and how they are celebrated, visa laws, property ownership laws and rights, how to go about finding housing plus many survival health tips, some learned the hard way!

Mexico Living and Travel has been prepared with the collaboration of many north of the border residents of Mexico, who represent a broad selection of people from the United States and Canada. You will enjoy the variety of observations, thoughts, and attitudes expressed in various chapters, which are the consensus of those persons.

The purpose of this book is to help make your adventure to Mexico as worry free and pleasant as possible.

General Index of Chapters

Editors Note: The above General Index of Chapters lists the general topics covered. Please turn to the designated page for a more detailed index of information covered in the individual chapters.

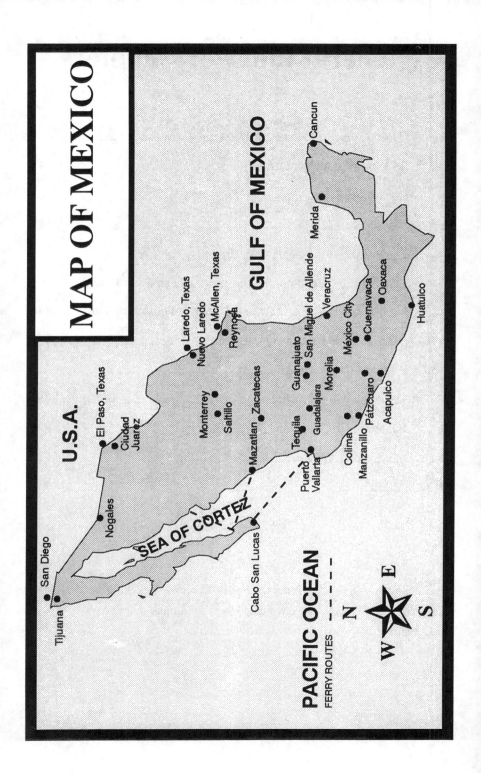

I

General Information about Mexico

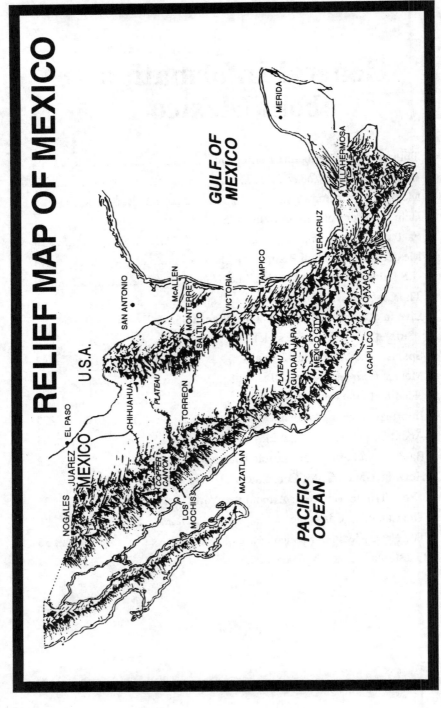

RELIEF MAP OF MEXICO

Things to Consider
Before Retirement

Couples considering retirement should share in the responsibility of any and all decisions in taking such a big step. Priorities of both partners as to what they are looking for in retirement should be discussed and given much consideration.

We have seen many divorces and separations occur simply because the plans were not decided by both partners in a mutual agreement.

Persons considering a retirement in Mexico or in any foreign country especially must ask themselves many questions pertaining to their health, their financial situation and their ability to adjust to a new and different culture as well as coping with a new language.

Any move can be stressful and especially so to those who are in a fragile state of physical or mental health. People who have psychological and emotional hang-ups to begin with will not find that the problem disappears simply because they are in a new environment, just as those with drinking problems or any other weaknesses will still have the problem in Mexico unless they seek available aid and support of a group such as the English speaking A.A. chapters in Guadalajara and Chapala.

Retirement may be just as much a disappointment in Mexico as in the United States for couples who cannot tolerate the constant daily togetherness that retirement brings. In Guadalajara and Chapala many groups of various interests welcome all new members and this is helpful to couples who share different ideas of what they want to do to fill their days, while also offering many activities for couples to enjoy together.

One's financial situation is another concern. Do not come to Mexico expecting to find employment or to start a business in order to supplement your income; it is illegal. Therefore, if your monthly fixed income is not as great as you would like, be prepared to learn ways, and there are many, to stretch your budget. For instance, by sticking to available fresh fruits and vegetables and less expensive cuts of meat, instead of the frozen or pre-prepared imported foods that are on the market, seeking out the many free events that are available for entertainment, looking around and asking advice on reasonable living quarters, and above all, not worrying about keeping up with the Joneses, you will find that there are many others in your same financial situation whatever it is, and you will learn from their experiences different ways to make the most of what you have.

Some retirees enjoy the best of two worlds by taking advantage of Mexico's Central Plateau region where it is cooler, than remaining in the hot, humid climate of states such as Arizona, Texas and Florida during the summer months, while others flee to Mexico to escape the snow, ice and freezing temperatures of northern states in the winter. This is a happy solution for many, especially those who are hesitant to leave their family and the accumulation of personal "things" for a more permanent time, or, who are worried about the possibility of not adjusting to such a change.

We and thousands of other couples found that retirement in Mexico has offered a wonderful opportunity to learn and experience new areas that we might not otherwise have had and that add to a happy and fulfilling retirement.

Living in Mexico Today!

People who are looking for comfort, security and friends to share common interests find Mexico to be their retirement choice, particularly Guadalajara and Lake Chapala. We know of no place where the climate is as good as here, perfect almost year around for any out-of-door activity, whether simply strolling through the interesting colonial streets to see and learn about the beautiful historical buildings, or to browse in quaint shops, stopping to relax at outside cafes where mariachi musicians provide music typical of Mexico.

For the sport enthusiast almost every day is perfect for golf and tennis, a definite plus.

Temperatures in Guadalajara and Lake Chapala range midday no higher than the low 90s in May and June, the hottest months, with nighttime temperatures in the 60s. During December and January, the two cold months, the midday temperatures are in the 70s, with nighttime lows in the 50s. This makes air conditioning or indoor heating unnecessary. The days are always warm and the nights are cool with low humidity, making it agreeable to anyone's comfort zone.

Visitors and retirees in Guadalajara and Chapala will find many excellent restaurants as well as recognize old familiar fast food chains. When shopping one will find favorite brand names of food items, clothing and household articles that, when added to Mexico's own excellent variety of fresh fruit and vegetables, delicious pork, chicken, beef and fish, will contribute to a sense of well-being.

Another plus for retirees in Mexico and also a top concern with all of us, is the fine medical care available at reasonable cost. There are modern hospitals, excellent English speaking doctors, low pharmacy prices and the knowledge that many United States insurance companies, along with Blue Cross and Blue Shield insurance, are honored here for reimbursement. Many North Americans take advantage of the Mexican Social Security Insurance which is available to them for a very low yearly fee. After passing the medical review and a waiting

4

period of six months you are eligible to receive full medical coverage. All medical bills including doctor, dentist, hospital and drugs are paid. This is a real safety cushion for those who fear a long term illness which could be very costly. Health care such as nursing homes and private home care is much more reasonable here than in the United States. This knowledge makes a great difference in one's feeling of security while in a foreign country.

Many North Americans have commented that they feel safer in Mexico than in their home state, and we feel that this is generally true. While there are petty crimes committed, the terrible violent crimes that we see so often in the United States are rare here. North Americans are safe while traveling in Mexico, and find it pleasant and inexpensive to do so both by train and bus. Flights to and from Mexico are made daily with Continental, Delta and American Airlines, with AeroMexico, AeroCalifornia and Mexicana routes adding to one's convenience.

Comfort, security and good friends are of great importance and are excellent reasons for a Mexican retirement, however, in many instances the overall cost of housing, hotels, restaurants, gasoline, mail and calls to the United States have reached north-of-the-border prices. This has discouraged some people although we feel that the primary attractions of Mexico, including climate, combined with new and exciting interests to explore, which are priorities for most retirees, still exist, making it a sound choice for retirement.

Mexico in Transition

When we arrived in Guadalajara in 1985 to begin our new life as retirees in this new and different country, we probably saw our last glimpse of a city caught yet in old traditions, customs and ways of living handed down by generations. However, even then there were stirrings indicating the early stages of modernization and a new way of life.

Guadalajara was and remains a beautiful city full of fascinating historical buildings, picturesque parks with statues and fountains and, of course, friendly people.

There are still street markets or tianguis, street vendors selling simply everything, occasional mariachi music from a nearby restaurant and also the clip-clop of horse-drawn carriages or calandrias, filled with tourists who want a leisurely ride through the city streets.

These things charmed us when we arrived and are a part of Mexico we hope will never change. But change is here in a big way, bringing with it more and more of the familiar things we left in the United States, both good and bad!

During our years here we have seen tremendous growth in every direction: super-highways are replacing the old winding pot-holed roads; malls and plazas are going up everywhere and are comparable and in many cases superior to those in the States. A walk through the malls or along the streets will show many familiar store names, although highly geared to the younger crowd (please remember that 50% of Mexico's population is under 19 years of age!) Fast food chains are well entrenched, and are very popular with Mexicans, although prices are somewhat higher than those in the United States, but with the same taste and excellent service (the similar cholesterol content is free!).

Department stores boast brands familiar to us all in cosmetics, clothing, appliances and other household items, large and small.

The latest big attraction to come to Mexico are the self-service stores such as Walmart, Sam's Club and Price Club, where you will find that about 40% of products sold are from the United States. These huge stores offer similar low prices and are popular with Mexicans as well as North Americans who flock to them for shopping. Mexicans like to buy in large quantities (big families!) and do not shy away from luxury items.

There are many other changes since our arrival, and many are good since they offer familiar things that we perhaps had missed, but also along with these changes have come a few less desirable ones.

With the tremendous growth of Guadalajara has come an increase in population. Streets can no longer handle the tremendous amount of motor vehicles as efficiently, and pollution has become quite serious, especially during the thermal inversions that make their appearance during winter mornings. Cellular phones are very popular, and can be a nuisance when someone at the next table in a restaurant is thoroughly enjoying a long, loud conversation! So far we haven't mentioned the cost of living increase, but that too is part of a changing Mexico, although costs are still very reasonable compared to the United States.

Fortunately the violent crime rate is still low compared to its U.S. counterpart. That's one "import" we can do without.

If one is looking for the truly "Old Mexico" it is still easy to find and a delight to enjoy. By driving only an hour or so you will find small villages whose people reflect their serene way of life. You can relax in the town's square (every village has one) and watch as the women and girls walk quietly by carrying huge filled baskets on their heads - the older women invariably draped with a black shawl, and usually wearing an apron. Children play together doing simple things as children did before all the sophisticated games and toys appeared, the men ride by on horses or mules carrying supplies needed for their day's work, and then the church bells ring signaling that all is well. Modernization hasn't come to these small villages yet and perhaps for most it is better that way.

The highway system has improved tremendously. During the last couple of years, the Mexican government allowed private contractors to built and operate (for 20 years) toll roads. These roads have greatly reduced travelling times between major cities, but are quite expensive. They are usually four-lane, with some two-lane sections through areas where a four-lane highway was not economically feasible. The Guadalajara-Manzanillo ($20 U.S. toll), Guadalajara-Lagos de Moreno ($12 U.S. toll) and Guadalajara-Mexico City ($60 U.S. toll) are a few examples of these highways. To get to Puerto Vallarta, you can now use a stretch of the Guadalajara-Tepic highway for about $25 U.S. This road has cut travelling time between these two major cities from six-seven (if you're lucky!) to a little under four hours. Mexicans balked at first over the price of these toll roads, but today anybody who can afford them uses them, most of all for personal safety. We highly recommend them! Seldom do we see livestock and other dangers along these major highways, a big problem when travelling secondary roads.

Major streets in Guadalajara have been widened, and computer-controlled traffic light systems have been installed, greatly improving the traffic flow.

Finding unleaded gasoline is no longer a problem when traveling throughout Mexico, except in the smallest of villages. *Magna Sin* and *Premium*, the unleaded regular and high-octane gasolines, are available at all major filling stations. Gasoline prices are now higher in Mexico than in the U.S.

Guadalajara has grown tremendously: the city has extended in all directions, except northward, where there is a 2000-foot canyon. Areas that were open fields are now filled with houses and apartment buildings. Cows no longer graze within eight blocks of the Plaza del Sol shopping center, the largest in Latin America when it was built, on the southwest side of the city.

When one crosses the border into Mexico, the immigration and customs people make you feel welcome. Government employees have undergone intensive training programs, and have come to terms with the fact that courtesy goes a long way in any situation: please treat them with similar courtesy and things go much smoother. We no longer witness the hassles that used to exist, and tourists easily obtain an FM-T visa when requested.

Cable TV. in English is available in most residential areas of Guadalajara. VCR tapes may be rented at stores throughout the area. A prohibitive tax on satellite dishes has been removed, making these more affordable.

Prices and the over-all cost of living are no longer the tremendous bargains that they were in 1985, but they are still more economical than in the United States, particularly for personal services, medical and dental services, prescription drugs, utilities, auto repairs, etc. Rents and real estate prices have escalated, just as have those in most major cities in the United States.

There have also been many changes from a homemaker's point of view. For instance, certain items which were (in 1985) impossible to find in Guadalajara are on the shelves of the stores everywhere, although at slightly higher prices than north of the border. The on-going food lists that we all keep to take on our next trip to the United States have become much shorter, and in some cases have been eliminated. Even frozen foods, from waffles, sweet rolls, vegetables and fruits, pizzas and various desserts (yes, even Sara Lee!) are quite easy to find. Most supermarkets have a complete section of imported canned and frozen goods, cake mixes, etc., that were unheard of when we first came!

Women will be happy to see some familiar labels on clothing in larger department stores, such as Leslie Fay, Calvin Klein and Liz Claiborne, as well as name-brand cosmetics, such as Max Factor, Helene Rubenstein, Clinique and Lancôme. It is also easy to find old stand-by brands in appliances, like Maytag, Amana, Whirlpool and Sunbeam, with their factory guarantees and service included. All of these "little" things add a feeling of "sameness", which is important when adjusting to a foreign country.

Prices certainly have climbed since our arrival, especially on some things that a woman would definitely notice, such as the cost of hair care, clothing, shoes, anything leather, and silver or gold jewelry. At the same time the quality of life has improved, if you compare it to U.S. standards. Inflation has been a terrible problem for a number of years, but the situation seems to be slowly stabilizing.

Other changes we have noticed with pleasure, since our Spanish leaves a lot to be desired, is that more English is spoken by waiters, clerks and office personnel, especially among the younger people who are learning English as a second language. This also helps in adjusting to life in a foreign country, although an effort should be made to learn at least basic Spanish for your own benefit and pleasure as well as a courtesy to your Mexican hosts.

Mexico is full of tradition; of old customs and life style, but many things are changing, giving way to the modern way of living. This contrast is evident when one observes the beautiful, modern shopping malls or plazas (equal to those in the United States), located just a few blocks from a *tiangus* (open market), where everything from food, clothes, shoes, house wares and plants are sold. One will see change in mode of dress reflected by beautiful young women dressed in the latest high fashion, complete with modern hair style, make-up and accessories, as they walk beside an elderly lady wearing the traditional dark dress with a black shawl draped over her head and shoulders.

Driving along the road one can't help but notice the jumble of electrical wires strung in every direction with no apparent thought to possible danger. Yet, modern microwave receivers, cable television, cellular telephones and modern computer equipment are very much in evidence.

We have been amused to see the little donkeys, sometimes hitched to a wagon pulling another loaded cart or old vehicle; these we call "tractor trailers"! Often also, we will see a person riding a horse leading two donkeys loaded with wood or agricultural products; these we call "double trailers"! Horses, donkeys and mules are still a very common means of getting around, as well as for transporting goods. It is amazing just how much can be piled on top of the poor creatures! Meanwhile the very latest cars, sports utility vehicles, motorbikes, trucks and deluxe buses are here to stay and are very much a part of the new Mexico.

Restaurants of every type are in abundance, from the old traditional roadside taco or pollo (chicken) stand, some on wheels, other more permanent with thatched roofs and tables, to the superbly beautiful restaurants that offer the favorite dinner choices found in the United States. Entertainment can be anything from Mariachi music, sometimes interchanged with current U.S. favorites, native dancers or classical musical performances. All delightful!

Some pertinent facts of interest to persons who are considering Mexico as a place to visit or retire are as follows:

Mexico is the third largest county in Latin America with thirty-one states, along with the Federal District in Mexico City (comparable to Washington, D.C.). The country elects a president to serve six years. There are three branches of government: the Executive, Judicial and Legislative.

Both the United States and Canada have embassies in Mexico City. The Guadalajara U.S. Consulate offices are fully staffed and offer many types of assistance.

Throughout Mexico, the Roman Catholic Church is predominant, however, in Guadalajara and the Chapala area, there are also Protestant Churches where English is spoken, as well as Catholic services in English.

Familiar companies such as AT&T and MCI now offer long distance telephone service. You choose your long distance carrier. Local telephone service is still controlled by the *Teléfonos de México* monopoly, which, despite repeated campaigns to improve service, don't seem to be getting anywhere. For calling the United States or Canada, simply dial 001, then the area code and desired number. If you wish to place an international, operator assisted long distance call, dial 090. For long distance calls within Mexico, dial 01, the area code plus the number. Dial 020 for operator assisted calls within Mexico.

We are pleased with many of the changes which have taken place during our years here, the things which add to our comfort and well-being, but we hope that Mexico can manage to retain at least the best part of the tradition of the old Mexican Culture.

Help For Your Foreign Retirement

With retirement comes many possibilities and options to consider. For a large number of people, the idea of retiring to a foreign country, in this case Mexico, is an excellent choice and they are happy with that decision. For others it may not be a viable choice at all. Many factors are involved, and they should be fully considered.

Since moving to Mexico we have discovered that some people adapt more easily to living in a foreign country than others. Some love living in Mexico but others stay only for a few months or years and return to their homeland. We know of no scientific personality studies that predict the success for living in a foreign country. This would be an excellent doctorate study for an aspiring sociologist or psychologist. We have, however, observed certain common characteristics that seem basic to successful living in a foreign country.

In order to help you decide whether you are a good candidate for retirement in Mexico we have compiled a test that might be helpful in determining your degree of adaptability to a new life in a new and different country. Read it, grade yourself and decide. Good luck!

M.R.T.A. Mexico
Retirement Adaptability Test

Using the figures 1 to 3 or **Below Average**, **Average** or **Above Average**, ask yourself the following questions and rate your answers accordingly: Couples should take the test separately.

ARE YOU?	Below Average	Average	Above Average
1. Open to new adventures	1	2	3
2. Flexible in your life style	1	2	3
3. Enthusiastic to trying new things in a new and different culture	1	2	3
4. Able to make and enjoy new friends	1	2	3
5. Willing to learn at least basic phrases in a new language	1	2	3
6. Healthy enough mentally and physically to leave family, friends and favorite doctor except for occasional visits	1	2	3

7.	Confident enough to be in a "minority" position or a foreigner in a different country	1	2	3
8.	Independent and self confident enough not to be influenced by negative and often ignorant comments against a possible move to a foreign country	1	2	3
9.	Patient with a slower pace	1	2	3
10.	Usually optimistic	1	2	3
11.	Eager to travel to and around in a new country	1	2	3
12.	Open minded to a different type of bureaucracy with a different language	1	2	3
13.	Understanding enough to look at things in a different light without being critical and accepting the differences	1	2	3
14.	Financially stable without needing to work (In most cases it is illegal for a foreigner to work in Mexico)	1	2	3
15.	A retired military person or a person whose work has taken them to a foreign country or several states within the United States	1	2	3

Score Comments:

37-45 Great! Come on down
30-36 Will have a few problems
22-32 Perhaps some rough spots but not impossible
Less than 22 Forget it!

In the case of couples perhaps the lowest score should be used, however, you may wish to average the scores. Most important is that both persons be in agreement with the decision they make.

It is suggested that you ask yourself why you would even think about retirement in Mexico. Is it because of a sense of adventure that you have never explored?; the chance to learn about a new and different country and culture?; to learn a new language while meeting new and interesting people from all over the world?; or is it simply that you are unhappy with the old routine and are ready for something different?

These are all good reasons for considering Mexico as a retirement choice, as well for the excellent weather you can expect to find year-round. Although the idea that you can live like a king for practically nothing is no longer the case, we find that whatever one's income is it will go further in Mexico and will provide a better quality of life for less money than elsewhere.

Once you decide to take the big step, prepare yourself for a new lifestyle in Mexico. You will find that many things are different. For instance, meals are served later and are taken more leisurely, making dining out a very social time. Driving in the city is a bit nerve racking until you get used to the noise, speed and traffic. Paying utility bills is no longer a sit down - write checks to mail affair, but sometimes a time consuming trip to different offices to pay in cash. On the other hand you need not be tied down to the usual boring house and lawn care chores since maid and gardener service is quite inexpensive, leaving you time for things you really want to do.

Social events are plentiful and you will meet others with common interests. Many types of entertainment are offered, and you probably will find more to do than back home. Check out the American Society and Am-Mex Club in Guadalajara and the Chapala Society in Ajijic at Lake Chapala, that offer a wide variety of social activities and excellent libraries.

If Mexico is a possibility then it is very important to gather as much information as you can from others who have had some experience in Mexico, as well as from any written material that is available. Word of mouth is the best source, and you will hear the negative as well as the positive side. If at all possible, a stay in Mexico for as long a time as you can manage is advisable, in order to learn first hand what you might expect as far as housing and living expenses and medical care and costs as well as other day to day expenses you would incur. After getting as much information as possible you must weigh the pros and cons carefully. The final decision is yours!

Fact and Fallacy

We are often pre-conditioned to form strong ideas about everything concerning politics, religion, people of other color or nationality, and life in other countries. Needless to say, most of these opinions are pure fallacy, based on few facts or on unfounded rumors. We've found that the "scare stories" we heard about living in Mexico were just that: "scare stories"!

For instance, before our retirement in Guadalajara friends warned us of an impending Mexican revolution, so we were psyched up to expect the worst when just after our arrival we heard and saw a truck going down our street with a loudspeaker announcing "something". Naturally, the announcement was in Spanish, which we didn't understand, but when we noticed several people leaving their houses and gathering in the street, all the dire warnings flashed back. "They were right, it's a revolution!" we thought. Thank goodness we didn't start packing right away, because after watching the activity outside for a few minutes, we realized it was just a produce truck advertising

13

fresh fruits and vegetables, and people had come outside to make their purchases. So much for the revolution!

Another "fact" which we keep hearing from our stateside friends is based on their concern for our safety. Apparently there are countless rumors about all the drugs and crime in Mexico. The fact is that in the years we have lived here we have seen less cause for concern than from what we hear on the news from the States. Women and children feel safer on the street here than we would in our former home state. There is crime in Mexico, as there is in every part of the world, but for the most part the horror stories are highly exaggerated due to excessive publicity of isolated events.

The mere word "Mexico" often brings up the topic of food and water, and whether or not it is safe for consumption. Everyone knows of an "Uncle Charley" who got sick while visiting Mexico. We can only say that from our experience it is generally not a problem, and Uncle Charley probably didn't use common sense as to where, when and how much to eat and drink, and paid the price. Naturally there are safety precautions one should take in any foreign country, such as drinking bottled water, making sure fruits and vegetables have been properly washed and, of course, one should eat only in well established restaurants, never at the sidewalk or open stands. In the time we've lived in Guadalajara there has been only one instance that we can trace a bad case of *turista* back to a certain restaurant, and it has since been closed. One might pick up a "bug" occasionally, but with proper care this is no more problem than it would be anywhere.

Another fallacy concerns driving in Mexico. The fact is that *bandidos* are not on every curve or road waiting to rob gringos but, as with driving anywhere, one should use caution about not picking up hitchhikers or stopping on isolated roads. The real danger is often due to animals (and please watch out for the small and old human variety near the villages, too!) running across the highways, an occasional unmarked hole on the road surface, or a stalled vehicle blocking the way. Mexican drivers **do** get a bit impatient with stopping for red lights or with slower drivers, but one learns to tune out the blasting and just wave them by. After all, we are here to enjoy life at our own pace. We are not in the fast lane!

Our point is simply this: don't believe everything you hear from uninformed sources. Find out the facts for yourself or from folks with experience to judge from.

Mexico's Climate and Retirement Choices

Most people from the United States who have visited Mexico have only visited the border towns of California, Arizona, New Mexico and Texas, probably when they were in the military service. Most likely they have formed the opinion that the climate of those towns is typical of the entirety of Mexico. They also judge the country by its border towns. These people fail to realize that Mexico has many climates, depending on the latitude and altitude of where one happens to be located in Mexico. It is difficult for some to visualize that about 600 miles south of the Texas border lies a mile-high plateau extending across central Mexico, where the temperature seldom rises above the low 90°s in summer, and winter temperatures are moderate, usually rising into the low to mid 70°s each day, and falling to the low 60°s at night in summer and the low 50°s in winter. Here are old colonial cites with beautiful tree lined streets, colorful shrubs, trees and other plants, many plazas and parks with benches and fountains, where one can take time to enjoy all the abundant beauty around.

It is in this central plateau that most retirees from the United States and Canada choose to locate for living year around or a part of each year, because of the near perfect climate, plus the interesting, beautiful area. The **Guadalajara/Lake Chapala area** is the most popular (with an altitude of 5,200 ft.) and has the largest group of United States citizens living outside of the United States. Also popular with retirees are **San Miguel de Allende** (6,100 ft.), **Morelia** (6,300 ft.), **Mexico City** (7,200 ft.), **Cuernavaca** (5,000 ft.), and farther to the southeast, the delightful city of **Oaxaca** (*Wa-ha-ca*)), whose altitude is 5,100 feet.

There are many other delightful cities and towns within this plateau area that have been chosen by retirees for various reasons, such as, to mention a few of them, **Zacatecas** (8,262 ft.), **Aguascalientes** (6,000 ft.), and **Guanajuato** (6,725 ft.). This section of Mexico is south of the Tropic of Cancer (the parallel of latitude that is 23.50° north of the equator, and the northern most latitude reached by the sun on June 21st of each year). These cities lie along the same general latitude as Hawaii, and one will find many of the same plants and trees, such as the hibiscus and various palm trees.

The temperature within the central plateau area varies according to the altitude; in cities with altitudes of 6,000 feet and above, one will occasionally experience temperatures below freezing at night during the winter months, therefore there may be the need for some sort of a heating system in order to be comfortable. Unless it is cloudy, daytime temperatures will generally be

15

pleasant. The amount of rainfall varies considerably within these areas, some having much green vegetation during the summer months, while others are relatively arid. At higher elevations one will find pine and oak forests. The central plateau generally is not humid during the summer, in spite of the fact that almost all of the rainfall for the year is between June and October, the greatest percentage of precipitation falling during the month of July; daily activities are not hindered by the rain because it falls during the late afternoon and night. Many retirees, from states such as Florida and the border states, enjoy the central plateau's great climate during the hot summer months in the United States.

Mexico's Pacific coast offers an excellent climate during the months from November to May, and is ideal for those persons who only want to live six months or less in Mexico each year, and who love oceanside living with beautiful beaches and a spectacular rocky coast. In June the temperature is hot, and when the rainy season begins, the humidity becomes unbearable for many, with the exception of a few hearty "gringos" who live along the Pacific coast year around. Most "gringos" in those areas either return to the North, or head for the central plateau region. The oceanside fringe along the Pacific coast that has the nicest climate and warmest currents for the longest period of winter enjoyment starts in **Las Varas**, just 60 miles north of **Puerto Vallarta**, and ends to the south in **Manzanillo**. This strip, recently baptized *"Costa Alegre"* ("Happy Coast") by the Tourism Department, is dotted with many, although less developed, small towns and villages, such as (from north to south) La Peñita (home of one of the largest trailer parks on the Pacific Coast), Rincón de Guayabitos (a full-service subdivision), Lo de Marcos (an ecologically sound development), Sayulita, Punta Mita, Huanacaxtle, Destiladeras (the whitest sand on this stretch of coast), Bucerias (practically a suburb of Puerto Vallarta), Punta Pérula, Chamela (a federally protected ecological reserve), Careyes, Tenacatita, La Manzanilla, San Patricio Melaque, Barra de Navidad, and Santiago.

Mazatlán is also a beautiful coastal city, 6 hours north of Puerto Vallarta, but subject to cold and overcast days during the winter months. South of Manzanillo are the well known resorts of **Ixtapa, Acapulco, Puerto Escondido, Puerto Angel** and **Huatulco**. However, these are much warmer and generally not considered for retirement, but more for winter vacations.

Other beautiful resorts in Mexico are **La Paz** and **Los Cabos** (Cabo San Lucas and Cabo San José), on the south tip of the Baja California Peninsula; **Cancún** and **Cozumel** on the Yucatán Peninsula, facing the Gulf of Mexico. These are also somewhat hot and humid in the summer, but are excellent choices for a winter getaway. **Mérida** is another interesting Yucatán peninsula city, located a few miles inland from the Gulf.

When choosing a retirement location, climate is high on the priority list of many people. It is probably the single most important reason taken into account by most people who retire in Mexico. It is a country with many climates, the majority a BIG step above what's available north of the border, and one has many options open when retiring...it depends on individual preferences as to the location one would select.

Other things that retirees consider, of course, are convenience to airports and distance to the United States; cultural, recreational, shopping and medical facilities; opportunities to socialize with persons with similar interests, cost of living and preference for living in an urban or rural envioronment. Also important is your desire to learn a new language, and the culture of a country a little different from "back home."

U.S. Sunbelt Residents Please Take Note

Guadalajara and Chapala and many other locations in the Central Plateau area of Mexico are delightful in the summer months because of the mild high altitude climate. This may be a surprise to many people and is a common misconception among people north of the border who have not traveled in Mexico. Many people will swelter in the hot humid summer months almost anywhere in the United States, particularly in the Sunbelt extending from Nevada and across Arizona, Texas, the "Deep South" and Florida when they could enjoy the wonderful mild climate in Central Mexico. It is only 600 miles south of Texas.

It is true that July and August are the rainy months, however, it will probably be less noticeable than "back home" since most of the rain comes in the late afternoon and at night. The summer and early fall months are a good time to move to Mexico since rentals are more readily available when the "snowbirds" are up north.

You'all come down this summer!

The Cost of Living in Mexico

It is well known that the first reason for retirement in Mexico is the wonderful climate. The second reason, cost of living, is also important. Though it's generally less than in the United States, there are a number of factors to consider.

Your basic living expenses are determined by such considerations as the amount and type of food consumed and size and quality of housing required or desired. Automobile ownership, long distance telephone calls, medical and dental services, trips north to the border and other travel, insurance, domestic and garden help, dining out, entertainment, club fees, etc. are other expenses you need to consider. Your cost of living will depend on your lifestyle, but whatever your income, it will go further in Mexico.

The principal types of expenses that are less in Mexico are public transportation, automobile and house insurance (fire risk is very low), real estate taxes, prescription drugs, medical, dental and hospital expenses, medical insurance (IMSS), domestic and garden help, household and automobile repairs, personal services, utilities such as electricity, gas and telephone, and fresh fruits and vegetables.

Comparatively, rentals may cost less than those along the West or East Coast of the United States, and more than in the Midwestern United States or in small towns. As in the United States, rentals are higher in or near large metropolitan cities than in small towns or rural areas. In the central plateau region of Mexico, heating and air conditioning are not required; therefore utility costs are very inexpensive.

Foreign retirees in Mexico are not subject to Mexican state and national income taxes. Americans are, however, subject to U.S. federal income taxes.

Many books written about Mexican retirement promote the low cost of living in Mexico, although inflation in recent years has made things less a bargain than they were when we arrived in Mexico several years ago. In reality it is basically one's personal lifestyle which dictates whether or not retirement in Mexico will be a bargain.

We have found that traveling in Mexico, eating out in better restaurants and staying in decent motels is usually more expensive than in the United States; this is probably due to the lack "middle-of-the-line" prices and quality in food and accommodations. Also gasoline for your car is more expensive than in the United States.

Although the authors live on $1000 each month (*not including rent*), many couples would not be happy with our modest lifestyle. Our three large rooms, two-bath condominium is adequate and comfortable for us but perhaps would not be satisfactory at all to many people.

One's willingness to shop at outdoor tianguis markets will reduce food costs and rent costs may be reduced considerably if you live away from the popular American retirement neighborhood areas.

You can expect the initial of cost of living to be higher than after you have lived in Mexico for a period of time and learned to use some ingenuity in your day-to-day expenses.

It is difficult for us to understand why so many people on small pensions or Social Security will struggle with miserable climates, high utility and medical bills when they could live so much better in Mexico.

Each calendar quarter "Mexico Retirement and Travel Assistance" publishes the *Newsletter*, a magazine designed to keep you informed with news about Mexico. This includes the MRTA Cost of Living Supplement that lists current prices for about fifty commonly used items. The current price for this is $10.00 U.S. for a single copy or $30.00 per year for a subscription. Send your check drawn on a United States bank or a Canadian Postal Money Order payable to M.R.T.A., 6301 S. Squaw Valley Road, Suite #23, Pahrump, NV 89048-7949. Add $3.00 U.S. for Canadian orders.

Live in Mexico on $300 to $800 Dollars a Month? Sure, If This is Your Lifestyle

"Once upon a time" a couple could live in Mexico on $300 to $800 dollars a month. Popular books are available that will tell you that you can still live on such a low budget. However, they do not tell how you will live.

To inject a little humor (and prove our point) the following sketches give suggestions on how to cut costs when living on $300 to $800 dollars a month!

Limit your entertainment expenses

When you eat out go to a cheap restaurant

Rent low cost housing

Use low cost transportation

Do your own laundry

21

Many years ago, a young city boy named Johnny would visit his grandmother every summer far back into the Appalachian Mountains in the Eastern United States. Invariably when he visited his grandmother would say "Johnny, if there is anything you want let me know, and I will tell you how to get along without it." If you are thinking about living in Mexico on $300 to $800 a month there are many things that you will have to learn to do without!

Seriously, one could probably live on a such a low budget in one of the small pueblos a short distance from Guadalajara, but there would be no drastic changes (for the better) in your lifestyle. We have found that most North Americans are not willing to give up many comforts to which they are accustomed. It is true that the majority of Mexican families survive on less money a month: but that's just the point - **it's survival**! However, we maintain that whatever your income, you will live better in Mexico!

Spanish, the Language of Mexico

The official language of Mexico is Spanish, however, you will find many Mexicans who speak English, or at least know a few English words. The Mexican people are very warm, receptive, and helpful. Those who know some English often want to practice their second language with you. Not knowing Spanish is not ordinarily an overwhelming problem.

Living here you will learn a few Spanish words and phrases each week, but knowing a few basic words before you come will be helpful. If you learn to speak Spanish it will enrich your life in Mexico. All you need for starters is a sense of humor, a little patience, and a good phrase book. You might want to buy some cassette tapes to help. Some people learn more easily by ear than by sight. Tapes, with their guidebooks, offer both. Here are some suggestions:

Mexico Retirement and Travel Assistance markets **a Spanish Language Guide** that is excellent for a basic starter. It offers help with pronunciation and phrases you will need for checking into your hotel, ordering in a restaurant, shopping, numbers, colors, a motoring vocabulary including parts of your automobile, as well as many useful expressions. To order send a check for $7.00 drawn on a United States bank or a Canadian postal money order for the equivalent amount to M.R.T.A., 6301 S. Squaw Valley Road, Suite #23, Pahrump, NV 89048-7949.

Barron's Spanish at a Glance is a phrase book and dictionary divided in sections for special situations such as: when you arrive, at the hotel, getting around town, food and drink, shopping, medical care, driving a car, etc. Always carry a paperback edition in your car or purse when you first come to Mexico. It may be purchased at Dalton's or other popular bookstores in the

United States, or write to Barron's Educational Services, Inc., 113 Crossways Park Drive, Woodbury, NY 11797. They also have a ninety-minute cassette tape, by the same name that includes a small pocket phrase book.

Barron's Getting By in Spanish consists of two cassette tapes and a small book. This is especially helpful for learning Spanish conversation. You may learn to speak Spanish but you must also listen to the replies. Same address as above.

Educational Service Teaching Cassettes - Spanish Language 30 contains two cassettes, a phrase dictionary and a study guide that can be carried in your pocket. It is concise and helpful. Try your favorite bookstore or write Educational Services, 1730 Eye St. NW, Washington DC 20006.

The New World Spanish-English Dictionary is available in a paperback edition and it is very complete. Published by Signet Books, New American Library, Inc., 1633 Broadway, N.Y., NY 10019.

If you are seriously interested in learning Spanish, a good Spanish textbook to buy is **Madrigal's Magic Key to Spanish** by Margarita Madrigal, Doubleday & Company, Inc., Garden City, N.Y. This book teaches you how to convert many common English words into similar Spanish words, giving you a large Spanish vocabulary at the onset.

Also helpful for the serious Spanish student is **501 Spanish Verbs** published by Barron's. See address above.

After you arrive in Mexico you will find there are many Spanish language courses offered. Some are free and others are rather expensive and are geared to the intensity of your interest (or needs).

The **Mexican-North American Cultural Institute**, located in Guadalajara at Enrique Díaz de León No. 300, offers several courses at a nominal cost. Some of our friends have learned excellent Spanish from their Mexican friends.

Mexico Retirees -
A Special Breed!

If you are thinking of Mexico as a possible retirement location, you should take several things into consideration. Talk to anyone who has lived there and who has firsthand experience; read material that is available, and if possible, learn some fundamental Spanish. You can pick up more later. Last, and perhaps most important of all, be open-minded to the differences that you will encounter.

We have discovered that the happiest, most contented retirees in Mexico share certain similar personality traits, such as sense of adventure, an eagerness to learn about a different country, its culture and language. Essential also is the ability to adjust; and let's face it, life here is different in many ways, and of course, one must have patience - lots of patience! The ability to relax and live one day at a time with the knowledge that there will always be a *mañana*, this is the attitude of the happy retiree!

It is certainly recommended that potential retirees take a vacation to Mexico, especially to the Guadalajara/Lake Chapala area to "test the water", so to speak. Spend at least one or two months, longer if possible, before deciding to take the big leap. We did not practice what we are now preaching since our decision was made after just one week. But having lived in Guadalajara since 1985, we are still pleased with our decision and have no regrets.

If you do decide to make the move, be prepared to have patience, be adventurous and come ready to adjust to the problem of finding a house or apartment close to your expectations. In many cases getting settled finds one in a situation similar to what we had thirty-five or so years ago living in a small house or apartment, in some instances with no telephone, dishwasher, disposal, limited laundry facilities and no T.V. You can bring or buy a T.V. and it is no problem to have a cable or satellite dish installed. So, with this in mind, consider yourself lucky when you do eventually find an apartment or house, especially if it has a phone and stationary tubs for laundry! (Forget the dishwasher and disposal, unless you're willing to pay premium rent prices!) With this major accomplishment completed you can begin to acquaint yourself with living in Mexico and all that it entails - good and bad!

Be prepared for the way things get done here, and remember, have patience and accept the fact that most Mexicans seem to be in a slower time frame and have a different sense of time awareness. We soon realized that since we could not beat it, we would just join it. After all, unless it's a matter of life or death, and since we are retired, what difference does it make if appointments are late or missed ? (The same thing happens in the United States.) Things eventually get accomplished, and life goes on!

The housewife who depends on frozen dinners and desserts, certain brands of U.S. foods or special cuts of meat might have a problem. However, a large selection of frozen and convenience foods are appearing on the supermarket shelves, and the large American chain discount stores are opening their doors in the principal cities of Mexico, with reasonably competitive prices. If one is creative and adventurous there is an abundance of exotic vegetables and fruits to use, along with the familiar ones, and these are inexpensive year around. We have never found more delicious pork than in Mexico, and other meats. fish and poultry are equally as good, although they are cut somewhat different-ly than we are accustomed to. Obviously, we eat a much healthier diet now since we use more fresh vegetables and fruits. The extra hygienic measures to prepare the fruits and vegetables become routine and, as a matter of fact, should be followed even in the United States.

Newcomers should definitely go to a local *tianguis* (open- air market) held in various locations of the city each day. The more creative cook will be delighted to choose meat, poultry, fish, vegetables and fruit for dinner at reasonable prices, as well as finding about anything else needed for the house. It's great fun if you don't mind the crowd and confusion!

Wherever you go be sure to carry currency and coins of various denomina-tions. The vendors rarely have change for larger bills and thus one must adjust to carrying their own change!

Tianguis, mariachis, bullfights, rodeos and cobblestone streets, especially in the smaller villages, are as typical of Mexico as the sombrero, margaritas and tacos. If noise and crowds are a problem, your best bet is to concentrate on the quieter aspects of this fascinating country, such as the many historical sites, the serenity of the magnificent Cathedral, churches, museums, the fun of shopping for native craft work, the many thermal spas (*balnearios*) or trips to nearby villages, which also provide interesting experiences.

Adjusting to Mexico may perhaps be more difficult for women, but the fact that here one can easily afford to pay for housework, laundry care, garden work and other services goes a long way toward making up for things one might miss!

For most people Mexico is a happy retirement option. Still, we realize that there are those who would not be content here, who prefer things to remain "status quo" with no surprises, who prefer to be surrounded by family, old friends, and familiar things and places. For those people it would be a mistake to make the move. Others, however, who can enjoy the somewhat different way of doing things, who want the availability of excellent, reasonably priced medical care, near perfect climate, good entertainment, opportunities to explore new interests, and all without ruining their budget, will find that a Mexico retirement is the perfect answer!

Heading to
the Promised Land

by E. Wright Sargent

My wife and I retired in June of 1991 and immediately put our three years of research to work and headed for the "retirement paradise" we had found. We were going to that promised land. Ideal weather! Fresh fruits and vegetables! Flowers! Dry air! Golf! Entertainment! Arts and crafts! WOW! Is there no end to it? Soccer matches, bull fights, ballet, the zoo, the planetarium, the restaurants, the music, the charros and the people were all pleasurable opportunities to learn and enjoy. BUT - we are ahead of ourselves. Let us back up a couple of steps.

My wife and I had taught in New England for a combined total of seventy-three years and decided we deserved to get all the gusto we could out of retirement living. For three years we read everything available about "Retirement Edens" both home and abroad. Eventually we agreed on five priorities.

First, there had to be great weather. No more ice, snow, mist, hail, fog, sleet, cold, dampness, salted roads, overcoats, flu and fuel bills. We found two really outstanding places for near ideal weather conditions. There was Guadalajara, Jalisco or Nairobi, Africa. We chose Guadalajara, Mexico since we could drive to or fly in and out of there easily.

Second, we wanted a variety of fresh fruits and vegetables year round to ensure a healthy diet.

Third, we wanted to be able to exercise everyday by walking, golf, tennis, etc. Here, even in the rainy season you can get your exercising in before the late afternoon showers.

Fourth, we had a desire to be among friendly and happy people. We felt we could forgo pushy folk in a hurry to go nowhere. Give us the optimists and the grateful.

The fifth reason was that Mexico was and is affordable. This was so very important to retired school teachers with no huge retirement income.

How does this relate to the Guadalajara area? It had the five points we were seeking **plus** the presence of over 40,000 English speaking American/Canadian/European retired people in the area. You don't have to speak Spanish to get started and settled down in the Guadalajara-Lake Chapala haven.

So, we headed on down with less than sixteen hours of an evening school

Spanish course as communications background. We also entered during the dog days of August via Nogales, Arizona/Mexico and drove fifteen hundred miles to Guadalajara. This was the most difficult part and we were not prepared for the poverty, dirt, heat and pot holes, to say nothing of dealing with the government officials at the border when your Spanish is non-existent. But, we would have to say that the enemy of all gringos - MOCTEZUMA - and his harsh revenge, diarrhea, was the crusher... despite pills and not drinking the water.

We had our Mexican car insurance and our daily routes laid out. We never drove at night and usually averaged only 250-300 miles a day and where we stopped for meals and lodging were all planned ahead of time. In these matters we found AARP, Sanborn's Insurance and AAA information most helpful. The big problem that we ran into was eating too much of the excellent Mexican food. We drank only purified water and brushed our teeth with it as we still do. However, resisting the succulent and inexpensive sea food as we made our way down the Pacific Coast was impossible. We also were getting a little tired from wanting to see and do everything possible in our new and exciting "retirement country". This was an open invitation for Moctezuma to teach a gringo to be careful. We had to spend a couple of days in the resort city of Mazatlán getting our traveling legs under us and finally limped into Guadalajara, September 2nd wondering about "Eden" and hoping to stop losing weight the hard way.

Once we arrived in the city everything fell into place. We joined the American Society, a group of English speaking folk from the United States and Canada who are glad to answer your questions and show you their very busy schedule of events. We went to weekly meetings of a group that had outstanding speakers on topics of interest about Mexican history and culture.

Next we enrolled in the Spanish Language School nearby and studied there two hours every day for five weeks. This was a most rewarding experience as we learned a little Spanish and many things about living and managing in the big city as well as more about the history and culture of Mexico. We also met interesting people who have become our new friends.

We found that it is not necessary to learn Spanish because of the large number of English speaking people in the area. Many people don't care to pick up the language and get along fine. But for us it's important to learn the language and we are going back to school for another five weeks once our visitors leave. What made the school extra great was because we took field trips to places such as the market, butcher shop, theater and fiestas. Also, the school is like a big caring Mexican family.

You probably are wondering how two hicks from the small town of Rye, New Hampshire could live in a large city. Guadalajara, five thousand feet above sea level and with five million people is a sprawling city of roses and fountains and perfect weather. The city has dozens of self contained "little towns," plus modern shopping centers with many small American-like grocery stores and delis.

We love it because we live in an upper middle class residential area with mostly beautiful and friendly Mexicans. We are able to walk to Pizza Hut, McDonalds, Kentucky Fried Chicken, Dunkin Donuts, VIP's, or New York, New York (these last two are good restaurants serving American style food) if we want. There is a pharmacy open 24 hours a day that is not four hundred yards away. A few steps further and we can have excellent Chinese, Italian, Swiss or Japanese food. There are numerous Mexican restaurants that also serve a hamburger, grilled cheese, or fries and the best pork in the world; some even have a mariachi band.

We have friends who enjoy bridge, tennis, little theater, painting, golf, arts and crafts, book clubs, horseback riding and volunteer work. Theater, ballet and symphony are performed at all levels from the world famous Teatro Degollado. You can obtain inexpensive tickets to dress rehearsals or watch the very capable college students perform folkloric dancing on Sunday mornings or Wednesday evenings. We were here five months before we even got time to visit the zoo, which is the fourth most visited zoo in all of the Americas, and you need several days to see all the animals.

You are always welcome at the American Legion, the American Society or an open AA meeting. We have excellent medical care from an English speaking, New Jersey born, American trained doctor and Blue Cross takes care of most of the bill.

P.S. It is true that one of our friends paid $10 a pill in the States and here it costs only one dollar. So, come on down, if you've got a good attitude.

INFORMATION ABOUT MEXICAN VISAS

By John Bryant

In Mexico, there are ten basic types of entry visas, with several variations of each. People retiring in Mexico need to be concerned with just three of these:

* The FM-T or standard tourist visa.
* The FM-3 *"no inmigrante visitante"* visa.
* The FM-2 *"inmigrante rentista"* visa.

The FM-T is a 180-day tourist visa and is the most common document used for entering Mexico. This visa is obtained easily upon entry into Mexico at the office of the *Delegación de Servicios Migratorios* at your border entrance point. You will need proof of citizenship, such as a passport, birth certificate or voters registration. FM-T holders are not permitted to work in Mexico, the exception being writers and artists, who may practice their profession but cannot sell their work in Mexico. There is no charge for a tourist visa. Proof of income is not required.

Should you know definitely that you wish to move to Mexico permanently and want to bring your furniture and personal property then you should obtain an FM-3 or FM-2 visa, prior to going to Mexico. You should contact your nearest Mexican Consulate for detailed requirements and detailed instructions. A list of consulates is available from the Mexican Embassy at 1911 Pensylvania Ave. NW, Washington, DC 20006. A more permanent type of visa, such as a FM-3 "no inmigrante" visa or an FM-2 "inmigrante rentista" visa is more complicated to obtain.

We recommend that a first time arrival obtain a tourist visa. Find out the advantages and disadvantages of each type of visa and then determine which is best for your economic situation and lifestyle. It is more important to enjoy the many pleasures and benefits of living in Mexico and to find out if you like living in Mexico. Talk to persons who have lived in Mexico for a few years and find out which type of visa they have.

Persons arriving in Mexico by commercial airlines will be given a FM-T tourist visa form prior to landing, and this should be completed before arriving at the airport gate. Should you have questions, consult one of the airplane attendants.

When arriving in Mexico with a foreign-plated motorized vehicle, and after obtaining your FM-T tourist visa, you will need an official windshield sticker for your vehicle (Mexican-plated vehicles do not need a sticker.) This is obtained from the office of the *Aduana* (Customs tax collector). In border cities the Aduana is usually located within a few blocks of the office of the Delegación de Servicios Migratorios, where you obtained your FM-T visa. You will need a major United States credit card such as a Visa or MasterCard, original auto title, auto registration and your FM-T visa. (You should purchase Mexican auto insurance prior to entry into Mexico, as your United States auto insurance will not be valid.) You will need to complete some forms, a simple process, and after paying a fee with your credit card with billing to the United States, you will be on your way, provided, of course, there was not a long line ahead of you. Your vehicle sticker is valid as long as your visa is valid.

FM-T holders must leave Mexico before or at the time their 180-day visa expires, and take any foreign-plated vehicle they might have brought with them out of Mexico. Vehicles with Mexican plates are not affected by the regulations mentioned here. According to law, foreign-plated vehicles may only remain in Mexico for six months of a given year, and during the other six months the vehicle must be kept out of Mexico.

Persons with a FM-T (tourist) visa may fly out of Mexico temporarily (although this is frowned upon) and leave their vehicle in Mexico. The new FM-T visa will not be extended for the time absent from Mexico and the time spent out of Mexico will not extend the vehicle's stay in Mexico. The vehicle will still have only a 180-day permit starting on the issue date of the original visa given at the border. To leave the country leaving the vehicle behind, a return airline ticket must be presented. A copy of the FM-T visa should be made, as it will be needed when the bearer returns to Mexico. No one is allowed to drive the vehicle during the registered owners absence, since that person is the only authorized driver (NEVER, NEVER lend a car to anyone under any circumstances - it could be confiscated during one of the spot street revisions that the government holds regularly). Upon returning to Mexico your new tourist visa will be validated for the same time as indicated on your original visa copy.

In order to encourage more use of long-term FM-2 and FM-3 visas, and particularly to limit the use of FM-T visas by long-term foreign residents, the Mexican Immigration may not always issue an FM-T visa for 180 days upon your request, and may give a lesser amount of time. To obtain a visa valid for 180 days you may need to visit the nearest office of the Delegación de Servicios Migratorios and request an extension to 180 days.

Usually this is no problem, however, if you are a long-term resident you will be encouraged to obtain a FM-3 or FM-2 visa if you are eligible. The procedures for obtaining these visas have been simplified considerably.

In Guadalajara, the office of the Delegación de Servicios Migratorios is located on the third floor of the Palacio Federal, AV. Alcalde #520. between Hospital and Juan Alvarez streets (telephones 614-9749 and 614-5874.)

Usually there is an Immigration officer in the Lake Chapala area on Tuesdays and Thursdays at the La Floresta Hotel, La Floresta, Ajijic, telephone (376) 6-1192.

About U.S. Taxes

by Liz Monty, CPA

U.S. citizens and aliens considered U.S. residents residing in foreign countries are subject to the same income tax filing requirements as citizens residing in the U.S.

Who must file? A return must be filed by U.S. residents living abroad who have at least a specified minimum amount of gross income.

When to file: Although tax returns for individuals are due on the fifteenth day of the fourth month following the close of the tax year (April 15th for calendar year taxpayers), taxpayers who are U.S. citizens or residents living outside of the United States and Puerto Rico on the regular due date have an automatic extension of two months to file (until June 15th, for calendar year taxpayers). While no formal request for this additional time is necessary, the taxpayer's return must state that he or she was living outside of the United States on the regular due date. If a joint return is filed, only one spouse is required to be living outside the United States.

Although there is a two-month extension period to pay the tax owed (unless the IRS specifies otherwise) the postponed due date does not relieve taxpayers from paying interest due on any unpaid portion of the final tax liability. Thus the interest is calculated from April 15th.

If additional time is required to file a tax return, a two month extension (until August 15th) is available by filing Form 4868 "Application for Automatic Extension of Time to File U.S. Individual Income Tax Return". This extension, however, will not excuse the taxpayer from all penalties unless he or she has paid at least 90% of his or her ultimate tax liability by the time the extension is filed. An additional extension to time to file may be requested by filing Form 2868 "Application for Additional Extension of Time to File U.S. Individual Income Tax Return". Use of this form will usually allow a taxpayer to obtain an extension until October 15th.

There is no extension of time for making estimated tax payments with Form 1040ES which are due on April 15th, June 15th, September 15th, and January 15th, respectively.

Where to file: Taxpayers who reside outside the United States should file all returns with the Internal Revenue Service Center in Philadelphia, Pennsylvania 19255. Taxes are payable in U.S. dollars and foreign bank checks must be drawn on U.S. dollar accounts. Claims for refunds or amended tax returns should be filed in the district where the related return was filed.

While these are the basic filing requirements for U.S. citizens living abroad, there are many complex rules relating to the special foreign earned income exclusions, moving and travel expenses, residences and other issues to be thoroughly considered and discussed with your tax advisor. If you believe you may have issues involving substantial amounts of tax you may want to contact your tax consultant.

Banking and Financial Transactions in Mexico

In Mexico, banking facilities equal and often exceed those in the United States. Although there are fewer drive-in banks, most banks have computerized operations, automatic teller machines and reasonably efficient service. Don't be shocked by the guards carrying automatic rifles - they are for your protection, since banks are very vulnerable during hold-ups. But, unlike the United States, there hasn't been a bank failure for years. Mexican banks were nationalized a number of years ago to allow the government to get a grip on the economy, and recently have been re-sold into private hands. Savings and Loan Associations do not exist in Mexico.

Basic banking practices are pretty much the same as north of the border; among the services offered are deposit accounts, checking accounts, savings accounts and certificates of deposit, along with safety deposit boxes (more expensive than in the United States) and trust department services, etc. Peso and international credit cards, such as Visa and MasterCard, are offered to preferred customers by most banks after making a credit application.

Cashing personal checks drawn on United States or Canadian banks may be time consuming and a hassle even if you have many times the amount of your check on deposit with the bank. Usually they are sent for collection, taking a month to six weeks. Use of checks for commercial transactions is much more limited in Mexico; most stores will not accept a personal check for merchandise you are taking with you, unless you're a very good client. And do not depend on your bank in the United States to wire funds to you at a bank in Mexico. Your funds may not be received for several days, and you could encounter expensive long distance telephone calls.

Tourists and newcomers should bring traveler's checks and their Visa and MasterCard cards. Traveler's checks and/or currency may be exchanged for pesos upon proper identification (passport, driver's license, etc.) at bank counters in major airports, banks, and currency exchange houses (*Casas de Cambio*). The larger *Casas de Cambio* tend to work with a smaller buy- sell margin, usually offering a better deal than the banks, but watch out for the smaller, "store-front" dealers that abound in tourist areas such a Puerto Vallarta; you could loose up to 10% on a transaction. It's best to check the rates offered by these different establishments, especially when dealing with larger amounts of money.

Traveler's checks and United States currency are usually readily accepted "as is" in most major hotels to pay a bill, and they will almost always exchange small amounts for pesos, though the exchange rate will not be as good as banks or *casas de cambio*.

Many Americans sell their dollars to affluent Mexicans - both seller and buyer get a better deal than in a commercial exchange house. Another possibility for selling dollars is to Americans returning to the U.S. and wanting to get rid of surplus pesos.

Instead of going through the hassle of trying to cash your personal check, you may obtain pesos with your Visa or MasterCard at a Mexican bank. Some banks will accept either card while others will accept only one. To avoid interest charges, mail your personal checks to pay off your "plastic" loan immediately. Mexican bank service charges for this service may amount to 5% or more of the amount of the transaction and your Visa or MasterCard may also have a service charge.

Other credit cards do exist in Mexico, such as Diner's Club and American Express, and these companies offer you the same service as in the United States. However, many commercial establishments are reluctant, or absolutely refuse, to honor these credit cards. Always ask beforehand which cards are accepted.

Because the Peso is a floating currency, and fluctuates daily against the dollar, the dollar amount charged against your credit card in the United States may be different than the amount calculated at the time of the transaction. Also, in this type transaction, the exchange rate will not be as favorable as with pesos.

Many banks offer an account called "Cuenta Maestra" ("Master Account"). With this account, your money is invested in a trust fund that pays an exceptionally high rate of interest. In addition, your investment has complete liquidity with checking privileges and a debit card. The debit card may be used in thousands of commercial establishments throughout Mexico, even in grocery stores. With *Cuenta Maestra* account you may transfer funds from one investment to another, whether it be checking, investments, credit cards or certificates of deposit. This account is ideal for people interested in traveling in Mexico, or anywhere in the world. Some banks have English speaking employees, and offer specialized investment and trust services for foreigners.

Most people use the services of the bank most convenient to their residence. Smaller banks give the best personal service. An English-speaking branch manager will be most helpful. Some North Americans use the financial services of Allen W. Lloyd, deposit brokers.

One popular information service says "if you want to get rich in Mexico, invest in Mexican pesos." With high interest rates you may get figuratively rich in pesos, but in true purchasing power related to Mexican inflation, and to the continuing and major unpredictable devaluations of the peso in relation to the dollar, you may or may not make a profit. Look for a devaluation just before or after a new president takes office each six years. The Mexican economy has stabilized appreciably in the past few years. Although there are good investment instruments in Mexico, we recommend a person considering retirement in Mexico leave the bulk of his funds in U.S. dollars, particularly at the outset of your move to Mexico. For the convenience of having pesos when you want them, and for emergencies, you may wish to put six months to a year's worth of living expenses in a certificate of deposit, or a Cuenta Maestra as mentioned above. For longer-term investment, if you are interested, we suggest you contact a reputable Mexican *Casa de Bolsa* (stockbroker). They offer a variety of mutual funds and other investment instruments.

If you are considering retiring in Mexico, arrange to have your Social Security, pension and dividend checks sent directly to your present United States bank checking account

If you are moving to Mexico permanently, you may want a mail forwarding service in the United States as a central mail collection point for your bank statements, insurance policy premium notices, and other important correspondence. Mail will be forwarded to Mexico, and you only have one address to change in your home country should you move. Also, when you return to visit for a few weeks, you can keep current with your mail. Several mail-forwarding companies now offer this type service, particularly from larger cities in the United States. We have used the mail forwarding services of "Keepin'n Kontact Co.", 6301 S. Squaw Valley Rd., Pahrump, NV 89048-7949 for many years and have been completely satisfied. It is a small privately owned and well-managed company. Fees are reasonable. We have not been satisfied with the mail forwarding services of the large franchise companies operating in the United States and Mexico.

With a reliable mail forwarding service, you may maintain your home country credit cards. It will be necessary to anticipate when your payments are due and mail your payments in advance. You will be able to maintain your good credit history and avoid late charges.

How the United States Consulate May Help You During your Trip to Mexico or Around the World

The United States Consulate General in Guadalajara is a branch of the United States Mexican Embassy in Mexico City, a function of the State Department. Consulate personnel say "We are from the United States Government and we are here to help you". They prove this in many ways. They will witness and notarize official U.S. documents such as real estate property transfers and affidavits, renew passports, or replace a lost or stolen passport. They can obtain your Social Security and Veteran benefits, provide you with Internal Revenue Service forms, and act as a registration service for U.S. citizens living in Mexico (helpful but not required). The primary benefit of registering with the Consulate is that you can be contacted in case of a family emergency in the United States, or your family may be contacted should you have an emergency here. In case of death while in a foreign country, the Consulate will assist your survivors in obtaining a death certificate and other official documents and help with the arrangements. Should a child be born to an American citizen in Mexico, the Consulate will register the birth.

The United States Consulate does not provide attorneys or legal or personal expenses for citizens who become involved in criminal or civil litigation. However, should you be arrested or get into trouble in Mexico, insist upon your right to communicate immediately with the Consulate. A duty officer is always on call and will help you in getting the necessary help. The Consulate is not a collection agency for debts owed in the United States. You may register to vote in the United States through the Consulate office.

The Consulate also provides a list of physicians, surgeons and dentists, as well as a helpful publication entitled General Information on the Guadalajara Consular District. The Consulate is located at Progreso No. 175; telephone numbers are 825-2700 and 825-2998. The offices are closed on all U.S. and Mexican holidays; however, a duty officer is always available - 24 hours a day, 365 days a year - to help U.S. citizens in trouble. In case of an emergency when the Consulate is closed, call 826-5553. If the duty officer is not available, leave your name and telephone number and he or she will return your call. You may fax the Consulate at 825-19-51

The Canadian Consulate

The Canadian Consulate is located in Local #30 inside the Hotel Fiesta Americana, near the Minerva Circle (Av. Vallarta and Lopez Mateos). It is open daily from 8:30 a.m. to 5 p.m., telephone 615-6215 and 615-6270, FAX 615-8665. After hours you may call the Canadian Embassy in Mexico City at 01-800-70629. Officials furnish many of the services to Canadians similar to those provided by the U.S. Consulate to Americans. One of the principal purposes of this consulate is to promote trade between Mexico and Canada. The Canadian Consul suggests that Canadians register with them so they can be located in case of family emergencies. In addition, they can notify you of special Canadian events and cultural activities.

The News Media in Mexico

With very little effort you can be better informed in Mexico about what is going on in the world than you are in the United States. You will have more time for reading and television.

The **Mexico City News**, published daily, is a complete, compact, tabloid size newspaper. It has news from Mexico, the United States and the world; financial news, including a daily N.Y. Stock Exchange listing; economic, business and Washington news; editorials by noted columnists and sports from the U.S. and around the world. It also carries features such as T.V. listings, Ann Landers, the arts, and comics, including Doonesbury, Garfield and Peanuts, as well as political cartoons. The Sunday edition has an excellent travel section.

You can buy the **Wall Street Journal, U.S.A. Today** and many popular magazines at newsstands and various stores that have newspaper and magazine sections.

There are several Spanish language T.V. channels, and some offer English language movies, particularly on the weekends. Major sports events in the United States are broadcast on Mexican T.V. with Spanish commentary. Many Americans buy a satellite dish and receive United States programming. To receive the major networks it is necessary to have a descrambler and buy special decoding on an annual basis that is much like cable T.V. in the United States. Cable T.V., carrying the principal U.S. channels, is now available in some areas of the major cities in Mexico, and is a fast growing business.

If you like up-to-the-minute news, bring a short wave radio. You can receive American programming from the powerful Voice of America and from other stations around the world. Occasionally you will receive broadcasts

36

from El Paso, Dallas or Houston, if the weather conditions are right. Local radio (AM and FM) has excellent classical and "easy-listening" music.

Questions Frequently Asked

We have two children. Are there schools available? How is the school system in Mexico?

Yes, there are private schools, with classes in English, available for your children in both Guadalajara and Chapala, and other large cities that have sufficient population of people from the United States and Canada. Tuition costs vary between schools. It is very difficult to enroll your children in Mexican public schools, as studies received outside the country must be revalidated, a complicated process. If your child starts with the first graders of primary school, there is no problem. Mexican schools tend to concentrate on the basics of education and there are less "frills". As in the United States, the quality of education can vary greatly from institution to institution. Educational programs are set at a national level; there are no "easy" courses for underachievers just to give them a certificate - the typical ninth grader here has already seen the "standard" high school courses offered in the U.S. and Canada, and understandably, the failure rate is extremely high.

May I borrow money from a United States bank to buy a house in Mexico?

Banks in the United States will not ordinarily lend money for purchase of a house in Mexico. Several United States mortgage lenders and brokers have an active interest in financing houses in Mexico for retirees from the United States or Canada. Individual mortgage lenders have different criteria for lending funds such as verifiable annual income, net worth, credit rating, ratio of loan to appraised value, type of construction minimum and maximum amount of loan, and interest rates. Various fees are charged such as origination fees, appraisal fees, title search, title insurance, trust set-up fees, annual maintenance, Mexican Notary fees, and various taxes. Property will be held in a Mexican bank trust (fideicomiso) for the borrower's beneficial interest.

May I bring my pets and horses to Mexico? Are there grazing lands available?

Yes, you may bring your pets to Mexico, provided they have had recent vaccinations and you have proof of this. As in the United States, many landlords will not rent to people with pets, and this could make your house or apartment search more difficult. There are many places to ride horses in Mexico, and stable facilities and grazing lands are available.

37

A burning question - how about smog in Guadalajara?

Yes, as with any large city, Guadalajara does occasionally have a smog problem, particularly in the central city. City fathers have started a vehicle inspection program that will improve the engine emissions situation. Chemical pollutants are not a major problem here in Guadalajara, as the amount of heavy industry is very small in proportion to the size of the city; the principal contaminants are ozone and suspended dust particles, that seldom go beyond "acceptable" levels. We live in an area on the Northwest side of Guadalajara where the air is clean and pure and we are practically never aware of any smog.

It is my plan to try to work in Mexico - is this possible?

It is illegal to work in Mexico unless you are a writer or artist, and your work is sold outside Mexico. With special visas one may teach English or practice specialized technical professions that are needed here. Mexico is now more liberal to foreigners who wish to organize corporations.

Which is more economical to rent: a house or an apartment? I will not have my furniture.

Rent prices largely depend on the section of the city and whether it is a furnished or unfurnished house or apartment. Unfurnished housing is usually less, and quite often one can find very good buys on complete household furniture packages that may work out well. Rent prices vary greatly, and the best results of house or apartment searching are by "word of mouth", and bulletin boards in supermarkets. Classified advertising in Mexican newspapers may be helpful.

What are the chances of an earthquake in Guadalajara?

Two major earthquakes have occurred in Mexico in recent years. The first one, in September 1985, happened shortly after our arrival in Guadalajara. The damage and death rates were devastating, mostly in Mexico City, which is literally built on top of a swamp, and in Ciudad Guzman, Jalisco, which sits on a major fault. The second quake, in October 1995, affected the Pacific coastal areas: poor construction, mostly with no heed to any modern building code, accounted for 95% of the damage and injuries. The resulting tidal wave was the finishing touch to this disaster, but people recognized it in time and got to higher ground, with no loss of life. These earthquakes *were* felt in Guadalajara, and caused a lot of panic, but Guadalajara's underlying bedrock is not as prone to movements as severe as in other parts of the country, and damage was minimal. We recommend total common sense and a cool head in case of an earthquake: no matter where you are, if you feel an earthquake, get outside! Follow evacuation instructions if you are in a large building, and get to clear ground, staying away from trees, power lines, walls, etc. If you are at the ocean, stay well clear of the water, but observe it carefully; a seaquake will first suck out the tide, and then slowly keep building and building up to form the tidal wave – you have sufficient time to get to higher ground if necessary. Don't panic, but don't ever think, "Oh, this will stop shortly" These precautions must always be taken, as they could save your life.

May retirement checks be mailed to Mexico?
Yes, however we suggest that your Social Security, pension and dividend checks be sent to your bank in the United States for direct deposit. Mail service to Mexico at times may be very slow, particularly in the months of December and January. Direct deposit is safe and sure!

Is paradise lost? The prices for many items appear higher than in the United States. Books say that you can live on $300 to $800 per month!
Yes, prices rise constantly in Mexico. M.R.T.A. publications do not promote travel or retirement in Mexico based on ridiculously low cost of living figures. We are sure that more publications are sold with spectacular claims about low cost of living, however, we wish to remain honest and straightforward even if we never sell the most books nor have the most subscribers.
Gasoline at over $1.50 per gallon is certainly no bargain. Rents may or may not be a bargain depending on where you come from. Practically all services in Mexico are much less than in the United States and good medical services are affordable. Fresh fruits and vegetables are generally available at low costs. Utilities are not expensive since one seldom needs heat or air conditioning. Our kitchen oven provides all the heat we ever need, and ceiling fans provide "air conditioning." Our living expenses are just $1000 monthly; however, we do not pay rent since we own our condo. We live well but not pretentiously. We have a satellite dish that provides us with a greater variety of programming than we ever had with cable in the United States.
Having accomplished most of our professional and social goals before retirement, we have no need to "keep up with the Jones's" or impress anyone with a sophisticated life style. We just enjoy simple living and the relaxed life style that Mexico provides, plus outings with congenial friends who share our interests.

We notice that the wages for a maid quoted in your Cost of Living Survey may equal that of someone in middle management positions in Mexico. Why?
We have been aware of this also since our arrival in Guadalajara. One will pay higher wages for someone who works as a maid on an hourly basis than for a live-in maid. With a live-in maid you may become responsible for health care, food, clothes, vacations, and often may take on responsibility for problems in the maid's family. Being a maid in Mexico has a much higher social status than in the United States. A good, honest, hard working, dependable maid is well worth the money in Mexico.

Do other Americans make newcomers feel at home?
There are many clubs and organizations of every possible kind in both Guadalajara and the Lakeside area, so that with very little effort one can immediately find others who share common interests. These groups greet newcomers with enthusiasm.

How may I call Long Distance in Mexico?
Telephone service in Mexico is modern in most respects as in the United States. One may direct dial long distance to the United States or Canada by dialing 001, then the area code and number. For operator assisted international calls for your credit card or collect calls you should dial 090.
For direct dial long distance calls within Mexico dial 01 first, then the area code and number. You should dial 020 for operator assisted calls within Mexico. If you have an AT&T calling card you may use their U.S.A. Direct Service simply by dialing 001-800/462-4240. The operator will place your call for you. You may also place collect calls to the United States with the AT&T U.S.A. Direct Service.

May I bring my gun to Mexico?
When coming into Mexico do not plan to bring your gun. It is illegal to bring any type of firearm into the country, or carry any sort of weapon (this includes knives) on your person or in your car, unless you have a special permit. Although Mexico has crime, it usually is non-violent in nature, and it is not considered a national problem as in the United States. You will not need a gun to protect yourself, and courts do not pamper criminals. Although Rod and Gun Clubs do exist in Mexico, and are organized at a national level, they do not lobby for pistols and automatic weapons for everyone, like the National Rifle Association.

How about crime in Mexico?
Much has been written about pickpockets and purse-snatchers, so we will not elaborate, just be cautious in crowded situations and alert to anyone who seems to be watching or following you. Also never leave your personal belongings unattended for any time period. We have never had an unpleasant experience such as this - but as in any large city it certainly could happen to anyone. Many people ask about violent crime in Mexico - and we can only say that we feel safer in Guadalajara than in cities in the United States. A Mexican friend told us recently that although there are drugs here, it is not the severe problem as elsewhere by far, nor are violent crimes such as random gun firing, rapes and murders very common. Nowhere is the world the crime free place of years ago, but Mexico appears as safe as anywhere we know, plus it offers many, many plus factors which add to comfort and enjoyment of life. With this in mind plan your trip carefully and then come to see for yourself whether or not retirement in Mexico is for you!

Is personal safety a problem in Guadalajara?
(We have received several letters about whether or not Guadalajara is a safe place for the elderly, or for single women.)
We would say that this should not be a problem or worry. It is quite common to see elderly people, young girls and even children seemingly alone at night at bus stops or merely walking along the streets. As in any city, there are areas in which one would not venture alone at night, but overall we feel much safer here in Guadalajara than where we have lived in the United States. We do suggest that purses should be held close to one's body to not tempt purse-snatchers, and of course, valuable jewelry should be left in a safe place, not worn casually. Pickpockets and purse-snatchers are around, but other more serious types of violent crime are not as prevalent.

II
Important Travel Information

APPROXIMATE FLYING TIMES TO AND FROM GUADALAJARA OR LAKE CHAPALA

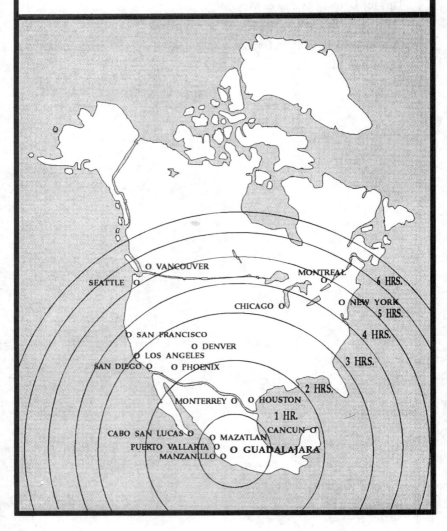

Be Prepared For Your Trip To Mexico

When planning a trip to Mexico, you may find the following suggestions helpful and a way to make your trip safer and more pleasant.

First, you should learn as much as possible about Mexico and the area you wish to visit; learn some Spanish if possible, and find out all you can about Mexican customs. In other words, be prepared!

As with any trip to a foreign country, it is wise to have a copy of your planned itinerary along with a photo copy of your passport information to leave with relatives or friends, and be sure to keep them advised of any changes. At the same time, make an extra copy to keep with you also. Shortly after your arrival in Mexico, make a copy of your tourist visa and keep the original in the safest place possible. You will need the original when leaving Mexico. If the original is lost, it may take a day or more to obtain another visa.

When packing for your trip, keep to the essentials, and leave any valuables behind in a safe place. In your carry-on bag you should bring a change of clothing, necessary medications and basic toiletry articles you would need in case of misplaced luggage. For those taking daily medication it would be wise to bring an adequate supply of what you will need, plus copies of prescriptions and a letter from your physician explaining the necessity of the medication. Also, a medical alert bracelet should be worn to indicate any major or life-threatening health problems. With the exception of tranquilizers and barbiturates, you can buy most prescription medicine over the counter in Mexican pharmacies. Just make sure what you buy is what you need.

When entering Mexico you will need your voter's registration and birth certificate, or a passport. If they should get lost or stolen, report it at once to the local police and the nearest U.S. embassy or consulate. A concealed money belt is excellent to use for carrying passports, traveler's checks and cash. Men would be advised to put their wallet in their front pocket and women should hold their purse, with a secure shoulder strap, under their arm, or use money belts or pouches. Be especially aware of crowded situations, as these are pickpockets favorite times to "work".

If you plan to drive to Mexico, you will need your auto registration card to show when crossing the border. If you are bringing a pet with you, it will be necessary to show health and vaccination certificates which have been issued not more than 72 hours prior to your entry. Do not bring illegal drugs or weapons (knives over 2" (5cm) included!) into Mexico. Firearms will be allowed only with a consular firearms certificate from a Mexican consulate (for sports competitions, principally). Don't take risks!

Driving in Mexico calls for awareness and caution. Learn the road signs (which follow international standards), and watch for livestock in the road, along with stalled vehicles with no lights. Avoid driving at night on unfamiliar roads.

During your stay in Mexico you probably will want to shop, but there are some items which you would not be permitted to leave Mexico with, such as Mexican birds, black coral jewelry, products made from sea turtles (their eggs included), and crocodile leather. Keep receipts for all purchases to show if needed. The U.S. Customs Service permits each U.S. citizen to bring back $400 dollars worth of merchandise duty-free. Amounts over that will be subject to a duty tax.

Mexico is a delightful country, and by following these simple travel tips, you will be glad you came!

Practical Advice for Travelers to Mexico or Elsewhere

Anyone planning to travel out of the United States should begin making their plans well in advance, taking many things into consideration, and one of the most important matters pertains to one's health.

Travelers going to any foreign country should make it a point to learn as much as possible about what to expect and what to avoid when deciding where and what they eat and drink. This article is targeted more specifically to Mexican traveling, but is applicable to any region in the world.

Most people have heard of the dreadful "Moctezuma's Revenge," referring to an intestinal disorder causing diarrhea and vomiting, from mild to intense cases. This condition exists in every country, but is grouped under the general name of "Traveler's Diarrhea", since it is caused by the introduction of a different type of intestinal flora (bacteria), dependent on local climatalogical conditions and latitude, which **can and will** be picked up during traveling. Don't think that Mexicans escape similar digestive maladies when they travel to the U.S. and Canada; this type illness is an intrinsic part of traveling.

Even though we usually blame "Traveler's Diarrhea" on the local water, (and it's true that one should definitely **not drink tap water, but only purified bottled water**), a major part of the blame should also fall on simple factors such as fatigue, travel stress, overeating, and perhaps excessive drinking, which do not allow the body to adjust to its new surroundings. With the difference in the altitude, eating different types of food at odd hours and trying to get in too much sightseeing in too little time, one's body can get completely out of sync, making it more vulnerable to becoming ill. Take it easy on over-indulging, eating and drinking **very, very lightly** the first few days, no matter how tempting the aroma of the exotic food and drink!

Treatment for such problems can be found in the form of Pepto Bismol, Imodium, and Kaopectate for diarrhea, and Dramamine to control vomiting. It's always a good idea to take along one or more of these over the counter remedies, just in case. In very mild cases, the problem can be relieved by getting extra rest, sticking to bland food as well as drinking a delicious and highly recommended tea called *manzanilla* (camomile), which has a powerful astringent effect and is very soothing. In extreme cases, especially if fever, dehydration (very common in the combined presence of diarrhea and vomiting), pain or very bad general malaise are present, a doctor should be called, and there are many excellent ones available in Mexico.

For the self-treatment of diarrhea, modern medical theories follow the old saying "better an empty house than a bad tenant". Never take a remedy for

diarrhea immediately; let nature run its course for a few hours at least, if possible, just in case you've picked up a massive bacterial or viral contamination; diarrhea is the body's natural defense mechanism to eliminate toxins, bacteria and other things that shouldn't be in it, and if the digestive system is "bottled up" artificially, it can lead to serious problems. Liquid stools are full of infection-fighting cells, so it's best just to let everything run its course, drinking lots of liquids to compensate for their loss. If you are so sick as to absolutely feel the need to stop the diarrhea to be able to travel or realize other activities, bed rest most probably would be more indicated than hopping on a plane or taking that tour. Use medications only in dire emergencies.

Another precaution to consider would be to check with your family doctor several weeks in advance, alerting him of your travel plans in order to have any immunizations that he suggests.

The choice of restaurants is especially important in the effort to stay well during travel. There are many excellent, clean places to eat where one can feel assured that sanitary methods are strictly enforced in food preparation. These are the places you will see other North Americans and health conscious Mexicans dining regularly.

Stay away from the sidewalk stands, open market food stalls and the little roadside restaurants when possible. They are simply not equipped to handle food properly. There are no bathrooms, no washing facilities or running water, let alone refrigeration. Usually you will see one bucket of water, which is used over and over for rinsing utensils and dishes!

Conditions such as we've described are very primitive and unsanitary and can lead to a sure way of picking up not only an intestinal upset but more serious cases of hepatitis, salmonella, typhoid and cholera. Keep in mind that any food to be eaten raw or unpeeled should be washed carefully with soap and water, and maybe soaked with disinfectant drops, such as Microdyne or

Halazone. Don't put all your trust in disinfectants alone; soap and running water are still the best disinfectants. **Unclean, contaminated hands are the** scientifically proven principal culprit in the transmission of the aforementioned illnesses. We worry tremendously about whether a piece of lettuce was washed and "disinfected", but never think about whether the waiter's and cook's hands are clean.

Sometimes disrupted travel plans, mechanical problems, etc., can leave one stranded for a period of time longer than one would wish to go without food. When forced to eat in dubious places, stick to certain types of food, such as beef, beans, tortillas, bread, cooked vegetables, fish (if at the seaside) and, in general, anything that comes hot out of the pot or off the grill with minimal handling by very potentially dirty hands. Avoid "like the plague" pork, chicken, sausage, cold cuts, shrimp and other seafood, and milk and its derivatives (cheese included) when on the road; these food groups are notorious for food poisoning and become contaminated very easily. Also avoid chopped fruit and vegetable salads; they're highly handled. Street stands are sometimes the better choice in small towns than the local restaurant or market, if they exist; if the food and the people handling the food look clean, everything probably is clean; just follow our food group suggestions. Cakes, potato chips, and other commercially packaged snacks sometimes are your only recourse to take the edge off your hunger - not very nutritious, but you can survive a few days on these "gourmet" delights if other food alternatives look bad. Better hungry than sorry.

These tips should be taken very seriously; any Mexican stuck under similar circumstances will follow them, and **won't get sick**. Twenty years of experience goes into these suggestions and we remind the reader of the old adage, "When in Rome, do as the Romans do."

It is very important for travelers who are on medication to take an ample supply of medicine with them, plus a doctor's prescription, preferably with generic names. Make sure you stay on the required medication schedule needed to take it just as at home. Any medication can be bought over the counter in Mexico, except tranquilizers and narcotics. Your American prescription is not valid to obtain these highly controlled substances, and Mexican doctors are very reluctant to prescribe them to unknown patients.

Traveling in another country is a fascinating and rewarding experience and can be made more so by individuals who prepare themselves before leaving home, by knowing what to expect and how to take care of themselves.

Do not let fear of becoming sick away from home limit your travels; just be informed and prepared, and with a little common sense, you will be able to enjoy the adventure.

Tips For Driving To And In Mexico

Many Americans drive to Mexico each year with little or no problems, contrary to the ever-persistent rumors of bandidos, unpassable roads and other discouraging happenings along the way. It is too bad that some would-be motorists miss this experience. With some planning and preparation beforehand, traveling to Mexico by car, van, motor home or any vehicle can be very rewarding, and gives one a better insight as to what Mexico and it's people are really like.

Your journey really begins before leaving your hometown as you have your vehicle checked out in readiness to go. A complete tune-up, lubrication, brake and tire check, and new tires, if needed, including a good spare. Don't neglect checking the windshield wipers, headlights, horns, batteries and even rearview and side-view mirrors. A good first aid kit in your car may be advisable. This may seem a lot of unwarrantable effort and expense, but "better safe than sorry" certainly applies in this case.

In preparation for your trip it is always wise to take along a few spare parts in case of a problem along the road. Parts such as extra fuses, spark plugs, water and air hoses, fan belts, brake and transmission fluid, extra oil, and even an easy to follow repair manual, plus a few basic tools.

Another part of your preparation includes proof of citizenship, such as your birth certificate and voters' registration, or passport, which will be necessary when you reach the border in order to receive your tourist papers and vehicle permit. You must show a valid drivers' license, car registration and original title: (have copies available also). Of course your vehicle must have current license plates. To obtain the vehicle permit you must pay $12.00 with a MasterCard or Visa Card (cash is not accepted). These cards are also excellent for emergency funds. Have plenty of pesos on hand for gasoline since U.S. dollars and credit cards are accepted in a very limited number of gas stations.

Now that your vehicle is in good shape and you have the necessary documents, you are ready to start to the border and begin your adventure. Once you arrive at the border and before crossing into Mexico it is important to buy Mexican automobile insurance since your U.S. auto insurance is not valid in Mexico.

Safety in driving is never more important than in a foreign country and Mexico is no exception. Use common sense; don't take chances with excessive speed or driving after dark, when potholes, stalled cars, cattle crossings and stones on the road are the potential problems, not *bandidos*! Often roads have no shoulders and there is no place to pull off in case of an emergency. Be alert to unexpected stops and drivers who might try to pass on curves or who tailgate. Keep your cool and ignore horn blasts by impatient drivers. Remember the saying "the life you save might be your own".

Highways and roads in general in Mexico have improved greatly over the past few years, and while there are some excellent new, but expensive, toll roads, the typical expressways are not up to U.S. standards. Highway maintenance is sometimes poor, resulting in potholes, detours, and narrow one-lane bridges. Again be cautious.

It is comforting to know that there are Department of Tourism "Green Angel" trucks that patrol highways twice a day from 8 A.M. to 8 P.M. looking for vehicles with problems. These assistance trucks are equipped to help in almost any situation and charge nothing for their labor, only materials used (an after-the-fact nominal tip is always appreciated - remember that salaries are very low in Mexico). The Federal Highway Police (*Policia Federal de Caminos*) will also give a helping hand in an emergency, and call the Green Angel truck on their radio.

There is only one type of gas station in Mexico, a Government monopoly called Pemex. All stations on Mexico's main highways and in major cities and towns have regular or high-octane unleaded gasoline (ask for *Magna Sin* or *Premium*). It is a very wise idea to have at least a quarter tank of gasoline at all times, as on some roads stations may be located much further apart than what you are used to. Also a gas station pump failure could be disastrous if it's the only one for miles around. Also gasoline can become a scarce commodity on long holiday weekends, Easter week, Christmas, etc. If you are planning to travel through very rural areas make sure you have enough gasoline before you

RELIEF MAP OF MEXICO

start out, and plan your trip carefully, consulting someone who knows the terrain. In some areas your only option to purchase gasoline will be at the local general store, usually sold in 10- or 20-liter containers, and there's no guarantee that they will have unleaded. When driving in Mexico it is a good idea to carry snacks, fruit juice and a good supply of drinking water. When driving through sparsely populated rural areas we suggest having breakfast and evening meals at the hotel where you stay, relying on snacks in between. The toll houses on the major highways, and most gas stations, have rest rooms and snack bars, offering a variety of standard junk food, not very nutritious, but perfectly safe to eat. Your pack of supplies should also include toilet tissue (an absolute must), handy-wipes and paper towels. No self-respecting Mexican would be caught dead on the highway without these basics. Knowing that you are as well prepared as possible, with a good supply of patience, you can relax and enjoy the exciting trip and beautiful scenery.

Driving in a city is often particularly frustrating for Americans. Although Mexican people are usually very patient people, when they are driving a car it is a different story! We have noticed that Mexicans will wait patiently in lines for practically everything but they will not wait for a red light to turn green! They will often honk their car horn for you to go even before the light has changed, which is greatly annoying but you soon learn to ignore it. You must always drive cautiously and defensively, however, in some situations you also must drive equally aggressively. You learn to anticipate anything and assume nothing.

Guadalajara has many *glorietas* or traffic circles that at first appear threatening; a good rule to remember is "he who is in front of you, or has already entered the traffic circle, has the right of way, and he who hits pays". Traffic circles are curved, so drive into them as such, not in a straight line. (Also remember that more likely than not the person who hits you is not insured).

Most rules of simple courtesy that you are accustomed to when driving do not seem to apply in Mexico. For example, it is sometimes best not to use a turn signal when changing lanes since often the driver behind will speed up and go into the space you planned to fill. Mexicans sometimes do not allow for what you would consider a safe distance from the car in front. Buses, taxis, and trucks really don't care who has the right of way: they make their own rules. With them it seems to be "me first - to hell with everyone else"! Size seems to be a predominate factor in determining the "right-of-way".

In spite of the seemingly reckless attitude of some Mexican drivers it is amazing how few serious accidents you will see. Mexicans are very creative in their driving as well as with their art forms! You will see "creative" driving in Mexico that you never dreamed of north of the border. This writer has been driving in Mexico for many years and fortunately has never been in an accident. Chances are you will be just as fortunate if you keep a cool head while driving. Who knows, you might soon be driving like a native!

(Editors note: Mexico Retirement and Travel Assistance has an excellent map package and a Spanish language guide to help you with your trip. Prices are $29.00 and $7.00 U.S. respectively. Order from M.R.T.A., 6301 S. Squaw Valley Rd., Suite #23, Pahrump, NV 89048-7949. An interesting and helpful book about driving in Mexico is "Mexico from the Driver's Seat" by "Mexico" Mike Nelson, who spends many months every year driving in Mexico. It may be obtained from Travelog and General Printing Inc., 2009 South 10th Street, McAllen TX 78502.)

MEXICO TRAFIC SIGNS

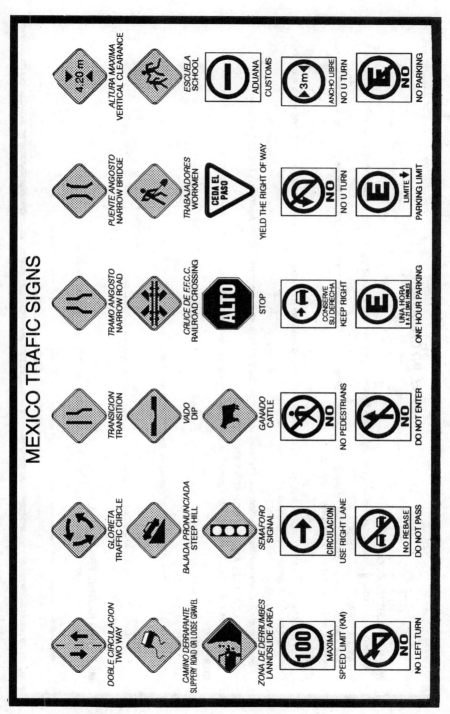

DOBLE CIRCULACION
TWO WAY

GLORIETA
TRAFFIC CIRCLE

TRANSICION
TRANSITION

TRAMO ANGOSTO
NARROW ROAD

PUENTE ANGOSTO
NARROW BRIDGE

ALTURA MAXIMA
VERTICAL CLEARANCE

CAMINO DERRAPANTE
SLIPPERY ROAD OR LOOSE GRAVEL

BAJADA PRONUNCIADA
STEEP HILL

VADO
DIP

CRUCE DE F.F.C.C.
RAILROAD CROSSING

TRABAJADORES
WORKMEN

ESCUELA
SCHOOL

ZONA DE DERRUMBES
LANDSLIDE AREA

SEMAFORO
SIGNAL

GANADO
CATTLE

STOP

CEDA EL PASO
YIELD THE RIGHT OF WAY

ADUANA
CUSTOMS

MAXIMA (KM)
SPEED LIMIT

CIRCULACION
USE RIGHT LANE

CONSERVE SU DERECHA
KEEP RIGHT

NO PEDESTRIANS

ANCHO LIBRE
NO U TURN

NO LEFT TURN

DO NOT PASS

ONE HOUR PARKING

DO NOT ENTER

NO U TURN

NO PARKING

UNA HORA
UNA HORA
ONE HOUR PARKING

LIMITE
PARKING LIMIT

53

GENERAL INFORMATION

WHEN TO VISIT MEXICO

Mexico is an exciting vacationland where you can enjoy fiestas, sports events, sightseeing, fishing, swimming and exploring all year long.

WHAT TO WEAR

Take low-heeled walking shoes, sports wear for traveling and at resorts, dresses and suits for cities and evenings, coats or sweaters for chilly weather and rainwear for occasional showers.

MEALS

American, Mexican or international cuisines are available. At higher elevations main meals are customarily served during early afternoon, followed by light dining in the evening.

ACCOMMODATIONS

Good hotels, motels, courts and inns display rates authorized by the Mexican Government at the front desk and in each room.

POSTAL, TELEPHONE AND TELEGRAPH SERVICES

Post Offices are found in all cities, towns and villages. Telephone and telegraph services are available in all important centers.

CURRENCY

Due to the fluctuation of the value of the peso, it is best to inquire as to the current value before taking your trip.

GALLONS AND LITERS

Gasoline is sold by the liter. There are about 4 liters (3.8) to one gallon

Gallons	1	5	10	20
Liters	3.8	18.9	38.0	76.0

MILES AND KILOMETERS

Distance is measured in kilometers. One mile equals 1.6 km. One kilometer equals .6 miles.

Miles	1	5	10	20
Kilometers	1.6	8.0	16.0	32.0

Coming to Mexico?
Don't Leave Your Manners Behind!

Good manners are important everywhere and especially in Mexico among all social classes. The possible exceptions where courtesy is not always observed seem to be where "time and space" are a factor, such as standing in lines for most business transactions, in banks, grocery store lines and other similar situations, lines where getting a seat is the prime objective, or when driving is the case. These situations are all entirely "each man for himself," and the good manners get lost in the shuffle. Exceptions such as those mentioned could be said about anywhere we might live, and perhaps just seem more noticeable to us here because of the otherwise extreme courtesy usually used.

In Mexico it is always polite to say *"por favor"* (please) when asking a request for anything, and certainly one must remember to say *"gracias"* (thank you) and *"de nada"* (you're welcome); even when the request is considered to be a routine chore or part of a job, these polite phrases are expected.

Greetings are also an important part of each day, and show that one has good manners, or is "educated." One should use the appropriate greeting for the time of day, such as *"buenas días"* ("good morning", before noon), *"buenas tardes"* ("good afternoon", until dusk), and *"buenas noches"* (good evening and good night). These expressions can also be used as a farewell, or of course, one may simply say *"adios."*

Using the correct form of address is something one should be aware of. For instance, girls or unmarried women are addressed as *"señorita"*, married women are *"señoras"*, boys or young teenagers are *"joven"* (pronounced HO-ven), a young child is *"niño"*, a man is *"señor"*, and in the case of an older man or women, it is a sign of respect to address them using *"don"* or *"doña"* before their full name.

When dining in a restaurant, unless one asks for the bill or *"la cuenta,"* it might be a long waiting period, since it is considered impolite to be presented with the check unless asked for. Dining is a very social, relaxing affair and should never be rushed.

If you are leaving a group it is customary to say *"con permiso"* (excuse me), just as it is polite to do anywhere. *"Perdón"* is also used for "excuse me". When someone performs an act of kindness or does a special favor it is proper to say *"muy amable"* (very kind of you).

Mexican people are very hospitable and generous, and will say *"mi casa es su casa"* (my house is your house) when they welcome you to their home. Quite often you will find yourself the recipient of a small item that you have admired.

55

Your good judgment should be used as to whether or not you should keep it. Remember, it's the thought that counts!

One common error made frequently by United States citizens is the reference to their being "American" or being from America. Mexicans are proud that they too are American, and sometimes feel the term excludes them. One should correctly refer to themselves as an *"americano del norte"* ("person from the United States") in order to avoid a touchy situation.

When traveling, it is well to keep in mind the simple courtesies that are always appreciated, while also allowing for the differences in customs and culture. **Good manners are never out of style!**

How to Travel and Live Happily in Mexico

by Ilsa Hoffman

Mexico is a beautiful country, with gorgeous mountains, lakes, beaches, deserts, courteous and very hospitable people, and above all, incomparable weather! Five hundred years of a mixed Indian-Spanish culture and traditions have made this country an exotic one, a land full of mystery. Although Mexico is not for everyone, it can be very appealing to those foreigners who are willing to leave behind their life style with more rigorous standards of excellence. Here are some simple tips for those who want to explore and enjoy the ins and outs of a foreign land, which is so near, and yet, so far.

1. It would be wise to leave your standards of efficiency behind and enjoy the pleasant contrast of being in a stress-free place where time has not so much meaning. *Mañana* (tomorrow) can be any morning of any week, month or year! Therefore, when a service required is promised for *mañana*, it does not necessarily mean it will be ready tomorrow.

2. Avoid the famous "Montezuma's Revenge" (strong diarrhea) by taking care of what you put in your mouth! Mexican food is not just *tacos*. It encompasses a large assortment of delicious dishes that nourish the Mexican people very well, but can be dangerous to the sensitive stomachs of foreigners, whose immune system is not used to the local bacteria or spicy food. Tap water is not safe for drinking. Drink bottled, purified, filtered, or treated water (drugstores sell drops for such purpose). Avoid raw vegetables and salads containing lettuce. Preferably peel fruits and vegetables, but if you want to eat the skins, wash them with soap and rinse afterwards with bottled water. Don't eat any dairy product that does not show a well-known brand name or say *pasteurizado*. Peasants around Guadalajara manufacture a lot of cheeses and dairy products with *leche bronca* (non-pasteurized milk).

3. Large cities have very good medical resources including hospitals with English-speaking doctors, but isolated areas lack them. Note that even the best hotel chains do not provide their guests with emergency medical care. If you want to visit a remote beach or mountain, ask your travel agent about emergency medical facilities. Also, have on hand a list of the telephone numbers of air ambulance services for possible emergencies.

4. After getting directions to find a place, be sure to double check by asking the same question to someone else. If both answers coincide, you are most likely on the right track. Be aware that Mexican politeness sometimes goes to the extreme of giving wrong directions, rather than not giving them at all.

5. Dress properly, according to the how you see local people dress. City people in this country usually don't walk around in shorts or tight sleeveless T-shirts.

Leave the beachwear for the resorts if you want to avoid wolf whistles. Also, avoid flirting or being very friendly to someone of the opposite sex when his or her spouse or partner is present. Mexicans can be quite jealous.

6. Make a copy of all your important papers (passport, FMT-tourist visa) to carry in your wallet, and leave the originals in a hotel safe or put them in a hide-in wallet. In the San Juan de Dios public market (also called Libertad market) you can buy very thin wallets (passport size) in which to keep your money, traveler's checks, credit cards, and documents. These wallets have a loop to pass through your belt and are worn tucked inside your trousers or skirt, so that they are readily accessible.

7. Courtesy is very important in this country. Mexican people are not as direct as Americans. In initiating conversations, Mexicans tend to "beat around the bush". For example: if you have a complaint about your hotel room, service, or food, do not bring the complaint up right away. Start by asking, "How are you today? Did you sleep well? How is your daughter doing in school?" When the person you are talking to sees that you care about him first, he will be ready to pay attention to your complaint. A good dose of politeness and patience always oils the wheels.

8. Avoid making unfavorable comparisons between your country and Mexico. This Mexico, my beloved land, is definitely another culture, not better, not worse, just different. Enjoy the differences and explore the country, but be careful about the places you visit. Most places are safe, but it is wise to check first with local people. Don't play "el valiente" (foolhardy), because you might find unwanted surprises.

9. Although the cost of living in Mexico and Guadalajara is less than the U.S., it is definitely no longer a steal. It is better to think of this city in terms of very nice weather, and also in terms of the multitude of experiences and adventures in the cosmopolitan/colonial setting, which Guadalajara offers to the open-minded tourist.

10. Tipping is very important in Mexico since wages and salaries are low and employees depend on the tips they receive. Always tip generously when you feel you have received service "beyond the call of duty" (15%), less if it was not particularly satisfactory (10%). Don't over-tip, 10 to 15% is enough, but if you don't tip at all, leave quickly, and don't go back.

11. And now the final and most important commandment of all: play it cool and stay out of trouble. For example, avoid hassles with traffic cops, immigration people, landlords, and sales or service people. You are in a different culture; your complaints might not be understood as your standards of justice might not necessarily correspond to those you find in Mexico. Also, avoid getting involved in heated arguments and indiscreet "affairs of the heart". Don't get drunk, and don't get caught with drugs, unless you are prepared to hibernate in an uncomfortable Mexican jail for some years. Keep a low profile!

Tipping in Mexico

In Mexico, it is always customary to give a tip to persons who offer services, and listed below are suggestions to help you decide who to tip and how much. These figures (expressed in U.S. dollars) are merely guidelines, and you may want to adjust them according to the quality of service, along with the possibilities of your pocketbook.

Restaurants - 10% of the bill is the norm. 15% could be used if the person who attended you was especially hassled with extra orders, etc., but is considered a little excessive by Mexican standards. Don't fall into the standard north-of-the-border problem of "so much for the bar attendant, so much for the food attendant" - just tip on the total and let them figure it out; tips are usually pooled and shared among all the employees, including the kitchen staff.

Parking Valets - In a public parking lot, if valet-attended, 30 cents (U.S.) is sufficient for the delivery of your car. If your car is taken away at a top-class restaurant or hotel, $1.00 would be in order when it is delivered. **Always demand a receipt for your car.**

Airport luggage attendants and bell boys - $2.00 for a loaded luggage cart. $1.00 for a single bag. In some restaurants and hotels, tipping is already included in the price for their normal services - this point will be made very clear to you at check-in or on the menu. If you wish to give more, it's a matter of personal choice.

Hotel maids - Tipping maids is not customary, unless a special service (extra towels, etc.) is solicited. $1.00 to $2.00 is normal, depending on the favor. A $2.00 to $3.00 dollar tip would be in order if you left a hotel room in bad shape; in a lot of hotels, these women are paid per room cleaned, and you could affect their salary terribly if they need to spend hours cleaning up.

Gas station attendants - no tip is necessary, except for special services - for a complete check (tires, oil, radiator), 75 cents to a $1.00 is customary. Some Mexicans still do give a very small tip, say 10-20 cents, for a fill-up, a persisting custom from years ago when these attendants worked exclusively for tips.

Beauty shop operators and barbers - 10% of the bill.

Taxi drivers - no tip is necessary - any luggage or parcel carrying or loading was very carefully calculated and included when you were quoted a price.

Public Sanitation Workers - On Mexican standards, this is a **must** - although they will take the garbage away if no tip is left, you will begin to notice small defects in the service, like a percentage of your garbage will be left thrown on the street, in direct proportion to the time that has passed with no tipping; 30 to 50 cents a week is the standard tip - don't give any more. If you dispose of an exaggerated quantity of garbage, like after "spring" cleaning or a big clean-up, a $1.00 to $2.00 tip should be offered, or they simply will not take it away. Like any sanitation service, fits are thrown when garden cuttings are put out, but offering a special tip like the one mentioned will usually smooth things over. This tipping scale should be used when municipal garbage trucks service your area - in certain private or access controlled subdivisions, garbage collection is already included in the subdivisions monthly charge, and no tipping is necessary. Find out from your neighbors.

Supermarket grocery-baggers - A full grocery cart of goods carried to your car should be tipped at 50 cents - an extra heavy load, $1.00. These kids will also wheel a load home for you if you live within a couple of blocks of the store, and then the tip should be doubled or tripled, depending on the distance. In some parts of the country, it is customary to tip 5-10 cents for bagging a small load, even if you are going to carry it, as a form of charity. If a boy or girl wants to work in the big supermarket chains for tips, he or she must prove that they are attending school. Never shop around one o'clock for a big load of groceries if you are going to need help carrying it and are in a hurry - the morning shift at school has just let out, and the afternoon shift is just starting, so usually there are no baggers. Also no training is given as to bagging techniques - so watch out, especially with the younger kids, that your bread or tomatoes don't land underneath the canned goods! Similar carrying services can be obtained at the public markets, and should be tipped aproximately the same.

Kids wanting to "watch-dog" your car when parked on a public street - don't laugh at this - it's not begging, or anything near it - these children are surprisingly responsible, and do perform a very useful function - this author once went to a soccer game, leaving her car in the care of a couple of the neighborhood youngsters - a tire went flat (a nail picked up on the way to the stadium), and these kids talked the stadium entrance guards into letting them in to look for me to let me know what had happened - they found me in a crowd of over 50,000 people. That's service! 50 cents per hour is more than sufficient.

Unlike the United States, where a pittance of a tip is considered the way to let a person know that you were not pleased with their services, in Mexico leaving **no** tip sends the same message. Tipping is **never** forgotten by Mexicans, as they know that salaries are a lot lower than you'd ever imagine (a day's work in Mexico is paid like an hour's work in the U.S. and other countries). Don't assume that the person helping you is a salaried "employee" - many times they are allowed to work exclusively for tips. This may include bell boys, waiters and waitresses, parking valets, airport valets, etc.

We would like to mention a touchy point at this time - not quite the same, but highly related - street sellers, performers and beggars. There is no welfare in Mexico - you work or you literally starve. These people seem pathetic and heart-wrenching, but unfortunately, are mostly professional beggars, commonly called "*Marias*", who drift into the big cities from the isolated mountain villages, and find begging a quick way to survive. Usually speaking no Spanish, the father works on a construction site as a watchman (salary and lodging included) and the wife and children go out for the day to see what they can pick up. The government frowns on "direct donations" to these people, and has tried to channel them into useful activities, but with little success. We have seen these professional beggars' children receive hundreds of dollars per family in an evening on the streets of Puerto Vallarta, up to $20.00 a "hit"! Your money would be better spent and put to better use with an established charity, such as "*Caritas*." But use your own judgment; is the person able-bodied? or is it an older or physically impaired person really incapable of labor? The latter really need the money, and a few cents will go a long way.

Foreigners have a terrible reputation as far as tipping in Mexico, and usually fall into two categories; either far too extravagant and way out of the ball park according to Mexican standards, or not tipping at all when it is really expected and needed, making the person look like a fool, or a Scrooge. **Never** ask the person offering any service what they expect for a tip; you will be taken to the cleaners. A maximum of 25% of what you would offer north of the border probably will be more than enough. I once saw a grocery boy asked by an American lady what he expected for a tip; without one blink of the eye, $5.00 was the suggested - and paid - amount.

We hope this article gives you an general idea about tipping in Mexico, and we have tried to cover most situations in which tipping is expected and customary.

III

Obtaining Housing - Rentals and Purchase

La Casa de Toña Mexico

Renting a House or Apartment

Perhaps the most frustrating thing you will encounter upon your arrival in Mexico is searching for a house or an apartment. Have patience. You will find what you want. Our suggestion is to stay in a <169>suites hotel<170> where you can do your own cooking. Take a relaxed look at the city, meet other friends, and start your search.

There are many ways to find houses and apartments for rent. In Guadalajara look in the daily newspaper El Informador, or visit the American Society office at Av. San Francisco #3332 in Chapalita and check their bulletin board. There are also bulletins posted at Sandi book store, at Av. Tepeyac #718, near the intersection with Av. Las Rosas, and Gigante and other supermarkets frequently have bulletin boards. More important - talk with other Americans - the best and least expensive rentals are found by word of mouth. In the Lake Chapala area the major real estate brokers, such as Chapala Realty and Sunset Realty have many rentals.

If you don't own or want to drive your car you can engage an English-speaking expert on rentals and real estate. The cost of this service is minimal. Another possibility is to use a tour guide or taxi driver. Determine the cost of their services beforehand. Help from these people may be well worth the money. There are guides usually found around hotels and motels. Ask the bell boys.

A house or apartment to suit your needs and budget will be found somewhere - it will just take a little time and effort. The writer's first apartment was completely furnished, in a nice neighborhood convenient to food stores and shopping facilities. It included a nicely furnished living room, dining room, kitchen, two bedrooms, den, two baths and balcony (porch) overlooking the street.

The months of May through October are best for house hunting since winter visitors (snow birds) have gone back to the United States or Canada, but good apartments and houses are always available.

Large cities in Mexico are like busy metropolitan areas in the United States with the usual heavy traffic problems. However, with lack of effective exhaust emission controls on buses, trucks and other vehicles, a certain amount of air pollution is present. This is noticeable especially on narrow streets in the downtown area and along busy traffic arteries. When looking for an apartment try to find one located a few blocks from a busy street (convenient but not contaminated). We have not found this problem to outweigh the many plus factors of retirement here. Having lived in or near large cities in the United States where air pollution also exists we are not particularly bothered by it.

Look for the following when renting in Mexico:

- Is there a telephone? If not, installation may be expensive and you may have a long wait.
- Are there adequate electrical outlets throughout? Wiring adequate for an electric heater? Fuse box or circuit breaker?
- Is the water heater automatic? Properly vented? Is the gas supply either two propane tanks with a valve to switch from an empty tank to the full tank (or a large-capacity stationary tank which is automatically filled under contract)?
- Location on busy street subject to noise, exhaust fumes?
- Are there screens on doors and windows?
- Is the neighborhood to your liking? Adequate trees, convenient to grocery market, pharmacy, and public transportation?
- Would you feel secure? Door and window locks adequate and in working condition? How about when you go to the States or take other trips?

Once you get settled into your house or apartment you can really begin to enjoy living in Mexico.

What About Rental Housing in Guadalajara?
by Ilse Hoffmann

As with any long distance move, finding good housing is of primary concern. However, suitable accommodations may be found in Guadalajara with some time, effort and patience.

One of the first steps many people take upon arriving in Guadalajara is to go to a "Suites Hotel" (equivalent to an efficiency apartment) for the first few days or weeks. Most of these "suites" are one bedroom apartments with a small living area, bath and kitchenette, offering a comfortable place to live where you may prepare breakfast and light meals, gradually become acquainted with the city, and take time to look for more permanent housing.

The suites are managed like a hotel with daily, weekly and monthly rates, furnishing linens and maid service. Most come with basic kitchen utensils and dishes. Some have secure parking areas, swimming pools and recreation areas; they are usually less expensive than a hotel, and of course much more comfortable.

We definitely recommend suites hotels for those looking to establish residence in Guadalajara, however, there are many hotels with standard accommodations and a full range of prices. Suites hotels are very popular with "snowbirds", and persons who visit Guadalajara for just a few weeks.

After you are settled in a suite or hotel, you will soon be ready to look for

66

more permanent housing. As in the case of any rental in any country, you should establish your high and low priorities for the following items: the amount or range of rent you are willing to pay; apartment or house; furnished or unfurnished accommodations; number of bedrooms and bathrooms; size of the living space; convenience to shopping areas, and other public services such as post offices, banks, laundries, entertainment and cultural centers, etc.; and finally, certain idiosyncrasies of Mexico, such as a telephone, gas installation, water supply and TV facilities.

The following is some general information that will be helpful to a newcomer to Guadalajara!

Telephone: The availability of a telephone is a huge controlling factor in deciding to take a rental or not. Usually, apartments with telephones are not the nicest or newest ones. This situation is slowly changing, but to get a line installed is still involves some waiting.

Unfurnished Apartments and Houses: An unfurnished apartment most likely will not include a refrigerator. Sometimes a stove is built in. The kitchen will have a sink and built-in cabinets. The bathroom, apart from toilet, shower and sink, may have a mirror only, but no built-in cabinets.

Furnished Houses and Apartments: Furnished houses are rare, except on a very temporary basis (like a house-sitting arrangement). The most common type of furnished apartment is the Suites Hotel, as we already mentioned, but some good furnished apartments are available, if you come before November. In January they are scarce.

Furniture: There are a number of solid wood Mexican style furniture manufacturers. One store provided a couple with furniture for a whole house (Two bedrooms with chest of drawers, two bed boards, and two night tables (mattresses are bought separately), upholstered living room set, dining room set with hutch, a TV bookcase and a desk) for $2,500 U.S. This kind of furniture can be easily sold in a "package deal"to other foreigners and even Mexicans, should you decide to move. This style furniture is very versatile and wear-resistant; it can be varnished, painted, or decorated a thousand ways, and its rustic style actually improves as it gets older. (see appendix for more on package deals.)

Bathrooms: Tubs are rare; nearly all bathrooms have showers only. They may or may not have cabinets for storage. Many places also have half baths (W.C. and sink) as well.

Condition of the Property: All rentals are "AS IS"; if the owner has any repairs in mind, they will be done before putting a rental on the market. This detail, of course, is a direct factor in determining the rent. One very nice thing about Mexican construction is its solidity: all concrete and brick structure; tiled floors, bathrooms and kitchens; hardwood carpentry; metal or aluminum window frames that rarely stick, and of course, never rot; electrical installations almost never are a fire risk (the wires are embedded in brick walls); etc. Houses and apartments are built to really last, and permanent damage can only be inflicted in the case of someone trying to "trash" a property. Any damage you see will be only superficial, and usually nothing a bucket of soapy water, a few nails and hammer, and a coat of paint won't solve.

In Mexico, there are no specific retiree communities, such as Sun City in Phoenix, where only retired people live. In Guadalajara, Americans are scattered throughout various districts, and live in all parts of the city, however, most live in the southwestern, western and northwestern areas. The eastern part of Guadalajara is not very residential, as it's full of industries. The residential areas are called colonias or fraccionamientos (subdivisions), and were developed as the city grew. There are over 300 colonias in Guadalajara; we have listed some of the most popular with foreign residents (and Mexicans, too) and a generalized description of each: an important factor for determining property costs (and rent prices) is if a subdivision is "open" (businesses are allowed anywhere), "semi-closed" (permitted only on principal avenues) or "closed" (absolutely no businesses) to commercial activity. Nobody cares to live next door to a loud machine shop, or have their driveway constantly blocked by inconsiderate people shopping at a store. Take this into account when you are renting. Some people have a very low tolerance for noise or a lot of people.

Colonia Chapalita: Chapalita was one of the first "residential subdivisions" created in Guadalajara, distinguishing itself from the barrios, or older neighborhoods or districts as they are called, with parks, wide avenues (side streets are very narrow), and an excellent urban infrastructure (open to commercial activity): almost anything you need is within walking distance. It's also the home of the American Society. As "a middle of the line" subdivision (not the cheapest nor the most expensive), it's a good basis for "ball park" rental prices; we will then compare these prices with other subdivisions.

- Boarding Houses in Chapalita can provide meals and a nice family environment. They run from $20 U.S. per person per day for bed and breakfast, and up to $30 U.S. per day per person for three meals a day.

- Furnished One Bedroom Apartments with a very small living room, kitchen and bath, suitable for single persons only or maybe a couple if they are not very demanding, rent for $300 per month. Most do not have a telephone.

- Furnished Two Bedroom Apartments with very simple furniture, basically the essentials, rent from $400 up. A fairly good two bedroom furnished apartment with telephone will usually be $550 or more.

- Unfurnished apartments are easier to find, but rents are not much lower, since the furniture is usually considered valueless in the owner's eyes. They range, sometimes with a telephone, from $350 to $500.

- Large unfurnished houses with three or four bedrooms, usually older and not in good repair, range from $500 to $700.

Colonia Providencia: This area is a much newer, more exclusive subdivision, with wider streets and a number of parks: semi-closed to commercial activity. It is more expensive than Chapalita, and a furnished apartment with a telephone will run $600 up.

Ciudad del Sol: Also a very exclusive subdivision, with wide streets and beautiful residences. There are a number of apartment houses, with rents running a bit higher than Chapalita. Although semi-closed to commercial activity, it's located next to Plaza del Sol, considered the largest shopping center in Latin America.

La Calma: Also a nice neighborhood, much newer than Chapalita, with good parks; however, no large shopping centers are really close, so shopping can be a problem on foot. Furnished two bedroom apartments with a telephone will start at around $500 U.S. Unfurnished apartments with a telephone are available at $450.

Las Fuentes: A cozy "suburb" (there used to be an undeveloped buffer zone between Guadalajara and Las Fuentes, but not anymore), with quaint cobble stone streets, compounds which hold 10 to 15 houses, beautiful garden areas, pools and other amenities. It is convenient, semi-closed to commercial activity, has good public transportation, and a brand-new shopping center nearby. There also is a farmer's market with fresh fish, meat, vegetables, fruits and flowers. The American Legion is located here, offering a lot of social activity. Rents can vary, as there are less desirable one bedroom apartments renting for $400 U.S., or very nice accommodations from $600 U.S..

Colinas de San Javier, El Country, Santa Anita, Ciudad Bugambilias, El Palomar: The most exclusive areas in town; practically 100% closed to commercial activity; the houses tend to be larger and more luxurious, very few apartments have been constructed, and rents are higher than other areas we have mentioned. There are very few furnished houses available for rent in these areas. American companies now establishing themselves in Guadalajara often rent houses in these subdivisions for their executives.

Near "The Arches" and Minerva Circle: Several large and very nice buildings are located in this area (the first apartment complexes built in Guadalajara). Well maintained, one and two bedroom furnished apartments, with a telephone, run from $450 up. Also a very nice furnished three bedroom, two bath apartment with telephone and TV cable could rent for $600. This area is considered 100% open to commercial activity.

Villa Universitaria, Monraz, Lomas de Guevara, Prados Providencia: These are all close to the Universidad Autónoma de Guadalajara, and there are a large number of buildings designed for students that rent inexpensive apartments, although generally in very poor repair. If you don't mind the noise, heavy metal music, parties, horns honking, etc., you will be able to find a nice spacious apartment before the semester begins in August or January. Villa Universitaria also has very exclusive residential sections, consisting of dead-end streets.

Puerta de Hierro, Santa Isabel, Atlas Colomos, Lomas del Bosque, Royal Country: are the newest subdivisions in Guadalajara, and very exclusive. They consist of a series of beautiful, tree-lined central avenues, with off-shooting closed compounds, each compound containing 20 to 50 houses. Security guards guaranty your privacy and safety. Houses will rent here for no less than $2,500 a month.

Downtown: Never judge a Mexican home from the outside: some surprisingly nice, very spacious apartments and houses can be found near the downtown area for a reasonable price, especially along Chapultepec Avenue, and on certain side streets. There are two or three bed and breakfasts for foreigners which run from $15 to $20 a day, with lower monthly rates available.

Deposits usually are required when renting an apartment or house. The custom is one month's rent for a security deposit and the first and last months rent, particularly if there is a telephone. Some landlords may not require the last months rent in advance. A co-signer (fiador) is often required.

Taking into account extra expenses to be encountered the first one or two months of living in Mexico one should budget extra funds.

As a rule of thumb one shouldn't pay monthly rent in excess of one third of his monthly income. Individuals who have income of less than $800 U.S. a month may find it difficult, though not impossible, to find suitable housing accommodations. There are always bargains to be found! After living in Guadalajara for awhile and getting to know the area and other people you will learn of these. Couples with $1,500 U.S. each month can make it and be reasonably comfortable, but with no luxuries or splurges.

In spite of the difficulties you may encounter in finding the ideal place, if you are willing to leave behind the amenities and luxuries that you used to have at home, and change any efficient-punctual-machine oriented styles for a more relaxed, human-oriented style, you will find that the wonderful weather and the social and cultural opportunities will provide a very challenging and worthwhile living experience in Guadalajara.

(Suites hotels that are popular with Americans are Motel Isabel, Hotel Suites Bernini, Suites Country Club and Margarita Suites. Should you want assistance in finding housing in Guadalajara telephone 647-3912.)

(Editors note: The prices of rentals quoted above were current at the time this book was published. They may be either more or less at the time of your arrival in the Guadalajara area.)

Rentals and Housing in the Lakeside Area
by Ilse Hoffmann

The Lake Chapala area, which lies some thirty-five miles south of Guadalajara, contains some of the most unique scenery and glorious weather to be found anywhere in the world. Whether one plans to stay forever or only for a few weeks, you must have, even in Mexico, a roof over your head.

What about housing in the lakeside area? Bottom line: cheaper than Guadalajara!

When first coming in and while waiting for jet/car lag to wear off, one can find many interesting and inexpensive hotels, motels, bed and breakfast places, and boarding houses in which to park overnight or longer. Some of them have mini-kitchens where you can at least make yourself the first morning cup of coffee and fill your body with some fuel to get ready for the house-hunt of the day. Such places are scattered all over the place, in downtown Chapala, Ajijic, San Juan Cosalá and Jocotepec, but also along the road that connects the lakeside towns.

Once you are settled in a decent hotel, you will soon be ready to look for more permanent housing. As in the case of any rental in any country, you should establish your high and low set of priorities for the following items: the amount of rent you are willing to pay; whether you want an apartment or a house; furnished or unfurnished; number of bedrooms and bathrooms; size of the living space; convenience to shopping areas and other public services, such as post offices, banks, laundries, entertainment and cultural center, etc.

Finally, and most important, since the telephone service in the lakeside area is still a major issue, you will have to set it as an important priority, the same with TV facilities (satellite antenna). This situation is slowly changing, but to get a telephone line installed is still a long wait and quite expensive.

Housing:

There are a considerable number of houses and apartments available in the lakeside area, either for temporary ("snow birds") or on a permanent rental basis. Some are owned by foreigners who place their houses on the rental market for several months of the year. The best idea in the beginning is to visit one or more of the several real estate agencies. Another suggestion might be to stop by the well-known Lake Chapala Society, drug stores, supermarkets, stationary stores that have a large bulletin board with a display of rental ads.

Furnished Accommodations:

Most of the houses along the lakeside available for newcomers are furnished, since landlords assume tenants are "temporary," who come only for the winter season with their suitcases. Some include most of the amenities of an American house: living room with fireplace, dining room, large terrace, two bedrooms, two baths (some with jacuzzi or marble Roman tub), kitchen with all electrical appliances (even dishwasher, microwave, washing machine and dryer, dishes, pottery, linens, etc.) plus telephone, pool and satellite antenna TV, maid and gardener services, all utilities included in the basic price. These houses have spectacular panoramic views of the lake, but there is a price to pay. Such houses are usually between $1000 and $2000 a month.

Less expensive accommodations and availability:

There are, of course, much less expensive rentals which start as low as $275 per month for a furnished bedroom, kitchen/den, and bath. The average range of rents for fairly nice furnished places along the entire lakeside area is between $400-$700. Unfortunately, it is very difficult to point out where to look for housing in the $275, $250, $400 or $700 range since houses and apartments are scattered all over the area. Therefore, the best idea is to pay close attention to any house accommodation tip you can get, whether it is through real estate agencies, local newspapers, bulletin boards, or best of all, word of mouth. Do not disregard any tip, since house accommodations are scarce during the winter season. Once you find something that more or less suites your taste, be sure to take it. As beautiful as Mexico can be, it will never be as ideal as your own home.

What to expect from an average furnished house or apartment:

Every house is different. Some are rented monthly, others for six months or a year, especially the larger houses, and a lease is required, along with first, last and one-month security (refundable) deposit when signing the lease, and also an additional refundable deposit for the telephone. Some houses and apartments are nicely carpeted, furnished, with dishes, pottery, linens and utilities payments included, even maid and gardener service, and the rent is surprisingly reasonable. On the other hand, you might find a nondescript place with ugly furniture and an even uglier price tag, but in a spectacular setting! It's eventually a case of setting priorities. Most furnished apartments or houses include Mexican rustic-style furniture (the basics) for:

Living room area: three-piece sofa set, coffee table, side table, one lamp and a small rug. No TV's, but you can rent or buy one.

Dining room: Table, six chairs, a small hutch with china for six.

Two bedrooms: One with two single beds, one with king size, a small chest of drawers, a chair, sheets, blankets, pillows, bedspreads.

Bathrooms: A sink (some have a cabinet with counter), a shower (very few have a tub) and a toilet, of course. Towels included.

Kitchen: Most have integrated cabinets, some pottery, cutlery, and dishes, with gas stove, sink and a small refrigerator. Very few have electrical appliances, mostly a blender, coffeepot and iron. Some have a washing machine, dryer, or even microwave, but that is if you are lucky. However, there is a number of laundromats around the area. Even maid service is so inexpensive that you may be able to afford a maid to pamper you.

Let's now start to visit some of the residential subdivisions alongside lovely Lake Chapala. Imagine now that you have just been greeted by one of the most marvelous vistas this side of paradise. Almost immediately you will encounter some of the best neighborhoods in the area. The following subdivisions are the principal ones in the Chapala area.

Chapala Haciendas: North of Chapala, with a great view of the lake. Like some people, the area is a little older, though it is very nice. Excellent water supply. Houses with parabolic and phone start around $600, fully furnished (Note: unless otherwise indicated, lakeside rentals come with all necessary furniture, dishes, pottery, etc.) There is also a hotel here which caters to the American/Canadian tourist trade.

Brisas de Chapala: Even better view of lake and mountains. Situated along an abandoned golf course. Secured area, cobble stoned streets. Rentals begin at about $450 for a very nicely furnished house with panoramic view, large windows, one bedroom, two baths, equipped kitchen, large patio and garden area. Rental includes gardener service and water. Tenant pays gas, electricity and maid. There is also a hotel there, but opinions vary as to whether it is open for business.

Las Redes: Before you reach the town of Chapala (right at the Pemex gas station just north of town), turn left and enter a divided cobble-stone street. Rather rundown area, but with excellent bargains. Example: 4 bedrooms, 3 baths, jacuzzi, phone, carpeted for $400 a month.

Vista del Lago: Fifteen minutes east of downtown Chapala. Sports and excellent nine hole golf course, with clubhouse. Enclosed security- protected enclave. Mini-estates sell as high as half-million dollars, with rentals to match. Smaller houses (many with satellite and telephone) can be had from $700+. On the road to San Nicolás, you will find on the left a couple of arches bordering the entrance with the name of the subdivision, one of the most exclusive areas, though a little far from Chapala and Ajijic social life. If you have a car and are a golf fan, you can do no better than Vista del Lago.

Chapala: Hub of Lakeside. Many military retirees. American Legion Post. Good restaurants, shops and services. Rentals from $300 up. Preferred area for foreigners with fixed and limited income.

Lourdes: Unlike its famous namesake in France, not the spot for the infirm or weak of will. Steep hill, cobble-stone street leads to local shrine. Nice view, clean area, well-furnished houses, one with 2 bedrooms, 2 1/2 baths, beautiful grounds, and a spectacular view of the lake, gardener included, for $750. Less expensive houses can be found in this small subdivision.

Riberas del Pilar: Few miles west of Chapala. Wooded, quiet, by the lake. Weekend retreat for many Mexicans from Guadalajara. Rents with phone and dish start around $500. One bedroom garden/compound apartments with pool start at $275, utilities included.

Chula Vista: The Beverly Hills of the area. Many homes have spectacular view of the lake and mountains, with a beautiful nine-hole golf course. Rentals start from $700, but in the lower area there are small, one bedroom apartments at $300. Potable water.

San Antonio Tlacoyapan: Typical Mexican town. Excellent bilingual school nearby. Relatively inexpensive. Rents start at about $300. Ideal for fixed income retirees or couple with school children. Not many rentals available.

La Floresta: Fairly new beautiful area close to lake with two hotels. Excellent security and large houses with cobble- stoned wide-arbored streets. Rents might start from $600 up. No small apartments. Best nursing home for Americans located in this area.

Central Ajijic: Favorite spot for writers, artists (painters/sculptors), and poets. (Excellent writers' group meets the 1st and 3rd Fridays of every month.) Boasts good Little Theatre and facility. Many cultural activities; fine shops and restaurants. Pier for boating. Homes run gamut from humble to palatial. Rentals, often with guest houses, satellite dish and phone start about $600. It's possible, however, to find beautiful, fully furnished houses for less, or even occasionally apartments, but don't expect to get that lucky too soon. Area much in demand.

Upper Ajijic (mountain side):   Great houses with spectacular view. Rents from $600 up. Condos go from $450 up. Areas of particular interest are Mission del Lago, Lomas del Lago and Lomas de Ajijic.

Las Salvias, Villanova and Rancho del Oro: Sits north of the highway, just west of Ajijic. Good view, nice, new large houses with satellite and some with phone. Price range starts more or less from $600 up. In Villanova there is a compound of small apartments with pool that start at $400.

La Canacinta: Rather secluded. Few miles west of Ajijic. Charming area $400 and up.

San Juan Cosalá: Famous for mineral baths. Two health spas and small casitas available. Just northwest of town, the Racquet Club subdivision has nice large houses. Prices vary depending on the condition of the house.

El Chante: Less than 10 miles west of Ajijic. Charming little town, great favorite with upscale Mexicans. Rentals run less than Ajijic, and often come with large gardens, as area is one of least congested along the lake. $400 up.

Jocotepec: At western extreme of Lake Chapala. More typically native than any other area. Excellent shopping, open-air market, charming plaza. Few really good restaurants, however. Very reasonable rentals which can start as low as $300 per month, usually fully furnished.

Roca Azul: "Blue Rock". Considered by some to be on the "wrong side" of the lake (south), though it's certainly on the right side for people on limited incomes. Rents are about 25% cheaper than in the Ajijic area, for the same package. For those who don't mind the drive back over to the north side, Roca Azul is probably the best buy. Also very pretty. $450 up for furnished houses.

Puerto Corona: Further along south side of lake. Planned development. Many foreigners, closely knit enclave. Rentals from $400 up.

Lakeside Highway rentals: Along the Chapala-Jocotepec highway, you will see signs advertising furnished apartments, houses or even beautiful villas for rent; therefore, don't disregard any sign you see along the highway.

We hope this information will make your house/apartment hunting easier, and your stay more enjoyable.

(Editors note: The prices of rentals quoted above were current at the time this book was published. They may be either more or less at the time of your arrival in the Chapala area.)

Purchase or Construction of Housing

As a foreign resident you may own real estate in Mexico through a bank trust or you may own real estate in your own name. There are advantages to owning real estate in a bank trust since it is simple to transfer upon sale, or in case of death, since a Mexican will is not required.

Mexico has restrictions regarding foreign ownership within sixty-two miles of the border and thirty-one miles of the coast. You will need help from a notary when you consummate a real estate transaction.

A variety of housing is for sale. Most construction is concrete, brick and stone. Very little wood is used except in mountain villages, where it is more plentiful and a traditional part of the architecture.

The same principles apply in buying real estate in Mexico as in the United States. They are importance of location, convenience, quality of construction, clear land title, etc. It is a good idea to delay buying a house until you have lived in Mexico at least a few months and know where you would like to live permanently. As with rentals, shopping and patience are essential.

If you prefer to build your own home, costs in Mexico are lower than in the United States, depending on specifications. Many excellent architects are available at reasonable prices. Most times the architect serves as the general contractor for construction projects.

Real estate taxes in Mexico are ridiculously low, and not an important consideration when buying real estate. Since construction is mostly brick and mortar, residential fire dangers are fewer, and maintenance costs lower.

Thoughts on Buying Real Estate in Mexico

When considering the purchase of real estate in Mexico, remember that you are in a foreign country where construction techniques are different, and the laws, customs and practices are unlike those "back home". There is no consumer protection agency that will touch real estate problems (these go directly to the Civil or Criminal Courts), so any transaction has to be done right the first time to avoid major (and we mean **major**) problems. We have purchased real estate in Mexico, and have had no trouble in most of the cases, but, unfortunately, we have suffered through bad deals involving losses of thousands of dollars. Our intention is not to be pessimistic, but realistic and enlightening as to some of the possible pitfalls.

Our purchase of a small condominium is one of Guadalajara's best residential neighborhoods was a success because the property has steadily increased in value, more than doubling since we acquired it. On the other hand, it has also presented many problems common to condominium living everywhere (noise level, parking problems, dictatorial administrators, etc.).

Another investment was in a beautiful new development located beside a lake (not Lake Chapala). The developer was a "bible toting, quoting" American who was grossly undercapitalized and did not have all of the government permits required. We never received a proper deed (*escritura*) that had been approved by a Mexican Notary and properly recorded. Our house stands half completed and is in a legal tangle that may take years in the Mexican courts.

Even though we encountered problems, we are optimistic that there are excellent real estate investments in Mexico. One must use the same basic principals (most of all, common sense) for selecting potential real estate to purchase as would be used in the United States. However, the legal procedures are different, and must be carefully investigated and followed. Owning real estate in Mexico is one of the soundest and safest investments you can make: property values held up with flying colors throughout the bad inflation and peso devaluation periods of the 1980's.

Since you may be new to Mexico it is wise to talk with other Americans who have purchased real estate. Try to determine what problems they may have encountered and learn from their experiences. Determine which Notary they used and find out if the transaction was handled professionally and if the fees were reasonable. Closing costs are generally a little higher in Mexico than in the United States (approximately 10-12% of the appraisal value of the property). Find out if the notary will return telephone calls promptly. Make contact with a prospective notary and discuss their services and fees. We have found that the attorney's ability to speak English is important, but more important is character, honesty and the motivation to follow through with the work to be done.

There are many good real estate agents that are eager to help you find the type of house you are seeking. You may wish to work with more than one agent. In Guadalajara there is no multiple listing service, however, one has been organized in the Chapala area.

There are many beautiful residential areas in Guadalajara and at the Chapala Lakeside with real estate prices within a range affordable for most potential buyers. Choose a good location and design that will be attractive to others (Mexicans and Americans!) and will have a good resale potential. Other things to consider are: who will be your neighbors? what's on the other side of that high-walled fence? (especially at Chapala Lakeside).

The degree of effort put into looking, comparing and pricing real estate should be many times greater than you would use in the United States. Do not be taken in by the quaint neighborhood with cobble stone streets, the beautiful bougainvillea and other flowering shrubs, or the view. Look at the structure of the house (usually excellent - Mexican construction techniques are very sound and solid), and for an adequate supply of water, electricity, closet and storage space, bathrooms, kitchen and telephone service. If the swimming pool is not heated it will have limited usage.

Buying Real Estate in Mexico and The Mexican Notary Public
by John D. Bryant

Even as a tourist you may buy real estate in Mexico. This may be owned through a Mexican bank trust or in your own name. With a bank trust (*fideicomiso*) it is simple to transfer title upon sale through a Mexican notary public. Beneficiaries may be named in case of death. A Mexican will is not required.

Should you decide to own property in your own name a deed, called an *escritura*, **must be prepared by a Mexican notary public.** In some states in Mexico it is now possible to name beneficiaries in the deed, but if this is not the case it is well to have a Mexican will prepared to avoid expensive legal fees and probate at the time of death.

There are great differences between the United States notary public and Mexican notary public. In the United States the notary public may be the local butcher, the new accounts clerk at the bank, the secretary at the office, or practice any other occupation.

In Mexico, the notary public (*notario público*) is a public official appointed by the State Governor. He has the capacity to attest and certify documents and business and legal transactions that require authenticity. He also provides for strict security of original records and documents.

Some of the requirements for becoming a Mexican notary public are as follows: 1. must be a Mexican citizen; 2. must be thirty-five years of age; 3. have a law degree; 4. three years experience working in a notary public office; 5. must take and pass an examination and 6. if he passes, in time the governor will give him an appointment. There is supposed to be one notary for each 30,000 people.

In Mexico, every legal document, such as deeds, wills, powers of attorney, constitution of corporations, establishment of trusts and other legal transactions must be made before a notary public in order to be valid. If the document is not notarized by a Mexican notary public it is not legal!

When buying real estate and you reach an agreement, go to the notary public first. The buyer chooses the notary public. **For real estate transactions you do not need an attorney.** The notary public is completely capable and legally authorized to carry out the transaction. In many cases an attorney will delay the transaction, charge you unnecessary high fees, and have absolutely no bearing on the situation, as it is not of his competence. Before giving any type of down payment or committing yourself to a deal, take a copy of the actual *escritura* (which should be given to you by the seller with no argument if everything is in order) to the notary public to check the deed's validity.

If buying property from a developer have the notary public check to see that he has his permits for the development and for construction. A beautifully engraved certificate or formal letter promising a deed at some future time is not a deed, but merely a sales contract. Have the notary public determine that the land is not *ejido* land (communal agricultural land). The right to use this type of land can be purchased, but always a risky deal, as it is not **your** property, you're only allowed to use it.

Insist on making all real estate transfer agreements before a notary public. Do not be pressured by someone who says that you need to put money down right away.

The notary public will need from both parties to the transaction proof of full names, marriage certificates, proof of dates and place of birth, official identification with photograph, such as passport or driver's license, and your visa to prove that you are in Mexico legally.

The notary public will need from the seller: 1. His deed; 2. Up-to-date tax receipts, water bills, subdivision (*fraccionamiento*) fees, and any other public utilities bill, paid up to the date of sale. The notary public will determine capital gains taxes through an official appraisal. The capital gains tax, if any, is paid by the seller, however, through mutual agreement may be paid by the buyer. Make sure you know how much this will be—the notary will inform you of the cost before the transaction, almost to the cent. Cash or money changes hands the minute the seller signs over the deed, usually in the notary public's office. The buyer ordinarily pays notary fees incurred, which also must be paid when the title is signed over.

The process is not over yet — the notary public must register the *escritura* in the *Registro Público de la Propiedad* (Public Registry of Properties). This should be done promptly, as the transaction is not valid until registered. A normal time frame for this is around two weeks.

Property within sixty-two miles (100 kilometers) of the border and thirty-one miles (fifty kilometers) of the coast must be held in a bank trust. You will need a permit from the Secretary of Foreign Affairs.

The buyer may choose the bank that will handle his trust, and may want to shop around to determine where he can get the lowest fees.

Most real estate transactions in Mexico are not fraudulent, and they are fairly rare and definitely not the norm. Any transaction done with a notary public should not have any problems, as **he or she** is legally responsible that everything is in order. People who buy real estate in Mexico often invest their life savings in their "dream" retirement home, and everyone should be aware of Mexican laws and be cautious. Sometimes people are so impressed with the natural beauty and climate of Mexico that they "throw caution to the wind" or "leave their brains at the border." This has been referred to as "margarita fever."

Another consideration: Is the property you are thinking of buying readily marketable should you decide to return to the United States or your native country?

We have found that most real estate brokers and developers are honest and above board. Should their sales techniques be like those of a "time share" salesman pressing for "an impending happening close" for the transaction, be careful.

Basic safeguards on real estate purchase do not exist in Mexico as in the United States. There is no credit bureau to check on the developer's financial condition; it may be difficult to locate liens and there is no title insurance. For the typical person off the street, you need a notary public to hold your hand right from the first steps of the transaction —a title search takes him at the most a few days. If there is any potential problem, the notary public will not foul his good name and will let you know immediately.

Chances are that you will never have a problem when buying real estate in Mexico. Just be diligent in doing your "homework" and be a little more cautious!

FINANCING HOUSING
By John Bryant

Traditionally purchase of housing in Mexico has been on a "cash" basis. It is not possible for foreigners to borrow money from Mexican banks to purchase real estate. A house in Mexico is not acceptable as collateral for a bank loan from the United States. Should you have other collateral such as securities, real estate, cash value life insurance, etc., you may possibly be able to arrange such a loan with your bank or stockbroker in the United States. We know a couple who financed a house with their Master Card and Visa cards; however interest rates are high in this case.

Since 1997 several United States mortgage lenders and brokers have an active interest in financing houses in Mexico for retirees from the United States or Canada. Individual mortgage lenders have different criteria for lending funds such as verifiable annual income, net worth, credit rating, ratio of loan to appraisal value type and quality of construction, minimum and maximum amount of loan and interest rates. Various fees are charged such as origination fees, annual maintenance fees, hazard insurance, credit life insurance, Mexican Notary fees, and various taxes. Property will be held in a Mexican bank trust (fideicomiso) for the borrower's beneficial interest. Mortgage lender services are very helpful to some retirees moving to Mexico.

Mailman's house in Glasgow

IV
Medical

Medical, Dental, and Prescription Drugs

The worry about the high cost of prescription drugs and medical expenses will never be a problem again should you decide to come to Mexico.

Doctors and dentists here are as competent as those in the United States or Canada, and many speak fluent English. A large number of them studied and trained in the United States.

Many Canadians and Americans come to Mexico for cosmetic surgery or major dental work. The savings will often pay a large portion of the cost of the trip and enable the patients have an enjoyable convalescence and vacation.

For some very unusual medical situations you might want to return north for consultation, surgery or specialized treatment. Some local doctors will refer you to medical care north of the border if the technology is not available in Mexico.

Hospital costs are less than in the United States. Unlike many hospitals in the United States, where care seems impersonal, here when you press the button for a nurse, one comes promptly. Mexican doctors and medical aides take a personal interest in your care and welfare.

Most major North American pharmaceutical companies have manufacturing facilities in Mexico and you can buy your prescriptions over the counter, except for controlled substances such as tranquilizers, barbiturates, etc. Practically all pharmaceuticals and drugs sold in the United States are available in Mexico. However, they may be marketed under a different name. Some European pharmaceuticals not yet marketed in the United States are available in Mexico. Most prescription drugs are sold in Mexico at a much lower price than in the United States.

Unfortunately you will not receive Medicare benefits in Mexico, or other foreign countries. When people with Medicare or military medical benefits need major medical attention they usually return to the United States. Unfortunately, this procedure is more costly for retirees living in Mexico, as well as for the United States Government.

Many private United States insurance companies will reimburse you for medical and hospital expenses incurred in Mexico. You should determine if your insurance company will pay for medical/dental care here. When living in Mexico you will be entitled to enroll in Mexico's National I.M.S.S. Health Insurance (this is described in a separate section).

MEXICO'S NATIONAL IMSS MEDICAL INSURANCE

By John Bryant

When living in Mexico, foreigners are eligible to apply for Mexico's national health insurance at the office of the *Instituto Mexicano Del Seguro Social,* nearest to their residence in Mexico. This is commonly referred to as IMSS insurance, or Seguro Social (Social Security) in Mexico. Once covered by this medical insurance, one is entitled to a broad range of medical services, including doctors visits, laboratory tests and prescription drugs, dentistry, eye examinations, hospital and surgical care as well as emergency and ambulance services. All salaried Mexican workers are covered by IMSS.

One may apply for this insurance at any time of the year. When applying you will be sent to a medical clinic to complete a medical review form, basic laboratory tests, a chest X-ray and perhaps a cursory physical examination. Should you have a preexisting medical problem this may be excluded under your coverage, or you may be rejected. At the discretion of the physician he may require a more extensive physical examination. With some preexisting conditions a waiting period of six months to two years may be required. Upon approval your insurance will start the first working day of the month following the month in which the application was approved. With some preexisting conditions, or in the case of certain dependents, a six-month to two-year waiting period may be required.

The cost of coverage is approximately $297.00 dollars each year, currently $2,470 pesos. The coverage includes the head of household, wife, children to age 16, or to age 25 if enrolled in a Mexican school, and parents. Dependents must reside in the same household. As with most medical expenses, these are subject to increase from time to time. With a peso devaluation related to dollars and increases in IMSS premiums in pesos your dollar cost for this coverage may have changed by the time you apply for coverage.

At time of application you will need two copies of your passport, FM-2 Visas or FM-3 Visa showing photos, marriage certificate translated to Spanish by an official translator if married, proof of residence such as utility bills and/or rental contract and birth certificates for children. You will need to apply at the IMSS office nearest your residence. Hours are 8 a.m. to 2:30 p.m. Monday through Friday. If you are not fluent in Spanish you may wish to have a translator with you when applying for IMSS medical coverage. Should you already have IMSS coverage, you should apply for renewal thirty days prior to expiration of coverage.

Throughout Mexico, the IMSS system is set up in three levels. Primary level care offers at least a small clinic with a family practitioner, and maybe an emergency room. In the big cities this type of clinic can be surprisingly large, some having over one hundred consultation rooms and a corresponding number of doctors and nurses. Secondary level care consists of a small hospital and outpatient clinic offering at least basic Surgical, Internal Medicine, Pediatric and GYN-OB services. Again, in large cities, secondary hospitals can have a number of other specialties, such as oncology, cardiology, etc., depending on the population density. Tertiary level care is offered only in Mexico's big cities such as Mexico City and Guadalajara. This is top-of-the-line, offering all the sub-specialties and taking care of the most complicated cases. Patients are sent from smaller clinics and hospitals to these giant medical centers. The IMSS also has nursing homes for the elderly, and Day Care centers.

In Guadalajara there are many IMSS clinics and hospitals plus the giant *Centro Medico de Occidente* specialty clinic for more complicated medical problems. There is no IMSS hospital in the Lakeside Chapala area, but there is a small clinic that handles family practice and emergencies; patients are transferred, at no cost, to the larger clinics and hospitals in Guadalajara, if their medical condition merits this type of treatment. This arrangement is similar in many small towns close to Guadalajara and throughout Mexico. Unless you have an emergency situation you may have to wait a few days for an appointment. Appointment times are usually at 8 a.m., noon, and 4 p.m., and when assigned you may have to wait your turn. Should you wish to see a specialist the physician to whom you are assigned will give you an appointment for these services.

Many foreigners in Mexico have IMSS medical coverage and consider it as "major-medical insurance" or a "safety net" to be used only for an expensive medical disaster. They use their own private doctor and dentist to handle routine medical and dental problems. A large number of doctors work a halfday shift at the IMMS, and attend their private practice during their free hours.

Medicare coverage is not valid in a foreign country. However, most Blue Cross-Blue Shield policies are valid as are many other private insurance policies. Before coming to Mexico one should check their coverage. Many private hospitals in Guadalajara will assist foreigners in applying for their United States insurance claims. Several United States hospitals, in border states, will accept Medicare as full payment for hospital services for Americans living in Mexico, and many people travel there for elective medical procedures. Several Mexican insurance companies offer medical insurance coverage to foreign residents living in Mexico; these should be evaluated carefully.

Mexico has established affordable national health insurance coverage, something not available to the average retiree living in the United States.

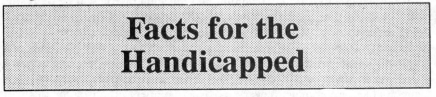

Facts for the Handicapped

We have received several letters inquiring about the facilities, or lack of them, for disabled persons coming to the Guadalajara or the Lake Chapala area. This is a real problem for many and so we have made it a point to speak with people living here who have first-hand knowledge and experience. Here are a few facts that may be helpful.

First, it seems to be the general opinion that the Mexican people are very anxious to help those needing assistance, and will rush to do so in any way possible. Wheelchairs are often difficult to maneuver, especially up steps, over curbs, around the cracked or otherwise torn up sidewalks that are common in the city, or on the rough cobblestone streets and narrow sidewalks in the Chapala and Ajijic area. The offer of help in these situations is greatly appreciated and is often compared with the sometimes-inconsiderate attitude of fellow countrymen in the United States.

The cost of personal aides for health care in Mexico is much less expensive and is more easily obtained than in the United States. This is a definite plus factor since it adds to the general comfort of the handicapped person. For many people, overall benefits of more freedom for getting about day to day and a more active social life would probably be impossible otherwise.

On the negative side it was recognized that there are many areas in which Mexico is sadly lacking in acknowledging the problems facing those in wheelchairs, or who are otherwise handicapped. Wheelchair ramps, street curb slopes, better tended sidewalks and streets, and especially building entrances and special facilities in public restrooms are just a few of the needs in which progress has been slow in coming to Mexico. Mexico is now following the United States' example in making changes for the disabled who require special facilities in public places. There are several groups now being formed whose voices will be heard as to what can and should be done to make life easier for the disabled. Progress is being made.

Want a "Lift"?
Check into Guadalajara!

In more ways than one, Guadalajara offers most of those things we are looking for to enrich our lives, new experiences to give more excitement, comfort and pleasure. The climate, of course, is nearly perfect, the city and surrounding countryside are beautiful and intriguing. You will be delighted with the handsome friendly people, the lower cost of living, and of great importance to all of us, the less expensive and superb medical care available. Whether your concern is with the usual ailments, dental reconstruction or oral implants, chronic disease, major or minor elective surgery, or, to give you a new lease on life, cosmetic or plastic surgery, many people of all ages, men and women alike, are coming in ever increasing numbers primarily for this very reason, to receive a sense of well-being with a more youthful appearance.

Plastic surgery of various degrees is readily available for less than the cost one would expect to pay elsewhere, and there are many fine cosmetic surgeons in Guadalajara who are extremely well qualified. It is no problem to locate bilingual surgeons who can advise you as to which type of surgery would be most beneficial in your particular case. The operation itself takes place only after a complete physical exam is made and your medical history noted, proving you are a good candidate for cosmetic surgery.

Once the decision is made, many plastic surgeons will give you a personal recommendation and put you in touch with various couples or single ladies living here who are willing to open their home to recovering patients. These people provide room, meals, transportation to and from the doctor's office each day as needed, as well as their sincere concern. This is a great benefit to those wanting security and privacy, and all for a very modest cost.

Anyone considering a face lift or other types of cosmetic surgery should certainly check into the advantages offered in Guadalajara, where they can recover in a beautiful climate with comfort and companionship while enjoying a delightful vacation to celebrate their new look!

When a Nursing Home is The Only Solution

In these times when families are scattered and one's life span is longer, we are seeing more and more elderly people living alone. Of course, as long as they are able to take proper care of themselves and are in good health and spirits, this is probably what is best. However, many elderly people are not so fortunate and should not be coping by themselves.

When a person needs help above and beyond what immediate family or friends can offer, the benefits of a nursing home should be considered.

This is a very traumatic and often painful decision for all concerned, although it can be made less so by choosing a nursing home with care. Certain important features, that apply in Mexico and probably the rest of the world, should be checked out:

- Is the facility properly licensed (as well as in the U.S.A.)?
- Do the patients look clean and well cared for?
- Are there certified nurses on staff 24 hours a day?
- Is there a doctor available at all times?
- Are there proper provisions for emergency medical care?
- Are the bathroom and bathing facilities designed with a disabled patient in mind?
- What are the procedures of the facility in case of death?

- Are family and friends welcomed for visits, and invited to regularly planned social activities?
- Is the nursing home clean - no odors or other signs of neglect?
- Are there plans for safe evacuation in case of emergencies?
- Are meals nutritional, appetizing and low in sodium and fat?

These are a few important factors to think about when choosing a nursing home, and with a thorough familiarization with the situation, you also lessen any feelings of guilt you might have in taking action on this very important but sometimes necessary decision.

There are some fine nursing homes in Mexico, where the patients get excellent care. Individual needs are recognized and attended to in a clean, warm and friendly atmosphere by a competent staff.

Another important fact that must be taken into consideration when taking this difficult step is the cost; care facilities in Mexico are much less expensive than in the United States.

Putting a loved one into a nursing facility is indeed a painful choice, but by being very careful in picking the facility and knowing that good care will be given, the pain in such a decision can be somewhat eased.

V

The Popular Guadalajara/Lake Chapala Area

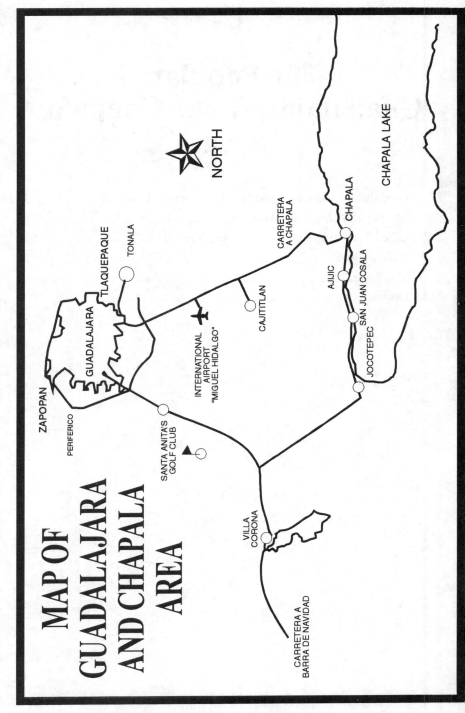

MAP OF GUADALAJARA AND CHAPALA AREA

NORTH

GUADALAJARA
ZAPOPAN
PERIFERICO
TLAQUEPAQUE
TONALA
SANTA ANITA'S GOLF CLUB
INTERNATIONAL AIRPORT "MIGUEL HIDALGO"
CAJITITLAN
CARRETERA A CHAPALA
CHAPALA
AJIJIC
SAN JUAN COSALA
JOCOTEPEC
CHAPALA LAKE
VILLA CORONA
CARRETERA A BARRA DE NAVIDAD

Guadalajara - Mexico's Most Popular Retirement City

Guadalajara, in the state of Jalisco, is located just two hours from Dallas and two and one half hours from Los Angeles by air. Its proximity to the United States is one reason why more U.S. citizens live in Mexico than any other foreign country and Guadalajara is the most popular area in Mexico for North American retirees. It is a place for everyone, with everything to make their lives more healthful, fun and rewarding.

Guadalajara is the second largest city in Mexico, with a population at five million. It is a central plateau city surrounded by mountains, at an elevation of 5,200 feet, four hours by car to the Pacific Ocean, and only minutes by air. It is in central Mexico, 620 miles from the nearest United States border.

Guadalajara is easy to get to. There are direct flights from Houston, Dallas, Chicago, Los Angeles and Miami, with connecting flights to all areas of the United States and Canada. Guadalajara is serviced by five airlines; direct flights are two hours to either Houston or Dallas, and two and one half hours to Los Angeles.

Train and bus service are available, or you may choose to drive.

Guadalajara is a great place to live and a great place to retire, as you will see. Although Guadalajara is a metropolis, it has the ambience and colonial charm of a much smaller city. It has verdant parks, wide streets, and private yards that are aflame with multicolored roses, purple jacaranda, bougainvillaeas, hibiscus, tulip trees and other semitropical plants. The possibilities for entertainment in Guadalajara are endless and limited only by one's level of energy and imagination.

If you asked any of the thirty some thousand North Americans who live here why they moved to Guadalajara you might get over thirty thousand answers, but there are a few reasons that show up repeatedly.

First, it's the land of eternal spring. Guadalajara's altitude contributes to one of the best climates in the world; no ice, snow, extreme heat, cold or high humidity. The average daily temperature is in the 70's. Nighttime temperatures in winter rarely fall below 50 degrees and daytime temperatures seldom exceed the low 90's in the summer. The sky is almost always a clear blue. High utility bills are unknown.

Because the city sits in the mountains the air is dry and clear. The mean December temperature is 62° and the hottest month is May, with a 72 degree average. Nights are always cool, in the 50's or 60's, for sound sleeping without air conditioning.

The rainy season starts in June and continues through September and into early October. This is the most pleasant time of the year. The late afternoon and nighttime showers clear the air and brighten the foliage. Rain may occasionally occur all day, however, this is extremely rare.

Average Temperature of Guadalajara (F°)

Month	Max.	Min.	Av.	Month	Max.	Min.	Av.
January	75	44	59	July	78	60	69
February	79	45	62	August	80	59	69
March	85	50	67	September	80	59	69
April	86	53	69	October	79	56	67
May	89	56	72	November	72	50	61
June	87	61	74	December	72	51	62

This information is based on observations registered since 1900.

The Popular Lake Chapala Area

While many visitors and retirees prefer settling in Guadalajara with its "big city" conveniences, there are others who are much happier living in nearby Chapala and the surrounding small villages.

Lake Chapala is about thirty-five miles from Guadalajara, with the large Hidalgo International Airport on the road between them. The Lake area has a delightful climate tempered by Mexico's largest body of fresh water. It's a little warmer in winter months and a little cooler during the hottest summer months when compared to Guadalajara. The beauty of the lake, plus the added spectacle of the mountains, offers the perfect setting for artists from all over.

The town of Chapala was founded in 1538. Tourism goes back many years, when the first steamboat appeared on the scene around 1868. Later, in 1905, the largest boat to be put in Chapala waters was named *El Turista*. During that period hotel accommodations gradually became available, and since that time more and more travelers are finding their way to take advantage of the climate, quaint villages, and of course, learning about the Mexican people, their history and their customs.

History buffs will find much of interest when exploring the historical old churches, such as the Church of San Francisco in Chapala, the San Antonio Church in the small town of San Antonio, and the San Andrés Church in Ajijic. Another place worth visiting is "el Baluarte", which was a fort during the War of Independence during the last century, although now in ruins. It is located on Mezcala Island, in the middle of Lake Chapala. There are tourist motor launches available to rent for a day's outing, and a picnic lunch will make the day complete!

Lake Chapala and nearby towns are very social and it is easy to be included in the parties, clubs or other groups. There is the Lakeside Little Theater group, that puts on excellent plays, and many of the restaurants provide live entertainment for dancing, along with fine food. A very active Lake Chapala Society was formed in 1955 and offers a variety of social and community functions, such as monthly luncheons with interesting speakers and a very good library complete with a "talking book" program for the blind. Other drawing cards to Lake Chapala are the English language churches, beautiful hotels, banks, and clubs with tennis and golf. There is something for everyone!

Unfortunately in the late 1980's and early 1990's Lake Chapala's water level receded considerably because water feeding the lake from the Lerma River was directed for industrial and agricultural purposes, and rainy seasons were well below normal. Steps have been taken to try to correct this, but without much success. Even so, the Lakeside area remains a beautiful place.

A modern new four-lane highway connecting Chapala with the southeast side of Guadalajara reduces driving time between the two cities to about forty-five minutes. This gives people residing at the Lakeside area better access to facilities offered in Guadalajara. The Chapala area is expected to grow since more people are beginning to commute to Guadalajara to work. Real estate prices in Chapala are somewhat higher the past years, and are expected to rise with a greater influx of North Americans.

For shoppers, Chapala and Ajijic are especially a real treat. There are many shops overflowing with original handicrafts, everything from leather, glass, ceramics, and, of course, the beautifully hand-woven articles. It is a rare visitor who leaves without a purchase!

A definite attraction to the Lakeside towns is the many thermal spas and swimming facilities. In the town of San Juan Cosalá one can enjoy thermal water swimming pools (hotel accommodations are available). In Chapala, the Hotel Monte Carlo has made its warm water pool available for a small fee. The Chimulco and Agua Caliente Parks at Villa Corona are also very popular. These are located about seventeen miles west of Lake Chapala. They have water slides, sports facilities, RV parks and a picnic area.

Lake Chapala: Is Small Town Living Your Choice?

For years, the Lake Chapala area has been consistently popular with many Americans and Canadians, whether they are merely visiting or have definite retirement plans in mind.

For those who prefer a country setting there are several small villages to choose from, especially along the more developed northern lakeshore. Many people find that Ajijic, Chapala, Jocotepec, and Chula Vista, to mention just a few, offer everything they are looking for in a place to vacation or retire.

The excellent weather, quaint cobblestone streets, churches (where English is spoken), and good hotels and restaurants are certainly important considerations. Numerous shops carry almost everything you need for day-to-day living; they try to pay special attention to retiree and visitor needs. Beautiful native crafts, jewelry, hand-woven articles, etc., etc., are also available. For the young at heart, the Chapala area offers golf, tennis, horseback riding, an active theater group, and various other clubs of interest. Something for everyone!

Retirees looking for a quiet lifestyle, and who enjoy doing their grocery shopping for perishable items in the many small markets, and who like the small town atmosphere where everyone is soon on a first name basis, will find these small "laid back" Mexican villages very appealing and satisfying.

All of this is available in the Chapala lakeshore towns. In addition, there is the convenience of being just thirty minutes from the Guadalajara airport and less than one hour from the city of Guadalajara and all of its big city services. The fine hospitals and medical services available adds extra assurance and peace of mind for those who need it.

"Lake Jalisco"
by June Summers

A cursory look down the prehistoric tunnel of time has re-revealed a large Pleistocene lake in the State of Jalisco, Mexico. This lake has tentatively been dubbed "Lake Jalisco". It covered Lake Chapala south of Guadalajara (Longitude 103° west and latitude 20° north), the valley of El Molino, Lake Atotonilco, and dry lakes San Marcos, Zacoalco, and Sayula. It also covered the city of Guadalajara (including Cajititlán), the cities and towns along lakes Chapala, Atotonilco, and the whole dry lake basin including Chapala, Ajijic, El Molino, Acatlán de Juarez, Zocoalco de Torres, Ciudad Guzmán to the site of Ciudad Tuxpan.

The general shape of the lake was an inverted "L". The extreme eastern point coincides with the town of La Piedad de Cabadas, near the Lerma River, from a source near Mexico City, flows into the lake basin.

The depth of water covering Guadalajara was 690 feet; Lakeside towns of

Chapala, Ajijic and Jocotepec was 820 feet; and Sayula by 1,340 feet. In the area called the "Atotonilco-Zacoalco- Sayula Basin" an abundance of petrified bones of prehistoric animals, such as mastodon, mammoth, horse, camel and other Pleistocene or pre-Pleistocene animals were uncovered.

Ancient human habitation sites were found, mainly on the shores of the dry lakes of the area. The valleys were apparent passageways for migrating prehistoric animals and people and the lakes appear to have been much as they are today...before the formation of Lake Jalisco and again following its drainage to its original condition. Now the valleys are inhabited by people as they were in historic times, and are believed to have been in recent and ancient prehistoric times.

Extinct animal bones are estimated to be 10,000 years old. People who lived in or migrated through the valleys, left evidence of prolonged residence, and that they were present in the area at the same time as the animals whose bones were discovered.

It has been speculated that "pre-man" might have originated - or at least lived - here, and that his development followed that of pre-man in other continents such as Europe and elsewhere.

It is believed that the basin was inhabited before the Spanish Conquest in 1519, and that the formation and drainage of Lake Jalisco required approximately 35,000 years. This would place inhabitants and animals whose petrified bones have been found in the area at approximately 35,000 B.C.

Imagine the majesty and splendor of this vast inland sea...a shimmering platter, ad infinitum, without limit...from horizon to horizon...from sundown to sunup...punctured by occasional mountain tops and reflecting the azure blue of an endless sky.

And the tops of today's mountains, mere islands, were inhabited with...what? It was the day of the small four-toed horse...the giant armor-plated slothes...armadillos the size of elephants...mastodons weighing tons.

How about our Neanderthal relatives...moving up from the Lake floor as the Lake filled up? Imagine Uncle George...hair blowing like a banner in the breeze..standing tall atop Mount Garcia. Wild, hairy, primitive Uncle George, standing stark naked, midst the mastodons.

And what did he see? By night, a moon that was like blood on the dark wall of Lake and sky...by day, a vast sea caressed by the wind and whipped into endless waves...a great span of water that began in sunrises and ended in sunsets...the waves running wild with iridescent pastels.

Then suddenly, the skies would darken and burst into silver raindrops. The Lake would sparkle with diamonds and sequins as the mountain tops disappeared in the mist. In a twinkling, the rain...a shimmering shield of crystal beads...would part. Then like magic the clouds would lift...the sun would smile...and we are all playing hooky again!

Why Lakeside?

E. Wright Sargent

Once we retired to Mexico from cool old New England , why did we decide on Lakeside living?

To begin with, we had eight months of living in the city of Guadalajara and it was great. What finally wore us down and kept us uptight was, first, the driving conditions, and second, the smog. Enough said!

Let's leave the negative now because we really did love our stay in Guadalajara and the positive factors far outweigh the negative.

Now, we'll shift gears to try and relay to you the nice things about the Lake Chapala area. Number one, of course, is the air - clean, clear and country fresh. The average temperatures are better even than in Guadalajara, being cooler during the day and warmer at night. This is because the large lake body, sixty-five miles long and eleven miles across, stabilizes the temperature a bit more. The altitude is a little over a mile high, about the same as in Guadalajara.

Next, we must mention the spectacular views, not only of the Lake but also of the hills and mountains that form a special lakeside valley. This must be seen to be appreciated.

Among other good reasons why many people have moved to Lakeside is because more English is spoken. Most stores and restaurants have someone employed who knows English, because there are more Canadians, Americans, British, and other English-speaking Europeans. As in Guadalajara, restaurants often provide menus in both Spanish and English.

Many people enroll in a Spanish class and try to communicate in Spanish. This is as it should be. However, it is not necessary and knowing this fact is comforting until you decide about Spanish classes.

If you are into "happy hours," Lakeside offers a wide variety of bars and restaurants, all hustling for your business. The American Legion is also available for "one for the road," or a simple *refresco* (soft drink.) It also offers many helpful services and has a good library. Some long-time Guadalajarans claim that the Lakeside area is a place just for drinkers, but this simply is not true. As is the case in any given group of people, I won't deny that some of them do have a drinking problem, but nothing I would consider out of normal proportions. For those who are interested, the Lakeside does have a very active AA group (with meetings in English) which gets together at least once a day.

The theater group provides entertainment for everyone. They put on a play every month from September to June, and welcome anyone who is interested in taking part at any level. Also at Lakeside are writers and readers groups along with a friendly volunteer organization that runs the Lake Chapala Society. The Lake Chapala Society has a huge library, VCR tapes for rent and offers many activities of interest.

For more athletic people there is tennis, horseback riding and golf, all readily available. Golfers will find the Chapala Country Club very pleasant. It is about seven miles east of Chapala and there are electric golf carts. The nine-hole golf course is surrounded by beautiful homes. Non-members are limited to playing once a week, but there are some membership openings. The Chula Vista golf course is less crowded and less expensive. It offers a spectacular view and a chance for plenty of exercise.

Lakeside is famous for shops, boutiques, artists, and *tianguis* that are always a delight. Here you can browse and buy native crafts and handmade clothing.

Last but not least, and for some, most importantly, I must mention the fact that house rentals are reasonable. In spite of rising rents there are still excellent finds to be had, so come on down!!!

Lakeside Beauty

by Bruce Allen

Lake Chapala, and the entire area it envelopes, has to be one of the nicest places on earth. Be it the climate, the people, or any of the numerous other reasons for being attracted to Lakeside, this part of the world certainly has a lot to offer. To anyone and for any number of reasons.

There is much underlying beauty that can be found here. My being a photographer might mean that the beauty in Chapala is easier for me to see than the average person. Do not assume, however, that a professional eye is necessary in order to appreciate all that surrounds us here.

Waking up in the morning brings new sights and sounds, no matter who or where you are. It's all right here for us to enjoy. Getting out and about in order to familiarize oneself and to get oriented to the Lake area is definitely the first step on your tour of beauty. It's that easy!

Do not arrive with preconceived notions. Keeping your senses open and ready to receive new experiences is all that is required of any newcomer or resident of the "Lakeside."

The fact remains that it won't take long to appreciate what we have here. As long as you realize we're in a foreign country, along with foreign people and customs (to us), one should have no problem adapting and starting to enjoy the wonderful way of life as we know it here in Chapala.

I wonder if the beauty of living in Chapala and the surrounding areas is one of the many reasons that make Lakeside living so attractive?

Is it the climate? Is it the people? Could it be the fact that both Mexicans and outsiders can blend together to form a melting pot of the best of all worlds? Possibly it's a combination of all the above and probably a few other reasons thrown in as well.

How many other places on this planet can offer what makes living here unique? It's incredible how quickly one is able to make the necessary transition that enables newcomers to feel at home and comfortable. Decades of living side by side have shown us that the Mexican community is friendly and flexible enough to constantly accept and welcome the ever changing foreign population.

Others that have come to this area before us have laid a solid ground for others who follow in their footsteps. Due to their enthusiasm as well as their respect for the local people and their way of life, we are able to be easily accepted into the mainstream of Lakeside living. This leaves less time trying to figure out how to fit in and more time to enjoy the life we elected to live south of the border.

VI

Things to See and Do in the Guadalajara/Lake Chapala Area

(Continued on Next Page)

What Do You Do With Your Spare Time?

This is a question we are asked quite often. Years ago it used to irritate me, especially when our five children were small. Caring for them, plus coping with a large house along with my husband's work and the endless meetings that went with it, meant that there really was no spare time! Now that our family is grown and our responsibilities are fewer we do have spare time, and it is precious to us.

In Guadalajara there are many clubs, groups, volunteer opportunities and social events of all kinds. Whatever your interest, you will find a welcoming club. There is no need to be bored. You can fill every day with activities if that is your preference.

Then there are options for those who do not feel the need to be doing something for "show and tell." If reading a good book, watching a favorite TV program, writing (whether letters to family or friends or articles to be published) or just taking a nap is your cup of tea, then do it. To the question "What do you do with your spare time?" just reply "Whatever I feel like doing."

We are not all busy bees with the compulsion to be accomplishing something every minute. Life is short, so be yourself and enjoy doing your own thing!

A Brief History of Guadalajara
by Professor Enrique Moreno

In the year 1530, the immense and unpopulated lands of Chimalhuacan, situated to the northeast of the Tarasco kingdom, were inhabited by nomad tribes of hunters and a few primitive agriculturists who lived in small settlements of huts. When the thriving and civilized Aztec empire fell under Spanish power in 1521, a few Spanish expeditions traveled through these territories.

However, it was Nuño Beltrán de Guzmán's army, formed by Spanish soldiers and Aztec auxiliaries that invaded the states of Jalisco, Zacatecas, Colima and Nayarit after having occupied Michoacán. They forced these tribes into submission and obedience to the King of Spain. Guzmán called these lands Nueva Galicia, and founded the settlement of Compostela in

Nayarit as the capital of the new Spanish province.

Meanwhile hundreds of Spanish colonists were arriving in Veracruz. They came with their horses, oxen and livestock, carts and farm tools, to obtain lands where they could establish large estates for grazing their animals with the help of civilized indigenous farmers and African slaves that they bought on their way through Cuba. The Mexican government did not want the new settlers in the Aztec Empire, which had been distributed among the conquistadors, and the newly arrived colonists were sent north, to the lands of the nomads conquered by Nuño de Guzmán and other Spanish captains.

For this reason, in 1532 the conquistador Don Nuño decided to found a city in the locality of Nochistlan (Zacatecas), where a group of newly arrived colonists from Spain were to settle. He ordered the new city to be called Guadalajara because he was originally from Guadalajara, a Spanish city situated close to Madrid, and whose Arabic name means "River of Rocks".

The first Guadalajara received sixty-three Spanish families and their servants. They started to breed livestock and farm the land, but the Indians were hostile, water was scarce, and the land inhospitable. Finally, in 1533, Captain Don Juan de Oñate ordered a move to the settlement of Tonalá, an old indigenous village. Here is where the second Guadalajara was settled, which was also ill-omened.

In 1535 the colonists were forced by Nuño de Guzmán, who did not care for the city of Tonalá, to move to a third Guadalajara which was founded in Tlacotán, close the great canyon of the Santiago River, next to its confluence with the Verde River.

Around 1540 the indigenous tribes were confederated under the command of the great chief Tenamaxtli. The Guadalajara of Tlacotán was burned and destroyed. However, the inhabitants had time to escape and take refuge in the allied Indian village of Tetlán. When the Spanish army arrived, the colonists could not agree where the city would be definitely founded. It was thanks to a brave woman, Doña Beatriz Hernández, that the colonists came to a decision. Guadalajara would be founded in the Atemajac Valley, next to San Juan de Dios Creek (now Calzada Independencia), without consulting Nuño de Guzmán, and trusting the king's approval. Doña Beatriz said: "The King is my rooster."

On February 14th, 1542, Doña Beatriz, the sixty-three colonists with their families, and Captains Oñate and Ibarra solemnly founded the present city of Guadalajara, this being over 450 years ago. The present-day metropolis celebrated its anniversary on February 14th, 1992.

(Professor Enrique Moreno was educated in Spain, and presently forms part of the Faculty of the Department of Philosophy and Letters at the University of Guadalajara. His TV-Radio program "Sobre Guadalajara" ("About Guadalajara") airs at 8 and 9 p.m. on Saturdays. He is also a renowned writer on cultural affairs and historical anthropology.)

Viewing The History of Guadalajara

The city of Guadalajara is located 5000 feet above sea level, making it a very pleasant place to be whatever the season.

Guadalajara is also a city modern enough to accommodate anyone's comfort needs along with a fascinating history going back four and a half centuries, making it a delight for history and architecture buffs.

A visit to this beautiful old city would not be complete without touring the special points of historical prominence, and we have selected a few of the most spectacular.

A good place to start your city tour is **The Cathedral**, on Av. Alcalde between Morelos and Hidalgo, whose twin towers are landmarks and often used as symbols of Guadalajara. The Cathedral was begun during the 1570s, and was not completed until half a century later. The result of this long period of construction is visually evident in the many architectural styles represented in the building, such as Gothic, Moorish and Neo-classic.

Just southeast of the Cathedral, at the corner of Corona and Morelos, is the **Palacio de Gobierno**, or **Government Palace**, built in 1714, that houses the offices for Jalisco's governors. Inside are famous murals by Clemente Orozco, two of the most famous being "*The Social Struggle*" and "*Dark Forces.*" This beautiful building is reputed to be the most historical building in a city full of history. It is in the Government Palace that one may read the words of Father Miguel Hidalgo engraved on a bronze plaque which decrees the end to slavery in 1810.

Just northeast of the Cathedral (Hidalgo and Liceo) is the **State Museum**, a building dating back to 1701. The museum exhibits religious art, paintings and pre-Columbian artifacts. Other buildings nearby, also of interest, are the **Palacio Legislativo** or **State Congress**, and the **Palacio de Justicia** or **State Court House**, the headquarters for the State Supreme Court.

The **Degollado Theater**, located across the plaza behind the Cathedral, is a special delight to visit. It is the stage for many cultural events such as the **Guadalajara Symphony Orchestra**, the exciting **University of Guadalajara Folkloric Ballet** performances on Sundays, and operas and concerts featuring internationally acclaimed artists. The theater, built in 1866, is located between Morelos and Hidalgo on Belén Street.

At the rear of the Degollado Theater is the **Plaza de los Fundadores**, or **Founders Square**. This is a 68 foot long bronze high relief sculpture which depicts the exact site of the first Guadalajara settlement. Visitors should take the time to study all of the detail shown on this great piece of art.

Plaza Tapatia, directly behind the Degollado Theater, covers nine blocks and is quite beautiful. There are fountains, monuments, sculptures, and gardens to delight tourists who enjoy relaxing amid the many buildings designed to blend with the post-revolutionary Mexican architecture.

The **Instituto Cultural Cabañas**, dating from 1810, is another magnificent building which stands at the east end of the Plaza Tapatia. It is one of the largest buildings and also one of the finest examples of neo-classical architecture.

Originally built to be used as an orphanage, it was later modified to become a center for cultural events and for a school to further education in music, dance, art and film. The Instituto Cultural Center is probably the best known for the dramatic murals by Clemente Orozco, dating from 1932. The famous frescos include the well-*known "Man of Fire"* and *"Four Horsemen"* as well as other complete originals and reproductions. One can spend hours just walking through the lovely patios, which are connected by numerous tile passageways.

These are just a few of Guadalajara's most famous landmarks;there are many others that also play an important part in the city's history.

There are numerous beautiful churches, plazas and parks to see, and, of course, the **Libertad Market** (known better by locals as **San Juan de Dios**) at Calzada Independencia and Juarez. The market is interesting for those who wish to browse or shop for the wide variety of Mexican handicrafts so colorfully displayed and available at a very reasonable price.

Guadalajara offers the very best example of traditional architecture along with up-to-date modern buildings. There is something of interest for everyone!

Shopping in Guadalajara/Chapala and Other Villages

One of the delights of Mexico, certainly for the tourist, is the excellent shopping in Guadalajara, Tlaquepaque, Tonalá and the nearby Lake Chapala-Ajijic area. Visitors and retirees from the "North of the Border" are seldom able to resist the native hand-made crafts, art work and beautiful hand-loomed and embroidered clothing displayed. Always very popular with shoppers are the unusual ceramic pieces and glassware, and few homes are without one or two sets of the very attractive dishes with hand-painted birds, flowers, butterflies and other designs, along with the beautiful glassware of various sizes and colors. It is fascinating to watch local artists at work and one may do so in many places in Tlaquepaque and Tonalá.

Guadalajara offers modern shopping centers, or *plazas*, where the very latest fashions can be seen, both in clothing and leather accessories such as belts and shoes, which few women can pass without buying - although prices in the plazas can vary considerably and are sometimes quite expensive. Shopping for shoes is a real treat due to the number of shoe stores where about every color and style can be found. One complete, modern plaza is devoted only to shoes! Larger sizes are more difficult to find, but with a lot of looking can be located. Our daughters never leave after a visit without at least three pairs of leather shoes and purses to match, which are also a good buy.

One of the best known markets - also the largest - is Libertad Market, located in the main center of Guadalajara. It is definitely the place for getting the best buys. One never pays the full asking price as it is expected that bargaining will take place - consequently often a purchase can be had for a little over half the original asking price. Libertad has a sample of every type of native craft work: beautifully designed wall hangings or rugs, *sarapes*, hand-made clothing, silver and gold jewelry, leather items, baskets, etc. It is certainly a "must" for everyone who comes to Guadalajara who likes to shop or simply browse. A word to the wise: the market and surrounding area have been known for centuries as *San Juan de Dios*; the market was renamed *Libertad* after it was remodeled a number a years ago (some Government official's splendid idea). If you want to get there by taxi or ask directions, refer to it as *San Juan de Dios*, or else you could get a very blank expression and end up who-knows-where!

Take a Ride in a Calandria!

One will find several picturesque horse carriages standing along the streets in the *Centro* (downtown) of Guadalajara; they are called Calandrias, and are part of the city's history dating back to the 1900s.

These horse drawn coaches were widely used for many practical purposes in their early years before cars and buses became the more popular means of travel. They were a means of taking care of the everyday necessary problem of getting from one place to another, or for parades and even funeral processions, and for transporting heavy materials.

In Guadalajara the number of Calandrias has dwindled to an alarmingly few, which are still used primarily to take tourists or sight-seers who prefer a slower, informative tour around the city. The polite, attentive drivers are very proud of their polished, comfortable coaches with folding roofs and lanterns, pulled by well groomed horses. Usually both the coach and the horse are gaily decorated with flowers, ribbons and bells.

The Calandria drivers are eager to tell their passengers fascinating stories, richly embellished with real or fictitious tidbits about the various historical buildings, famous people of the past and intriguing events, as they ride slowly through the streets.

Perhaps taking a sightseeing tour in a carriage is not as efficient or as inexpensive as the tour buses or cars which are available now, and which are a real threat to the continued existence of the Calandrias. One must realize that the drivers of Calandrias depend solely on tour fares for their livelihood. They spend long twelve to fourteen hour days hoping to earn enough money to feed their family, plus have money left to cover the upkeep of the horses and carriage.

The Calandrias add much to the calm serenity of this beautiful old city as sounds of the horses' slow clipity-clop passes by. It would be sad to see the Calandrias suffer the same fate as many customs do in the name of modernization and progress!

While in Guadalajara treat yourself to the delightful experience of being a brief part of the city's proud and colorful past.

Degollado Theater - One of the Cultural Events in Guadalajara

by Jack Cathell

At the end of Plaza Tapatia, you will see the beautiful facade of a building resembling a Greek or Roman temple. This is the Degollado Theater (*Teatro Degollado*), which opened its doors to the public on September 13th, 1866 with the opera "Lucia de Lamermoor"; performed by the Grand Italian Opera Company. And, since that evening, it has been Guadalajara's center of opera, symphony concerts, ballet, singers and other performing arts including, today, the outstanding program of traditional Mexican dances, costumes and music presented each Sunday morning at 10 a.m. by the Folklore Ballet of the University of Guadalajara.

The interior of the Degollado is full of Old World charm similar to the La Scala Opera House on Milan, Italy. And its dome and the proscenium of its stage are decorated by colorful murals depicting "Time and The Hours" and " Allegory."

Behind the Degollado Theater is a dramatic, sixty-eight foot long bronze mural, whose nine-foot figures depict the arrival of Spanish soldiers, settlers and religious leaders on the Valley of Atemajac, where Guadalajara is located. From the metal mural the spectacular "Plaza Tapatia." with its restored colonial buildings, fountains, arcades and promenades, extends out for seventeen acres.

Finished in 1982, this great Plaza is an ideal place to stroll, visit the colonial-style offices of the State of Jalisco Tourism Office, enjoy a Mexican snack, lunch or dinner...or just sit and watch "Tapatios" (Guadalajarans) from all walks of life and of all ages enjoy themselves within this tribute to them, their ancestors and their culture.

Spend a Day at the Zoo!

A major attraction in Guadalajara is the little publicized zoo which, although only a few years old, is already considered one of the finest in Mexico. Located a few blocks east of Calzada Independencia Norte, about five kilometers from downtown, it offers everything for a delightful day's outing, and is open Tuesday through Sunday. Just before you arrive at the Zoo proper, to the left is an impressive amusement park, full of fun things to do for the younger crowd.

Everyone will love the whimsical monkey statues sculpted by local artist Sergio Bustamante, which are at the entrance. From here, the very realistic landscaping and design of the entire area invite you to go on. To the left of the entrance you can rent baby carriages and wheelchairs for a nominal fee.

The zoo is HUGE and houses almost 350 different species; the reptiles and huge insects have their own pavilion, and small birds are housed in two aviaries which you walk through - a piece of newspaper or carton is recommended on your head, as the birds fly around freely. Elephants, gorillas, giraffes, etc., etc., are very much at home in their appropriate habitat. A train is available for all who prefer to ride; it slowly tours a major part of the zoo, with emphasis on the giant mammals.

The entire zoo is quite attractive and is kept very clean by the 150 or so full-time employees dedicated to the well-being of the animals and the success of this wonderful addition to Guadalajara.

Unlike many zoos, the Guadalajara Zoo is self-reliant with an independent administration. Many plans for future projects include developing breeding programs for the rarer species, and possibly converting newly available property into a game reserve.

A day at the Guadalajara Zoo is fun and should be a must on your tour and sightseeing list. Don't miss it.

Guadalajara's Grand Canyon

If you want to escape from the hustle and bustle of the city for some relaxation amid natural beauty, it's very easy to do, doesn't cost money and isn't far away. Visit the *Parque Mirador Barranca de Oblatos*, known to many as simply the "Canyon Park."

The park is located a few blocks from the Zoo on the northern end of Calzada Independencia. It is well-kept, very complete with picnic tables, refreshment stands, large playground, basketball courts and soccer fields, and a Greek-styled amphitheater where dance festivals and other events are held.

The park's biggest attraction is the spectacular canyon it overlooks. There are a number of *miradores* or lookout points from which to see the canyon, the waterfall and the river 2,000 feet below. There are many hiking trails around the canyon rim and, for the really hardy, a four-mile trail down to the river. A visit to "Canyon Park" makes an entertaining day. Take your camera to capture the scenic beauty *and* the happy Mexican families enjoying a day of fun.

The Instituto Cultural Cabañas

In the center of Guadalajara, at the far end of the popular Plaza Tapatia, stands one of the most historical buildings in the city, the Instituto Cultural Cabañas, with its impressive chapel, museum and many patios.

This interesting building was constructed between 1805 and 1810. It is neo-Classical in design and was originally called "The House of Mercy and Charity." Its early history includes the use as an orphanage and a retreat for those of all ages who were in need of refuge. The occupants were taught useful skills such as sewing, weaving, blacksmithing, carpentry and other trades that could be later passed down to their children which would enable them to be prepared to make a decent living.

The War of Independence, in 1810, caused the orphanage to be converted into barracks for soldiers, and also sheltered their horses. It was not until 1829 that the buildings were made available once again to the needy, however, this was to be somewhat temporary, since on two other occasions it was again taken

111

over to be used for military purposes. The site also served as a jail and an asylum. Finally, around 1860, the Sisters of Charity reclaimed it for its original purpose and later the government of Porfirio Diaz officially declared it a refuge for those in need.

The Instituto Cultural Cabañas offers much of interest, however, the main focal points include the Chapel, which is dominated by the magnificent art murals painted by José Clemente Orozco, a native of Guadalajara, the most famous of which are the *"Man of Fire,"* and *"The Four Horsemen of the Apocalypse."* In the smaller museum, the Museo Orozco, one will find drawings, prints and other paintings by this very talented artist.

Many cultural events take place in the Instituto Cultural Cabañas, such as concerts, art and photography exhibits, folkloric and classical dance performances and lectures.

Near the entrance is a small shop where one may find books, magazines and other material of interest, along with a Public Relations office which is very helpful in offering suggestions and useful information.

The Excellent Benjamin Franklin Library

If you like to read or need to do some research on a particular subject in the United States, you should know about the fine up-to-date Benjamin Franklin Library, located at the University of Guadalajara, Tomás B. Gómez #27, S.H., Guadalajara. This library was formerly a branch of the United States Information Service (U.S.I.S.). It is very complete, including over 11,000 volumes. The library is open to the general public from 9 a.m. to 8 p.m. Monday through Friday, and Saturdays from 9 a.m. to 1 p.m. The telephone number is 616-3152. You will find the staff friendly and helpful.

Services available at the library include: book loans, reference library, a periodical collection of over 140 titles, specialized bibliographies, automated catalog, and a video collection. Also available are several United States newspapers, including the *New York Times*, the *Wall Street Journal* and the *Washington Post*.

The Benjamin Franklin Library is an integral part of a larger network and can provide access to the Benjamin Franklin Library in Mexico City (which boasts 30,000 volumes, inter-library loans, over 400 periodicals, and database searches in the United States.

The library fills a great need in the Tapatio community for quick, reliable information services about the United States. It is at the service of the community, providing the transitional flow of information essential for mutual understanding in this complex world.

Obtaining a membership card is quite simple. You will need to prove your address and also give references. You need not feel "cut off" from familiar reading material, even while in a foreign country. The Benjamin Franklin Library can fill almost every need.

Tianguis and Mercados

To go to a *Tianguis* is somewhat similar to going to a huge overcrowded flea market or garage sale in the United States with an abundance of Mexican flavor thrown in! Every village has a day set aside each week when the local farmers, fishermen or anyone who has a product to sell comes to town to display and hopefully sell his wares. It is a very old tradition and part of the Mexican culture.

In Mexico some larger *tianguis* and *mercados* are located in permanent places, and smaller ones move from street to street, but they are always busy places and easy to find (just follow the crowd!) One can find everything from a wonderful variety of fresh fruit, vegetables, fish, poultry, meat, clothing, shoes, housewares, hardware and even stop for a bite to eat and drink if you're tempted!

Prices quoted in *tianguis* and *mercados* vary greatly from stall to stall, and it is an expected "part of the game" for the customer to bargain for a better price. I expect a gringo shopper comes out a bit on the short end of the deal, perhaps not if one knows their prices, but it is great fun to try your hand at the game. The vendors are experienced in separating the lookers from the buyers and do not spend much time on the former.

The noise of much haggling, the vendors advertising their bargains, plus children and sometimes dogs running all over the place in small crowded aisles, are somewhat overwhelming to many who would rather pay for probably poorer quality but in a quieter, more organized atmosphere, however, many housewives faithfully go to their favorite *tianguis* or *mercado* as often as possible, and thoroughly enjoy being among this tangle of people and products. For many it is the only way to shop, and has been for generations, for women carrying babies with small children tagging along, all with shopping bags to hold their purchases. These women know the stalls where they can get the best for less, and will favor these each time. One could learn a lot by either shopping with or following such women!

Tianguis and *mercados* have a secure place in the everyday life and the Mexican way of living, and those of us from north of the border should enjoy the experience of seeking them out whenever we can.

Mercado de Abastos - The Ultimate Farmer's Market

The Abastos Market, as it is commonly known by North Americans, is Mexico's second largest market of its kind (Mexico City has the largest), and is owned by the city of Guadalajara. "Abastos" means "provisions" or "supplies," and this is the central supply market for wholesale and retail businesses in the entire metropolitan area. Spaces or booths are leased to persons for 99 years, and consequently are passed down from generation to generation. The market has practically everything one needs, whether for cooking, cleaning, or small repairs; there are party supplies such as large *piñatas*, hardware, paper products and many other hard to find items, and even banks right there for your convenience!

We think everyone should go at least once, just for the experience. When you do, dress comfortably - especially shoes - and bring a large shopping bag...you will need it!

Abastos Market is located on the west side of Guadalajara on Lázaro Cárdenas Avenue. It is huge, and it is estimated that well over 100,000 persons shop there daily.

Vegetables, fruits, spices, seafood, meat, poultry, eggs and cheeses are on display, and you will not find better quality, or a fresher or wider selection anywhere. Prices on some items may be slightly higher than in other markets (when dealing at a retail, not wholesale level) but the quality is also much better. For the most part, however, you will find good bargains compared with the supermarkets, and it pays to shop around the various booths as prices can vary considerably.

Abastos is a safe place to shop. However, as in any crowded area, watch out for cars and trucks, and there is always the possibility of pickpockets, so it is wise to be aware of these details.

You will discover many interesting types of vegetables, nuts and spices, sold in bulk, and you will also find it is almost impossible to come away without filling your bag with these interesting and varied items. Happy shopping!

The Charros

Mexico is usually associated with bullfights, which are colorful and exciting. But many people find that attending a *charreada* or Mexican rodeo, featuring the daring *charro* cowboys competing on horseback with the fancy and complicated lariat rope tricks, is just as exciting and thrilling to watch.

In Mexico the "Day of the Charro" is celebrated on September 14th; the Association of Charros of Jalisco is now over seventy years old!

The *charreada* is a nationally recognized sport with specific rules to be followed during the competition, and is spectacular not only for the daring riding and lariat swinging tricks, but also for the beautiful and often quite expensive costumes each participant wears. Both men and women compete, with ladies riding sidesaddle at breakneck speeds! Charros usually begin training as small children. The expense, including costumes, horse, saddle and other items can total a very sizable amount.

The day we went to see the charro cowboys perform was another new adventure to us, certainly different from our usual form of entertainment, and we enjoyed it greatly.

Mexican families arrive early and are prepared to spend the entire day cheering on their favorites. During the events they snack on food brought from home or bought from vendors who circulate about the spectator section selling refreshments, both hot and cold, just as they do in the U.S. at sports events.

The crowd gets livelier as the day progresses, whether due to the heightening excitement or perhaps, in some cases, from a bottle. Part of the fun was in watching the audience and, in our case, watching one lady who quite obviously had been "refreshed" with several drinks and who felt compelled to stand up and loudly cheer, whistle and even break into song! She was having a grand time, but I can only imagine how she felt the next morning...

In spite of the huge crowd, excitement and spontaneous side show, there were no unpleasant incidents. It was just a fun day offering another view of life in Mexico. A day such as that is a good way to see an old Mexican tradition at its best.

Olé La Fiesta Machismo

by Adele Woodward

The bugle notes sounded loud and clear above the sanded arena of the vast amphitheater. Beneath a circle of flags the gringo tourists and the mestizos leaned forward in an expectant hush. Vendors peddling chips, soda, and beer paused in their endless treks between the rows. It was 4:30 p.m. on a sunny February afternoon in Guadalajara, Mexico, and the age-old struggle between man and beast was about to begin.

Red double doors in a five-foot wall opened to pomp and pageantry, as the band's pasodoble was buried beneath a burst of cheers. Led by the bailiff on horseback came three toreros, resplendent in their traje de luces (suit of lights), close-fitting outfits of silk and satin heavily embroidered in gold or silver. Each headed a line of three banderilleros and two mounted picadors, like a trail of flowers in gleaming pastels. Bringing up the rear were the ring attendants in white pants and bright red shirts, along with the red-tasseled mules that haul away dead bulls.

High in the stands the ring president signaled for the corrida to begin. The set was cleared. As a second bugle call rang out, a massive black bull burst from the toril.

To the aficionado bullfighting is not a sport, but an art form, a ballet that has been called a dance of death, and the bull is not always the victim. During his career every bullfighter will be wounded, more or less seriously; perhaps one in ten killed by up to half a ton of charging bone and muscle equipped with a pair of horns meant to disembowel its tormentor.

Although introduced in Mexico by the conquistadors in the 1520's, the bullfight, as we know it, began in the 1700's when toreadors first dismounted to meet the beast face to face. What had been a favorite sport of the aristocracy turned into fame and fortune for such peons as Joselito, Belmonte, Manolete, and Ordóñez from Spain; Gaona and Arruza from Mexico. They were among the greatest stars of their time, and two of them, Joselito and Manolete, gave their lives to the horns.

This afternoon the featured torero was Arturo "El Coyo" Díaz, who was about to receive his doctorate in tauromaquia (bullfighting). He had served his apprenticeship as a novillero, fighting the lighter, younger bulls in minor novilladas as he developed control and rhythm. Curro Rivera, one of Mexico's premier bullfighters, will confer the alternativa when he lends him his sword and muleta, and the right to kill the first bull of the afternoon. The third torero, Miguel "Armillita" Espinosa will be the witness in this drama that consists of three acts.

Act I: With shouts and waving capes, El Coyo's assistants took turns provoking the beast to charge this way and that, as the torero noted the way it ran, turned, hooked, and braked. Bulls are color blind. It is the moving object that lures them, and the matador controls the direction of the bull's charge through his handling of the cape. El Coyo stepped into the ring and, using both hands, began a series of veronicas with the large magenta and yellow capeto, drawing the bull close to his body as the crowd shouted "*olés*".

Picadors entered on their padded and blindfolded horses to stab the short steel point of heavy, eight-foot lances into the bull's hump. Again and again, the enraged and bleeding bull drove his horns into the protective padding until he knocked one horse and rider to the ground. The normal series of cape passes used to distract the bull became a genuine rescue.

Act II: Like nervous butterflies El Coyo's assistants darted in one at a time, to place a pair of banderillas in the animal's neck. They'd stretch their arms to full length to reach over the horns of the charging beast, then turn to run for their lives. The thirty-inch darts with their paper frills protruded from the hump, bright colored pins in a bloody cushion.

Act III: The bugle call introducing the third and last act hung in the air. This was the moment, *La Hora de la Verdad*, (The Hour of the Truth) the crowd has paid to see. La faena, the combination of passes that are a bullfighter's art, and his salvation.

Holding Rivera's muleta and sword El Coyo doffed his hat, the montera, and dedicated his first full-grown bull to the ring president. The muleta is a heart-shaped piece of scarlet flannel draped over a two-foot pointed baton with finger grips. Three times El Coyo brought the bull in close with a graceful right- hand pass. Three times the bull bumped him. On the fourth pass, the beast caught him and tossed him in the air.

Bulls are known to have a remarkable memory, yet once again, El Coyo tried the same pass. Once again the bull tossed him on his horns. Unhurt, save for pride, he set the animal up for the kill. In following the muleta the bull lowered his head, and El Coyo plunged the sword over the horns and into the hump.

Each torero was assigned two bulls. With his second animal, El Coyo included a series of five manoletinas, a pass where a corner of the muleta is held behind the back, in his faena. Judged on points for mander - mastery of the bull; parar - how he, the torero stands; and templar - timing, how clean the kill, El Coyo was awarded two ears.

Fighting bulls are supposedly bred from cows field-tested for belligerence, and bulls with top physique, vigor and tenacity. Although rare, a bull can be so exceptional the matador will request it be "pardoned". If granted, the animal is then retired to stud. Yet some aficionados claim these once proud descendants of savage cattle that were used in war as well as games as far back as 228 B.C., have shrank in size, strength and power.

Certainly one bull in Guadalajara, battered and bleeding from pikes and banderillas, stood and bawled like a bewildered child who does not know why he has been punished. That was no contest, and the matador kills quickly to end the misery.

The rest, though erratic in their charges, were competitive. Besides the bull that knocked down the horse and rider and tossed El Coyo, there was another who charged a horse so hard the picador was jarred from the saddle. It is bulls like these that test the skill of the matador, that make it a fair fight only one can win. That brief moment it appeared man might not be the victor was soon over.

To exultant Olés and cries of the crowd El Coyo circled the ring, as they showered him with hats, cushions, flowers and wineskins. This slim young man with the curly dark hair will go on to meet the bulls on arenas across the country until retirement - or the horns - stop him, for he is a matador. El Torero de Jalisco has danced the ballet of fear and death, and lived to dance again.

(Adele Woodward is a prominent freelance travel writer who resides in Tampa, Florida.)

Sports In Guadalajara
by Jack Cathell

Guadalajara offers a wide variety of sporting activities; its incredibly good weather rarely puts a damper on the fun. Your favorite sport can be practiced year-round. We will mention the various facilities available: there's something for everyone and for every pocketbook, ranging from free (or symbolic fee) public parks, to very exclusive (and expensive) sports and country clubs.

Golf, always a favorite, can be readily enjoyed. In or near the city are four-18 hole, "perpetually green" golf courses, complete with caddies and carts. All of these greens belong to very exclusive, very private clubs. Depending on demand, arrangements usually can be made to make use of these different golf courses, but with no guarantees as to accessibility, especially on the weekends.

Tennis is widely played in Mexico. Courts are part of the facilities offered by many metropolitan hotels, every private sports club, and a number of public parks. The public parks charge a nominal fee to rent their courts on an hourly basis, and an enterprising attendant will even have rackets and balls on hand to help earn himself a little extra income.

Basketball and volleyball courts can be found in most public recreational parks. Swimming pools are plentiful both in hotels and motels as well as in country clubs, and in open-to-the-public swimming centers (private and city-owned), which charge a very modest fee for the use of their heated (or sometimes unheated - check this out) pools.

The typical private sports or country club in Guadalajara offers a complete variety of facilities: swimming pool, tennis courts, soccer field, squash or racquetball courts, gymnasium, weight-lifting equipment, luxurious steam baths, showers, etc., all impeccably kept in prime condition. **These clubs are NOT open to the general public,** and are in great demand by health-conscious people. Some of these clubs charge a monthly fee (with almost no limit on the number of people attending), others are owned by shareholders (with a limited number of members). The most common arrangement for shareholder clubs, which are the nicest, is to rent out a share from a member who is not presently using the facilities. Renting is the only answer for visitors, as the cost of a share in one of these clubs can range from $10,000 to $30,000 U.S., not including the monthly "maintenance fee."

Jogging? You can set your own pace along the special jogging paths between the trees of *Parque de los Colomos* or around one of Guadalajara's tree and flower-studded parks close to where you are staying. Or, if you're really adventurous, you can take on the challenge of the 2.65 mile jogging trail down into and out of the *Canyón of Huentitán* where Mexican runners congregate every weekend.

Bowling enthusiasts will be delighted with Guadalajara's spacious air conditioned, well-lighted bowling centers that welcome you day and night; be sure to reserve your lane well in advance if you want to bowl in the evenings.

All of the afore mentioned activities have been "imported" to Mexico. *"Tapatios"* (native-born Guadalajarans) offer many spectacles that are innately Mexican, which you can also enjoy while visiting this centuries-old city. Ine of the most colorful of these is the *"Charreada"*, a unique kind of rodeo where elaborately costumed *"Charros"* and beautifully dressed *"Charras"* show off their magnificent horses and exceptional riding skills, and where participants compete in tests of their ability to rope, throw and tie horses, calves, and bulls. Most Charreadas include a special time slot for the general public called the "jineteada" (literally translated as a "ride"); this is mad-bull riding, recommended only for the very brave (or very foolish).

There are also the big *"Palenques" where, in an atmosphere of excitement, cockfights are held along with Mariachi music and "Ranchera"* (Mexican ranch) songs performed by stage and T.V. stars. Tapatios bet heavily on the fighting roosters of their choice, that are battling to the death in the sandy arena below. Many people don't bet on the cocks, but prefer to play the Bingo games offered as an alternate activity. The cost of entering the Palenque will vary according to the quality of the performers scheduled for a given evening; when a top-notch singer is billed, a ring-side or near ring-side ticket can cost from $100 to $200 U.S.

The *"Fiesta Brava"* (Bullfight or "Celebration of Courage") is also a spectacle close to the hearts of many Tapatios. Every Sunday during the bull fighting season they make the Plaza Monumental Stadium on the Calzada Independencia ring with shouts of "Ole!" when pleased with the grace or exhibition of valor by one of the participating bullfighters in his glittering "suit of lights".

Beyond doubt, however, the greatest favorite of all Tapatios, regardless of their social status, or income level, is *"Futból"* (soccer). Up to seventy-two thousand shouting, banner-waving fans pack the Jalisco Stadium during important games involving competing local and national teams.

We have hardly dipped below the surface with this brief description; one never need to be bored with such a variety of activity as is available in Guadalajara!

About Golf

The Guadalajara/Chapala area is a golfer's paradise, with four eighteen-hole golf courses and one nine-hole course in or near Guadalajara, plus two nine-hole courses at the Chapala lakeside. The climate is almost perfect for golf year around. The rainy season runs from the middle of June through October, with the month of July having the heaviest rains. However, most of the rain occurs in the late afternoon or at night, and rainy days are a rare occurrence.

Some of the courses are closed for non-members on weekends and holidays, and some are closed on Mondays. Also, most have special functions for members, such as ladies' day. Although there are very few days when the courses are crowded and reservations for tee-off times ares seldom needed, it is always a good idea to call in advance to make sure the courses will be open, or available, for play.

The **Guadalajara Country Club** (tel. 641-4045), the oldest and perhaps the most beautiful club, is located about three miles northwest of the colonial downtown area of Guadalajara, nestled in the middle of the Country Club subdivision, one of the nicest, most exclusive, subdivisions Guadalajara has to offer. This is a private club, and admittance must be through a club member, or perhaps through one of the major hotels. One of the pros is an American and may be helpful in arranging admittance. The Guadalajara Country Club is the "in" place, and among its members you will find the most prominent and important personalities of Guadalajara. The course is immaculately maintained, with fairways tight and tree lined. The club house is beautiful, and the outdoor patio is great for a snack after playing a round of golf.

The **Santa Anita Club de Golf** (tel. 686-0361) is a prestigious country club surrounded by a lovely residential development. The architecture of the houses bordering the course is sometimes as interesting as the course. Santa Anita is located about eleven miles southwest of the downtown on Highway #54, that turns into a four-lane expressway to the Pacific Coast. The course is located at the base of a hill and offers outstanding views of the surrounding countryside. Everything about Santa Anita is first class. Temporary residents of the Guadalajara area who like golf could look into the possibility of renting a membership to the club, which would include full use of all club facilities. Several American executives working for major U.S. corporations in Guadalajara, and a number of retirees, live in Santa Anita.

Just north of Guadalajara is the **San Isidro Country Club** (tel. 633-2044), located in a valley a few hundred feet lower in altitude than the city. The stream flowing through this valley is the same one that goes over the *Cascada de Cola de Caballo* (Horse Tail Fall) into the two thousand foot deep Oblatos

Canyon (don't miss this spectacle, best observed after a few days' heavy rain). The course is very hilly and the most challenging of the four major Tapatio courses. Views of the surrounding hills and canyon are spectacular. You may wish to use a cart on this course because of the terrain. The San Isidro Inn, located nearby, is available should you wish to spend a few days playing this excellently maintained course. The surrounding real estate development is less expensive than Santa Anita.

This writer was pleasantly surprised when he visited **Club de Golf Atlas** (tel. 689-0085), located just east of the airport highway southeast of Guadalajara. The course is somewhat less popular because of its location in the predominately industrial area of Guadalajara, however, the well maintained course is a delight to play, with narrow fairways between large trees. The 14th hole is spectacular, a par three 196 yards, with an excellent view of Guadalajara. The course is practically always free of other players, and guests always feel welcome. With the completion of the new four-lane Guadalajara/Chapala highway, this course is only a 35 minute drive from Chapala lakeside.

Just five miles west of Ave. Patria on Ave. Vallarta, along Route #15, known as the Nogales highway, is the nine-hole **Rancho Contento** golf course (tel. 621-6889). Although maintenance of the greens and fairways may not be the quality of the other courses, it is still a pleasure to play. Daily, weekly and monthly green fee arrangements are available, and the course is comparatively less expensive to play than others. It is the most popular course for retirees residing in Guadalajara. In Rancho Contento you will also find a very nice residential subdivision; though started by Americans about twenty years ago, only a few remain in residence.

The are two nine-hole golf courses in the Chapala lakeside area. The **Chapala Country Club** (tel. 5-22-55) is located just seven miles east of Chapala and is adjacent to the Vista del Lago residential area, on a hill just above the course. The course has a panoramic view of Lake Chapala, particularly from the tee at the third hole. There are two sets of tees for each hole that add variety when playing the second round. Maintenance is generally good except in the dry season, when fairways become somewhat brown for lack of watering. Green fees and membership fees are reasonable for most retirees. The membership consists mostly of retired Americans and Canadians who are quite friendly. Food at the Club House is good and reasonably priced.

The nine-hole **Chula Vista Country Club** (tel. 5-22-81) is located on the Chapala-Ajijic highway. The par 31 course is short but hilly with play beside and across a stream. There are many hazards along the course, which is a bit of a challenge for the amateur player. Views of Lake Chapala are beautiful from the scenic course. Most of the membership is Mexican, however, daily play for tourists is permitted.

124

A trip to the Guadalajara/Chapala area to play golf would be an adventure, but retirement here with the many things to see and do, in addition to golf, is a daily adventure.

For Pure Relaxation Find A "Balneario"

Near the Guadalajara and Lake Chapala area there are many *balnearios* (hot water spas) which are very popular with the Mexican people as well as those of us who are visitors in Mexico.

Some spas are more highly developed for use than others and offer a complete medically supervised health program. Others are somewhat off the beaten path and have only the barest of facilities. All, though, are a delightful way to unwind and ease pains and aching joints!

People who are looking for pure pampering, special massages and exercises, along with a vegetarian diet, and who don't mind being away from the telephone and television (there is none!) will find that the **Rio Caliente Spa** is a perfect solution. This spa is located about one hour west of Guadalajara in a beautiful rustic setting of pine trees. The slightly expensive rates include everything, and are well worth the benefits of a thoroughly relaxing visit. Rio Caliente is not open to day visitors which adds to the warm intimate atmosphere.

In the village of Chapala near the western edge of town is lovely **Villa Montecarlo and Spa**, owned by the University of Guadalajara. The spa is open to daily visitors who also enjoy the beautifully maintained grounds.

San Juan Cosalá Spa, between Jocotepec and Ajijic, is very popular and rooms should be reserved in advance. San Juan Cosalá Spa offers a variety of pool temperatures and private thermal pools. Daily visitors are welcome.

Going southwest about thirty miles, near the village of Villa Corona, are **Chimulco Spa** and **Agua Caliente Spa**. Both are especially geared to youngsters with a completely equipped playground, tennis courts, water slides and other fun water sports. Each of these spas has several warm water pools with lifeguards, along with picnic facilities and restaurants. Private pools and facilities for R.V.'s are also available.

Other very nice family spas are **Los Camachos**, north of Guadalajara, and **Río Escondido**, located around forty minutes southwest of Guadalajara, west of highway 15 at Santa Cruz de las Flores. Río Escondido Spa has recently been equipped with cottages to rent and a restaurant as well as the usual picnic area.

125

Throughout Mexico there are over five hundred spas, and there are dozens located in the state of Jalisco alone. From the very highly developed spas which offer many activities and health programs to those with just basic requirements, all are wonderfully relaxing fun for a day's outing or for a week or longer. Everyone should take the time to treat themselves in this delightful way.

Tlaquepaque

Tlaquepaque is perhaps the most popular community in the area for tourist shopping, and for a good reason! It is famous for the unique pottery, glass ware, hand-woven clothing, leather articles, and many other types of artwork and crafts typical of Mexico.

Independencia and Juárez streets, running parallel to each other, are especially attractive, but the streets that connect both are also excellent for finding great buys. It is fascinating to watch artists design delicate hand-blown glass items, or observe the fine craftsmen at work on original ceramic pieces. The main plaza faces a central courtyard complete with a bandstand for concerts. It is a treat to take a break at one of the cafes for a refreshing drink and to watch the activity going on around you. Groups of mariachis in costume wander about singing and playing their guitars, and of course there are always the colorfully dressed Indian women, usually with small children, who offer handmade articles such as yarn dolls, lace table scarves, and beads. Several streets are blocked off from traffic, making it more pleasant and convenient for shoppers.

Although Tlaquepaque is usually thought of for shopping, it is equally important for history buffs, offering the opportunity to see some fine examples of colonial architecture. Some buildings of interest include the Parish Church, constructed by Franciscan priests in the mid-1800's. Nearby are the Sanctuary and City Hall, and just a short distance on Independencia, is the Regional Ceramics Museum with a fascinating display of the ancient along with more contemporary works of local ceramic art. At Independencia #208 is the house and garden where the "Iguala Plan" was signed. This historical document was most important for the creation of an autonomous Mexico.

Tlaquepaque is filled with fine old colonial mansions, some of which have been renovated and are now used as the perfect showplace for Tlaquepaque's exquisite handicrafts.

There are many restaurants where one can stop for lunch. For us three of the best are *El Abajeño*, at Juárez #231, *El Patio* at Independencia #186, and *Mariscos Progreso* at Progreso #80. All offer excellent food, colorful and pleasant atmosphere, and fine service. We have been here for seven years and find that it is still fun to take a day and revisit this unique and picturesque town, for the same reason it attracts a constant stream of tourists - it simply is a delightful, interesting place for an outing.

Guadalajara West to Magdalena

After working for almost thirty-five years in an office environment, I greatly enjoy my freedom to be out-of-doors most of the time in a near perfect climate where I can appreciate the magnificent beauty of Mexico. Since we live on the northwest side of Guadalajara at the edge of the city, many of my explorations into the country (campo) have been along route #15, frequently referred to as the Nogales highway (a three-day drive to the Arizona border). Av. Vallarta, going west, continues into this road. The following are a few points of interest well worth exploring at your leisure. As a point of reference for measuring mileage, our trips west start at the intersection of Av. Vallarta and Av. Patria.

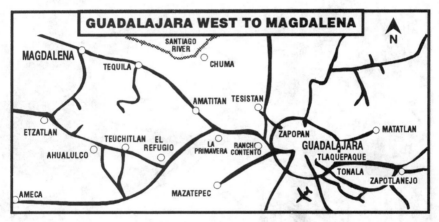

Our first point of interest, five miles out, is the residential area and golf course known as **Rancho Contento** (Happy or Contented Ranch). North Americans started this real state development several years ago. However, there are only a few North Americans residing there now. Within the development is a beautiful nine-hole golf course that is open to the public with reasonable daily and monthly rates. Usually you will be required to use a caddy. This golf course is great for old duffers like me!

The second point of interest is about ten miles for our starting point, turning of to the **Primavera Forest**. The sign is small and is on the west side of an elongated town called La Venta del Astillero. Make a careful left turn here, and after a few blocks through a village make a right turn for two or three blocks, then continue south. Do not be discourage by the dirt an gravel road, and the fact that you will need to drive across a small shallow creek; once there you will be delighted with the beautiful pine forest and spectacular view of the

Tequila Volcano and surrounding mountains! We usually continue on the main road toward a rustic resort called Rio Caliente (Hot River). The river at the point where the road crosses into the resort is so hot it will burn your skin! The resort entrance is a good place to park and take off on foot down stream looking for volcanic stones, plants and wild life. There are open fields that are popular for Sunday family picnics.

Following the highway westward, and within three or four miles, the divided highway forks, with the left road going to the interesting villages of Ameca and Etzatlán. This broad fertile valley is used for farming sugar cane. The right fork is the main road and it proceeds through *agave azul* cactus fields to the town of Amatitán, which is about twenty-five miles from our starting point. After you go through some curves, down a hill, and as you enter town, make an immediate right turn past a cemetery and under the railroad track to the **Tequila Herradura** factory. This brand of tequila is said to be the best in Mexico! The factory is located in an old Hacienda behind high walls with towers that still have rifle slots for protection of the property in days long past.

Leaving Amatitán, proceed eight miles west to the town of **Tequila** (approximately thirty-three miles from our starting point). There are several tequila factories with guided tours; however, my main interest in the town is the road that goes almost to the top of the **Tequila Volcano**. To find the road follow the signs pointing to the **Microondas** (Microwave relays). Find your way to **Calle** (Street) **Miguel Hidalgo** and proceed up the hill over the railroad tracks by the train station. The view from the volcano is spectacular and well worth the trip for people who are adventuresome. **Note:** *A warm jacket is advisable because of the higher altitude, and also a picnic lunch and extra water or soft drinks may be in order.*

The fifth point of interest is the village of **Magdalena**, forty-eight miles from our starting point in Guadalajara. Magdalena is known for **opals** that are mined in the nearby mountains. We parked at the main village plaza and were immediately approached by men sitting on the park benches to sell us opals. It was a good time to practice bargaining. There are also stores on the streets surrounding the plaza that sell opals and opal jewelry. One owner took us to a shop where we watched opals being ground and polished. The day before our arrival, a group of Japanese gem buyers had been in town and had depleted the inventories of most of the stores. Not being knowledgeable about opals and their price we made no purchases, but the trip to Magdalena was worthwhile.

More adventurous people may want to hire an English-speaking guide to take them to the opal mines a few miles west of Magdalena. The first time we went we purchased handpicks in Magdalena. After seeing the mines we were permitted to do a little mining ourselves. We broke open some stones and found some beautiful opals. We did not have the success of the professional miners but our guests were enthusiastic and had a good time. Many of the miners will offer to sell you stones – don't pay the asking price.

We recommend that you take a picnic lunch and plenty of water. Although there are probably good restaurants along the way we did not see any that appealed to us. When visiting small cities or towns we are very cautious about where we eat.

Obviously one cannot visit all of these points of interest in a single day or even in several days; however, these are just a few of the attractions of the *campo* around Guadalajara.

Los Altos - Northeast from Guadalajara

Setting out to explore the Los Altos regions of the State of Jalisco on a beautiful fall day, we were delighted to find that the *Autopista* (Expressway) to Lagos de Moreno, a distance of 122 miles from Guadalajara, is now complete. Seeing that the highway was finished we immediately changed our itinerary and decided to visit our ultimate destination, Lagos de Moreno, first and visit the towns of San Juan de los Lagos, Jalostotitlan, San Miguel el Alto, Tepatitlan and Zapotlanejo on our return trip.

The Autopista starts just west of Zapotlanejo. The first section of the highway is rolling hills for about twenty miles, then becomes a wide plateau with beautiful views of distant mountains and wide valleys - very colorful with pink and gold flowers - a spectacular sight! Much of the land is devoted to agriculture, such as corn, poultry production, and cattle grazing. After about forty miles of the plateau the terrain turns somewhat hilly again until you reach Lagos de Moreno. When you cross the new autopista from Aguascalientes to León, you will notice "La Mesa de Moreno" to the right, a geology textbook example of a mesa (table flat-top mountain) and to the left and in the distance are other mesas. Although green in the summer and fall, the land is more arid than Guadalajara, and you will notice more nopal cactus and mesquite and less corn and agriculture. We hope that you will agree that the twenty-three dollars in tolls for such a wonderful view of West Central Mexico, with no trucks and little traffic, is well worth the money. This road is also excellent for a trip east to León or Guanajuato or north to Aguascalientes.

MAP OF LOS ALTOS REGION OF JALISCO

Lagos de Moreno, a declared colonial historical monument, is well worth exploring. It is filled with wonderfully preserved old buildings such as the very ornate Cathedral, baroque in design with intricate carvings on pink stone, and as beautiful inside as outside. Of interest also is the Capuchinas Ex-Convent, now used for art exhibits and concerts, and the neo-Classical Rosas Moreno Theater, just to name a few of the many cultural and historical sites.

Lagos de Moreno also boasts one of the most picturesque main plazas, or *zócalos*, that we have seen in Mexico, It is delightful to walk or sit and be part of this lovely setting. There are lush palm trees, magnolias, large ficus, shrubs and a colorful variety of flowers throughout.

On our return trip to Guadalajara, twenty-seven miles from Lagos de Moreno, we found San Juan de Los Lagos, another very traditional area, full of what we think of as the "Old Mexico." The town is primarily famous for the year around pilgrimages to the Sanctuary of the Virgin , San José Church. There are markets well known for the beautiful local handicrafts as well as delicious candy.

Twelve miles from San Juan de los Lagos is Jalostotitlan, a very small town, which has several interesting churches, such as the Sacred Heart Church, Parroquía de la Asunción and the Guadalupe Sanctuary. There is also the usual town park, quite nice, and a few restaurants to stop for a sample of the local food.

San Miguel el Alto, a few miles east of the Autopista, boasts a unique main plaza with its pink stone arches on each side. There are many interesting shops where one can purchase everything from cheese to stone work and fabrics, as well as architectural delights such as "La Purísima" Church, which dates back to 1700.

Tepatitlán also offers a chance to explore several interesting old buildings, such as the churches and city hall of the 18th century, and for shoppers there are stores where one can just browse or buy embroidered handicrafts and other works of native art.

We found this city to be very clean and beautiful. It is located next to the Autopista, just forty-nine miles from Guadalajara. We learned that there is a small colony of about twenty-five Americans living in Tepatitlán, and could see why they were attracted here.

Last of the towns we visited was Zapotlanejo, just eighteen miles east of Guadalajara. This small town attracts many for shopping. There are clothing factories nearby which have several outlets for the products they manufacture. These items are found in all of the town's shops and can be a very good deal for those serious shoppers who will take the time to examine each item carefully for flaws. Keep in mind that dressing rooms and mirrors are almost non-existent (since sales are supposedly on a wholesale level), so take a friend with you whose honest opinion you can rely on before purchasing!

We did not visit the towns of Arandas, Teocaltiche, and Encarnación de Diaz. Arandas, a quiet commercial town, is noted for having the largest bell ever made in Mexico, located at the entrance of the Church of San José Obrero. It is called "the bell that never rang" because it was too large for the bell tower where it was to be placed. Arandas is also famous for its tequila, preferred by many connoisseurs over the town of Tequila's product. Teocaltiche is noted for the manufacture of *sarapes* along with 16th century churches.

Of principal interest at Encarnación de Diaz is the park with topiary art - shrubs formed into figures of animals, various people and other objects. We will visit these another time.

One should allow two or three days to see all of the Los Altos region. Each of these small towns has a special charm of its own, and all still retain the Mexican atmosphere that is rapidly disappearing from the larger cities.

Tapalpa
A Relaxing "Get Away"

This mountain village, located only two hours southwest of Guadalajara, offers an excellent chance to get away from the city life and escape to the mountains with cool fresh air. For those who like picnics, hiking, climbing and exploring in general, this is certainly an ideal choice.

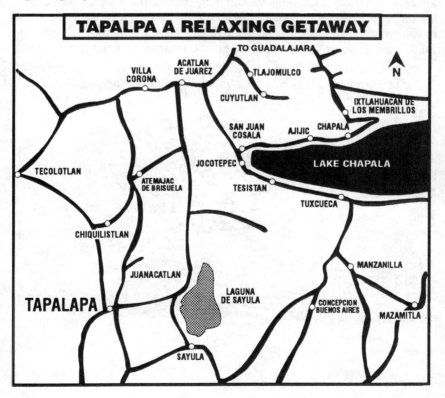

Tapalpa is a small pueblo once quite well known around the area for excellent *sarapes*, sweaters and rugs which were hand- woven from the wool of local sheep. Now those items are not as plentiful, and even if one finds them, they tend to be quite expensive. Shopping, in the usual "tourist" sense, is very limited, although Tapalpa is becoming famous for delicious cheese, honey, canned fruit, fruit liquors and jams. One should not come away without trying a sample of each. All Mexican villages have their main square, or *zócalo*, and Tapalpa is no exception. There one can sit to relax and watch as the local people take time out to stop and chat before going on about their business. The large church bell keeps everyone alerted, and life seems simple and satisfying.

Fifteen or twenty minutes west of Tapalpa, one will see the "Tapalpa Rocks" or *Piedras de Tapalpa*, which are huge boulders huddled together in an open field. The field is fenced off, so in order to really explore the rocks, it is necessary to park by the side of the road and go on foot. This is a favorite picnic place, and often there are couples and large families there to spend the day, eating and relaxing while the children, young and old, are entertained by the challenge to climb to the top of the boulders, which is usually easy to do since the rough surface of the rocks offers many "grab holds." Around this area are also many good spots for camping beneath the tall pine trees, which are on both sides of the road. (To find these rocks turn right at the sharp turn as you enter Tapalpa, after passing the Pemex service station on the left. The road is cobble stone and dirt, but the extra distance is well worth the drive.)

A day, weekend, or longer, spent in the mountains leaves one refreshed and with a sense of well being. **Visit Tapalpa, you'll be glad you did!**

A Day Exploring Mazamitla

Recently we decided to drive out of the city for a day to see some of the Mexican countryside. With some friends who were also in the mood for adventure, we packed a picnic lunch, filled the car tank, put on our most comfortable clothes and started out.

There are many great places to go for such an outing but we decided on one of our favorites, a small mountain village called Mazamitla, founded by the Tarascan Indians around 450 years ago. It is about 75 miles southeast of Guadalajara, and has an elevation of 7,200 feet above sea level, making it an excellent retreat when the temperature is at its peak before the rainy season in the city.

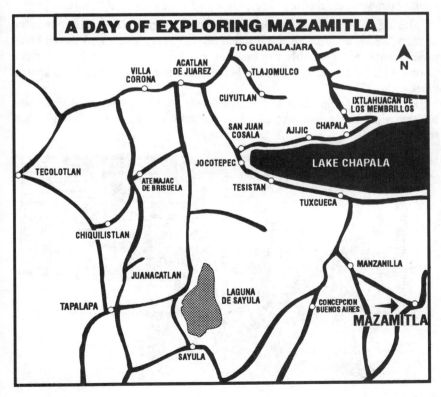

A DAY OF EXPLORING MAZAMITLA

135

The drive from Guadalajara along the south side of Lake Chapala, then turning south, takes two hours driving at a leisurely speed. The scenery gradually becomes different because of the sudden appearance of tall pine trees and other evergreens as the altitude increases, giving it a definite wooded effect. When we reached the village, we were all impressed at the cleanliness, swept streets, weeded yards, and the neatness of the houses and the buildings. There is a delightful park in the center of town with tall trees, flowers and clean benches, where we sat just to admire the beautiful church across the street, and watch the people as they went about their daily business. Because of the abundance of trees, many houses and buildings are built of wood, and others have a very decorative wooden trim, and entirely different look from the usual concrete block, brick or adobe houses we have become accustomed to seeing in Mexico.

Mazamitla offers very limited shopping in the sense that we usually look for; the stores carry only those items necessary for everyday living. (This fact pleased the guys, I'm sure, and is probably a factor in the appeal of the trip!)

We saw very few North Americans living in Mazamitla, but we find it very picturesque and the people seem quite friendly. For a weekend treat, or for a longer vacation, there are hotels and cabins available, which we all agreed would be a wonderful place to relax and enjoy the beauty of nature.

During our drive to our usual picnic place, which is a few miles out in the country beside a waterfall, we discovered that many lovely homes are being built. Some are probably for vacation or weekends, others looked more permanent. So apparently this lovely area has been "discovered" as a special treat.

For an enjoyable short trip which leaves you refreshed and gives you another view of Mexico, take a look at Mazamitla. I'm sure we will go back many times.

A Visitor Comes To Guadalajara

by Judy Crawford

A travel writer of sorts and an inveterate boll weevil (I really must find a place to retire one of these days), I finally could no longer resist a friend's promptings to visit Guadalajara, which he described as somewhere between Paris and Heaven. Now I live in a pretty idyllic setting myself, on an island in the Caribbean, but he's a fellow with a lot of travel savvy; so when the recent elections gave me a week off from my toil at the University of Puerto Rico, off I flew to Guadalajara.

I immediately found a nice reasonable hotel in the historic district, and located a marvelous restaurant only a few doors from the hotel. Being neither wealthy nor inclined by temperament to take "tourist" tours (people and their everyday surroundings interest me more than most of the usual sites), I began to explore the wonderful streets and plazas. Of course I had read in various guidebooks what to see, but the real pleasures were not even hinted at. Perhaps in Guadalajara they are so pervasive and so evanescent, it is not possible to list them. A stone sculpture exhibit graced one nearby plaza, while in another the Jalisco Orchestra played from a stage cleverly improvised over the lovely fountain at the back of the Degollado Theater. The well-kept greenery and flower beds did not sport a collection of paper cups, soiled Pampers, and beer bottles as they would have in other parts of the world. The profusion of fountains, of lovely accessible human scale, lured children to dip their hands, feet and toys. And the restroom in the magnificent government building, where I had gone to view the famous paintings of Orozco was so sparkling and clean than I actually took a picture of it! The shopping in the Mercado Libertad is well and rightly publicized, but shopping in the city itself, in all of the crammed and various little stores, produced in me increasing delight with the Guadalajarans themselves, as they and I tried to negotiate a sale in my much-less-than-perfect Spanish.

But my most valuable find was not in the stores, but in the bus system. Many of the city buses look like adventures about to happen, and with the exception of first class buses to areas outside the city, they are not for the timid. The buses are efficient (never did I wait longer than five minutes for a bus), easy to find, will stop nearly anywhere, and cost almost nothing (about 25 to 30 cents, depending on the type of bus service). On one occasion I mistakingly boarded a bus heading away from where I wanted to go and enjoyed a great trip all around the city before I arrived at my original objective. Although I did enjoy the ride, from then on I was sure to ask the destination as I boarded!

137

I estimate that I took about thirty local buses in the nine days I was in Guadaajara, and I found all of the bus drivers patient and helpful, and many of my fellow passengers extremely kind as well.

The buses that travel between Guadalajara and other towns leave from either the Old Bus Station or the New Bus Station (one can find out which buses leave from which station by asking at any hotel, and cheap local buses can take you to either one from almost anywhere in Guadalajara) and go nearly everywhere in Mexico. They range from spiffily new to cozily dilapidated. And every so often on the longer trips, the bus driver welcomes aboard an individual selling enticing snacks. This person rides along for as long as it takes him to sell coconut candies, cold drinks, or fruit to everyone who wants to buy, then hops off, and apparently catches a ride on another bus bumping along back to where he came from.

No where else that I've been lately has impressed me with such richness for the eyes and ears (and I am not even thinking about the well-known attractions of Guadalajara), and I can't remember ever having had more fun getting around. I am going to have to do it again soon. And I am going to send this report to my friend; he'll be pleased.

(Judy Crawford is author of an alternative travel book entitled **Low-cost Vacations With A Difference.** *It is available from Pilot Books, 103 Cooper Street, Babylon NY 11702. The newest edition costs $5.95.)*

The American Society of Jalisco

Over 50 years ago, the American Society of Jalisco was formed to promote better relations and understanding between Mexico and its neighbors to the North. Now a well-known and respected organization, AmSoc continues to be an important factor in the ongoing effort to strengthen relations between the two cultures.

As a private, non-profit group, an *"asociación civil,"* AmSoc's membership is open to anyone interested, regardless of race, religion or nationality. Myriad cultures, languages and nationalities form the roster of the Society.

The primary purpose of AmSoc is to provide for its members various social and cultural events, and other services for English-speaking persons residing in the city.

AmSoc offers many rewards for its membership. Activities include: speakers, lunch and dinner parties, new member cocktail parties, armchair traveler programs, cultural events and the traditional 4th of July picnic. Members receive special prices for some events and activities. They are

138

advised of upcoming events through their monthly newsletter, **The Voice**. There are over 400 members.

You are encouraged to join AmSoc either before you come or upon your arrival. When you join AmSoc, you will receive a directory of members and list of various organizations and special interest groups active in Guadalajara.

The American Society office is located at Av. San Francisco #3332 (off López Mateos), Colonia Chapalita. The telephone numbers are 121-2395 and 121-0887. They are open from 10 a.m. to 2:30 p.m., Monday through Friday.

Join the Memorial Society and then RELAX!

Even though death is never a popular subject to think about or discuss, it is inevitable, therefore the sensible thing to do is to prepare the best we can for necessary arrangements, and then resume enjoying life.

While in Mexico, for whatever length of time, it is very important to join the Memorial Society of Guadalajara, which also serves the Lake Chapala area. The procedure for joining is very simple, inexpensive and certainly worthwhile. Cost for a lifetime membership is around US $3.00, and for this small amount your personal information will be kept on file. This information includes; who should be notified, what your wishes are for your remains, and at death a Mexican death certificate is obtained to use for life insurance policies and other official purposes.

The Memorial Society was created in 1974. Services includes all paper work, various fees paid to the Mexican Government and the necessary final arrangements. Charges will depend on the service requested. Cremation costs US $400.00, and includes the urn, all paperwork and fees paid to four Mexican Government offices. If ashes are sent anywhere in the United States or Canada, add $50.00 for shipping and handling. Shipping of the Body by air to the United States or Canada costs US $1,200.00, including metal casket, shipping container, permits, insurance policy on shipping and other paperwork. Body donation costs US $100.00; the Body is picked up and delivered to the Medical School of the Autónoma University of Guadalajara, and all necessary paperwork is included. For burial in Guadalajara or the Chapala Area, the cost will vary depending on the type of service, casket and the cemetery used (US $500.00 up).

Forms for membership to the Memorial Society may be obtained in Guadalajara at the American Society office located at San Francisco 3332, Chapalita, at any time during their office hours between 10 a.m. and 2 p.m. The Memorial Society has a representative at the American Society on Thursdays, from 10 a.m. to noon. In the Lake Chapala area, membership forms may be obtained at the American Legion in Chapala.

All completed personal information on file with the Memorial Society should be updated as needed. The information is completely confidential and only the one-time membership fee is required. This is a very excellent service which all visitors and retirees should be aware of and should utilize.

To report a death, call San Miguel Funeral Home (Eduardo or Patricia Pérez, 825-1556 or 825-1355, or their answering service, 613-1228, *clave* (pager) 1214. They are available 24 hours a day. Or you may call San Ramón Funeral Home (María Eugenia López, 657-3267 at any hour, or 659-2222, 8 a.m. to 8 p.m.) If necessary, ask for someone who speaks English. If no one is available then call the other funeral home. Other phone numbers that may be called are 627-1724 or 627- 1843, ext. 112; 647-7737; 647-9924 or 121-2348. These last numbers are officials of the Memorial Society who maintain membership records. It is not necessary to call the police, the Red Cross or the Green Cross. If the deceased was an American citizen, you may also wish to contact the American Consulate at 825-2700, or at 826-5553 on weekends or holidays to discontinue Social Security benefits for the deceased.

Other information may be obtained at the American Society office, or by attending the monthly meetings held on the first Thursday of each month at 11 am at their headquarters.

ICMNA Offers Outstanding Service to our Community

The Mexican-North American Cultural Institute of Jalisco, or ICMNA, founded on 1949, probably has the busiest calendar schedule of any single non-profit organization in Guadalajara.

This excellent cultural center offers the opportunity of better understanding and communication between the two cultures. There are many educational, artistic and cultural appreciation programs available. Classes for those wishing to learn Spanish are readily available in all levels. For those more advanced students, lectures of interest are given weekly in Spanish on topics, which will further help understanding the Mexican way of life. Classes in English are also offered, since it is commonly recognized that the ability to speak, read and write the English language is rapidly becoming necessary in order to advance in the world today. Much thought, effort and training has gone into programs of teaching both the Spanish and English language, and there are extracurricular activities and events which are designed to aid in the progress of these classes, many which are free of charge.

Another excellent service offered by the ICMNA is finding Mexican families willing to open their homes to foreign students who wish to live with a Mexican family in order to be completely "immersed" in an environment where only Spanish is spoken. This program seems very effective.

The Mexican-North American Cultural Institute also makes good use of Guadalajara's numerous galleries, museums and theaters for learning and enrichment experiences. They offer a wide variety of cultural events, musical programs, theater productions, lectures, art exhibitions and many, many other opportunities for binational appreciation and enjoyment.

The ICMNA has a mailing list available for those wishing to receive a copy of the monthly calendar of events. Address: Enrique Díaz de León #300, Guadalajara, Jalisco. Tels. 825-4101 and 825-58-38

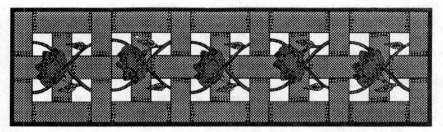

The Lake Chapala Society

by Melba Boudreau Wasey

Many years ago (in 1955 to be exact) a few retired Americans residing in Chapala, Jalisco were drawn together to form a small social club and memorial society. As their membership increased to include any English-speaking people in the foreign colony, they rented small quarters and opened an English language library as a non-profit organization. With all volunteer help and donations, it became very popular. For a small fee you could become a member of the Lake Chapala Society, which entitled you to use the library services and also attend their social activities.

As the years passed and the membership grew, the quarters that housed the library in Chapala became too small. Neill Jones, an American pioneer known for her philanthropic work among the Mexican community, offered the society a much larger building in the nearby village of Ajijic. In October 1983 the new library opened at 16 de Septiembre No. 16-A.

The librarian and helpers have cataloged all the books and have card index files. These volunteers must be admired for their work, as there are probably over eight thousand books. The library has been remodeled and expanded, the exterior repainted, and the tropical gardens restored to their former beauty.

At 11 a.m., on the second Wednesday of each month, a meeting is held at La Nueva Posada in Ajijic. New members are introduced and refreshments served. Usually there is an interesting guest speaker or other entertainment. Among the social events scheduled are a variety of parties during the year, such as the 4th of July barbecue. The happenings of the Society are included in a newsletter written by the society president and mailed to members monthly.

The library offers a unique service and is the only organization outside the United States to have "Talking Books" from the Library of Congress, Washington, D.C. A small cassette recorder is furnished, with taped readings of current books. You must be an American citizen and a Lake Chapala Society member. If you have a vision impairment or are physically handicapped, and have a legitimate certificate from a doctor, you will qualify. For more information visit the library any Thursday.

There are now over one hundred members in the new video "Tape-Worm Club", that opened in 1990. For a small donation you may borrow a VCR English language tape. There is a large selection of new and old tapes, including classics, drama comedy, suspense, etc. Drop by and take a look, you'll like the video "Tape-Worm Club".

The Lake Chapala Society also offers a "Post Life Planning Service" to its members. This service is similar to the Memorial Society, described previously.

Almost two thousand members are listed in the annual directory. The Spanish Language Library (*Biblioteca*) for children is located in an adjacent building to the library on 16 de Septiembre. The Lake Chapala Society took on sponsorship of this worthy cause. This popular *biblioteca* is open six days a week and is well attended by children of all ages.

Ms. Neill James, who is now deceased, permitted the Society to renovate the beautiful gardens on the grounds of her home adjacent to the Society. Ponds, fountains and stone statues were cleaned and long overgrown pathways were cleared, creating one of the most beautiful tropical gardens in the area. This paradise is open to the public and a walk through such a lovely place should be on your itinerary when in Ajijic. The North American community can be proud of the accomplishments of this fine organization.

The Lake Chapala Society provides a most valuable service for the community on the north shore of Lake Chapala, and should be visited by retirees and visitors.

Curtain Up on the Lakeside Little Theatre

by June Summers

Founded in 1964, by Betty Kuzell, The Lakeside Little Theatre is now Mexico's oldest English language theater. The first production, "From Kokomo to Mexico", was an original musicale written by Kuzell. It was presented at Chapala's old railroad station. Other early shows were presented on a variety of improvised stages, until the organization began renting the second floor of the Chula Vista Country Club.

When advised that their lease would not be renewed, Lakeside Little Theatre leaders decided to concentrate on giving the theater a home of its own. Fund raising for the new theater began and building plans were set in motion.

Ricardo O'Rourke donated a plot of land between Chapala and Ajijic. Ground breaking ceremonies were held on January 3, 1987. Meantime the Lakeside Little Theater continued its presentations on improvised stages around the community, and in the Chapala Haciendas Restaurant and Chapala Real Hotel in La Floresta.

Lakeside Little Theatre's gala and official opening of their new Theatre took place on January 15, 1988. The premier production in the new Playhouse was Woody Allen's comedy "Don't Drink The Water". All productions are of professional quality and the contributions of this organization are a plus in considering the Guadalajara/Chapala area as a place to retire. Kudos to Mexico's oldest English language theater. CURTAIN UP!

Do You Like Fishing?

Fishing is good at Barra de Navidad on Melaque Bay (southwest of Guadalajara) from December to March each year. Fishing boat rentals are reasonable in price. Barra de Navidad, on the Pacific Ocean, is a four and one-half hour drive from Guadalajara, and is an excellent place to spend a week or so in December, January or February.

For more information on fishing in Mexico, write or call:

Mexican Fisheries Department
2550 5th Avenue, Suite 101
San Diego CA 92103-6622
Telephone (619) 233-6956

Church Directory for Guadalajara and Lakeside Chapala

English Speaking Churches in Guadalajara:

All Saints Lutheran Church
Av. Tepeyac 4600, Guadalajara
Telephone 121-6741
Grace Baptist Church
Pedro Buzeta #970, Guadalajara
Saint Mark's Episcopal Church
Chichimecas 836, corner of Aztecas , Col. Monraz, Guadalajara
Telephone 641-6620
Saint Mary of Guadalupe Roman Catholic Church
Av. Tepeyac at Fray Juan de Zumarraga
Colonia Chapalita, Guadalajara
Telephone 629-9698 and 629-8459
Bugambilias Presbyterian Church
Callejón del Iris#50
Ciudad Bugambilias, Guadalajara
Telephone 684-5448

English Speaking Churches in the Lake Chapala area:

Little Chapel by the Lake
Chula Vista, Jalisco.
Telephone (376) 6-0726
St. Andrew's Anglican Church
Calle San Lucas , Riberas del Pilar, Chapala, Jalisco
Telephone (376) 5-3926
San Andres Roman Catholic Church
Marcos Castellanos #14 , Ajijic, Jalisco
Telephone (376) 6-0922
El Lago Community Church
Javier Mina #7, Ajijic, Jalisco
Telephone (376) 6-0509

Mexico Kaleidoscope of Color

Just as each turn of the kaleidoscope offers a new and delightful variety of color and beauty, such is the case of the following pages of this book. As you turn each page you will be treated to an exciting glimpse of Mexico and all it has to offer.

We have selected a wide range of scenes that are typical of this fascinating country captured in beautiful color photographs. As you turn these pages you will see a variety of beauty: spectacular mountain and beach scenes, the fascinating architecture of beautiful old buildings, typical village scenes and of course the exotic plants and flowers and many others.

We hope you will enjoy this colorful and stimulating taste of Mexico as you study the photographs and read our book!

THE CATHEDRAL IN DOWNTOWN GUADALAJARA

THE DEGOLLADO THEATRE IN DOWNTOWN GUADALAJARA

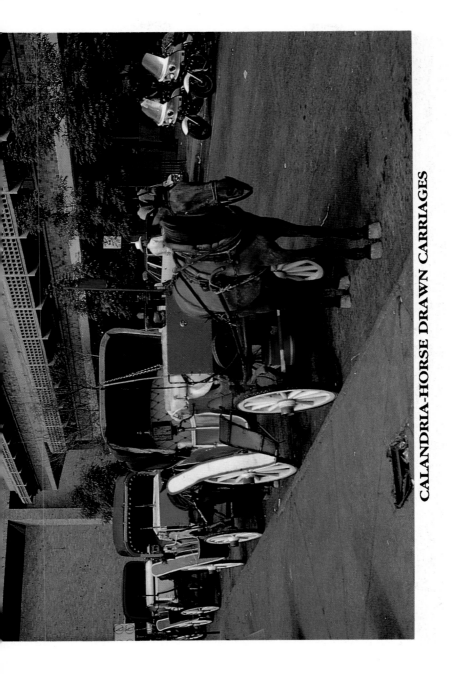

CALANDRIA-HORSE DRAWN CARRIAGES

COLORFUL MERCHANDISE AT THE LIBERTAD MARKET

BEAUTIFUL FRESH FRUITS IN A MARKET

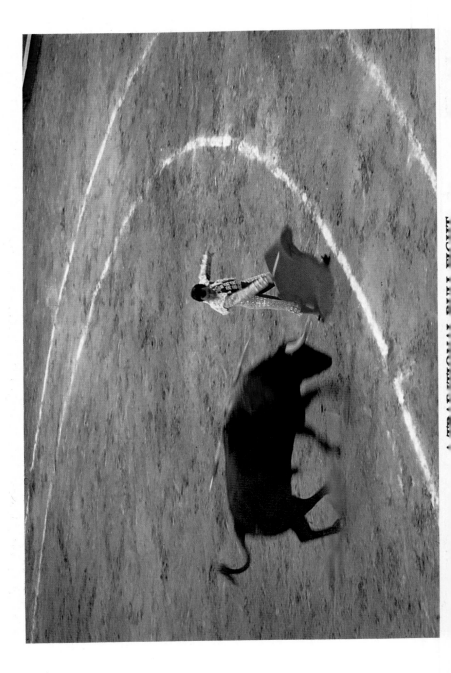

THE OBLATOS CANYON AT THE NORTH SIDE OF GUADALAJARA

AGAVE AZUL TEQUILA CACTUS NEAR VILLAGE OF TEQUILA

THE CHARROS (COWBOYS) PERFORMING

VIEW OF INSIDE THE BASILICA AT ZAPOPAN

HORSETAIL FALLS NORTHWEST OF GUADALAJARA

VIEW OF DOWNTOWN CHAPALA

VILLAGE SQUARE IN CHAPALA

SCENE AT THE LAKE CHAPALA SOCIETY IN AJIJIC

A BEAUTIFUL HOUSE IN AJIJIC (COURTESY OF CHAPALA REALTY)

STAIRWAY IN THE NUEVA POSADA INN AT AJIJIC

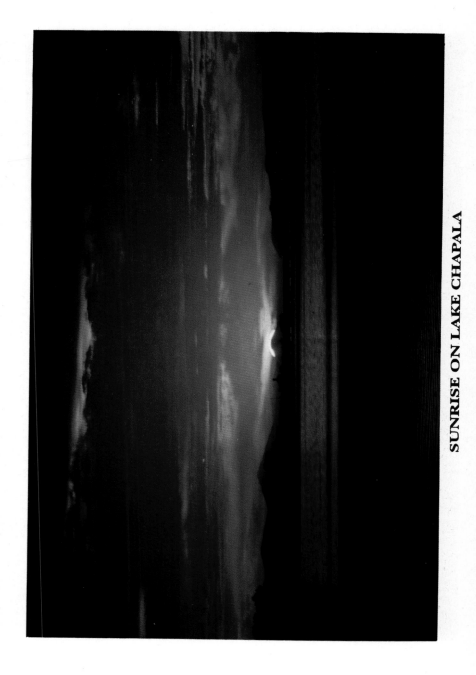

SUNRISE ON LAKE CHAPALA

FOLKLORIC DANCER AT A FIESTA

TURTLE ROCKS AND BALANCED ROCK NEAR TAPALPA

CHURCH ON THE SQUARE IN MAZAMITLA

LA PARROQUIA CHURCH IN SAN MIGUEL DE ALLENDE

GENTLY FLOWING RIVER AFTER THE CASCADE NEAR URUAPAN, MICHOACAN

A SCENE AT MELAQUE BAY

SECURING THE MORNING FISH CATCH AT RINCON DE GUAYABITOS, NAYARIT

VILLAGE OF AJIJIC ON LAKE CHAPALA

THE EIGHTEENTH HOLE AT LAS HADAS GOLF COURSE, MANZANILLO

THE DAYS CATCH AT CABO SAN LUCAS, BAJA CALIFORNIA

FRIARS ROCKS, BAJA CALIFORNIA

VII

Other Possible Retirement Locations

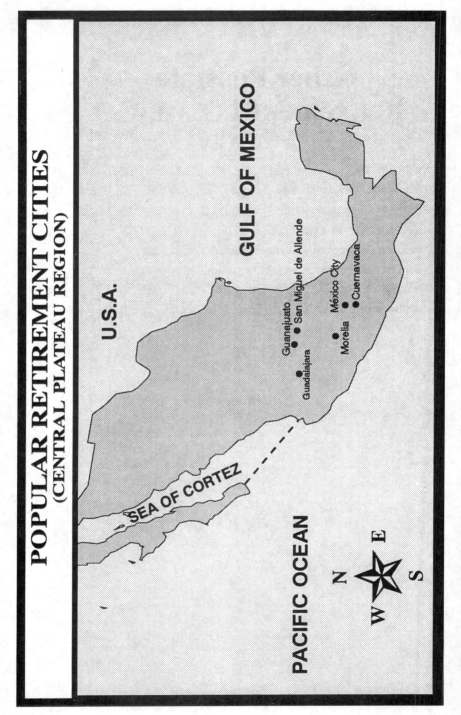

Visit Cuernavaca

by Florence Gilbert

My husband and I found Cuernavaca almost by accident. A friend, who had attended one of the many language schools in this city, recommended it highly when we said we were going to retire in Mexico, probably in Guadalajara. We were driving from Mexico City to Guadalajara four years ago when we decided to make the detour - and we're still here. For us Cuernavaca is the place to retire.

The first thing to impress you is the climate. At one mile high (just like Denver, Colorado, where we moved from) with a mean temperature of 72 degrees, how could anyone ask for more. We like to call ourselves golfers and we don't know any place else where you can play your favorite outdoor sport almost every day of the year. The rains normally come only during the summer and early fall months, then only during late afternoons or evenings. Only a very few times, in our experience, have they been heavy enough to make the golf course too wet for play.

When we arrived, we decided to rent an apartment at first. We bought a membership in San Gaspar Golf Club and were ready to buy a home close to the club a year later. Other courses in and around town include Club Cuernavaca, Tabachines, Santa Fe, Lomas de Cocoyoc and Hacienda Cocoyoc. A club interchange allows members of each club to visit each of the others on specified weekdays, a real perk. We are not tennis players but we did learn that there are several fine tennis clubs, complete with swimming pools and other family activities, in town. Probably the most outstanding are the Raquet Club and Delago Sports Club.

One of the first things I did was to pick a language school to study Spanish. Friends recommended Cemanahuac but there are many other very fine schools - Ideal, Multi-Cultural Institute, Cuauhnahuac, to mention just a few.

In those early days, we were making Mexican friends, mostly through our golf membership, but we were eager to meet other *Norteamericanos* as well. No one is sure how many "foreign" residents live in and around Cuernavaca, the capital city of the State of Morelos. The Navy League Directory of Foreign Residents of the State of Morelos lists some 600 names but the number of residents from other countries is probably more than double that figure. They come from many countries besides the United States and Canada but English is the predominant common language.

Anyone who wants to be part of this small community must visit the Guild House at No. 111 Tuxtla Gutierrez. It houses an excellent lending library. The all volunteer staff also has a tremendous supply of used books for sale. You can also visit the Thrift Shop, where all kinds of clothing and useful items are on sale, and The Pantry, for freshly baked goodies, jellies, spaghetti sauce - you name it!

Equally important, all the English speaking community organizations publicize their activities at the Guild house. This group includes the Guild itself, which works to raise funds for charities that benefit their adopted country; the Center of the Creative Arts; Association for the Protection of Animals; Navy League; American Legion; American Benevolent Society; and the Salvation Army. Membership in these groups let you act in plays, plan fund-raisers, attend lectures and go on outings guaranteed to raise your cultural I.Q. If you enjoy classical music, there are a variety of concerts presented throughout the year.

The official 1990 census places the metropolitan area, Cuernavaca, Juitepec and Temixco, at 451,000 and the figure is probably fairly accurate even now, but only on weekdays. It seems to double each weekend as literally thousands of well-to-do Mexico City residents, also known non-affectionately as *Chilangos*, visit their second homes in Cuernavaca or fill up the hotels in and around the city. We soon found out the city comes in two sizes - Monday through Friday and Friday night to Sunday afternoon.

One of the most popular resort hotels, about 20 minutes outside town, is Hacienda Cocoyoc. It has over 300 rooms, three large swimming pools, a nine hole golf course at the hotel plus easy access to its 18 hole golf course only minutes away. Its lush gardens and antique charm - it really was a colonial hacienda - make it the perfect place to get away from it all.

Then, on the outskirts of town, there is another favorite, Hacienda Cortés, where Hernán Cortés used to spend his leisure hours. You can close your eyes and imagine you see him, clad in armor, clanking his way through the ancient halls.

Inside the city, excellent hotels are everywhere. Pricey Villa Bejar, like something out of the Arabian Nights, is one of the most popular spots for small meetings, or family weekends. Less expensive but with a charm of its own, we have Hostería Las Quintas. One of its attractions is that it is within easy walking distance of the best store in town, Bio-Art, a treasure trove that offers gorgeous handicrafts, clothes, furniture, decorative pieces to enhance your home, jewelry, tableware - whatever your heart desires. It is the perfect place to find a unique gift for that special someone.

All of the hotels mentioned offer outstanding cuisine as well as lovely guest rooms.

The premier restaurant in town, Las Mañanitas, actually is a small hotel as well, but most people just go there to enjoy the magnificent gardens along with fine food and service.

Cuernavaca actually has two central plazas, almost side by side. Many *Norteamericanos* love to sit in the sidewalk cafes across the street and watch the colorful carryings on. Of course, while you sip your Cappuchino you will be besieged by shoeshine boys and street merchants hawking everything from dresses and hammocks to beads and birds. On weekends, one end of the Zocalo offers a great market with bargains on clothing, especially woolens, rugs, silver items, wall hangings and much much more. The huge city market offers bargains in all sorts of household items, foods, clothing, gorgeous flowers, and is close to the center of town. As a tourist visiting Cuernavaca, you probably would have flown to Mexico and landed in Mexico City. We have an excellent, almost new, airport outside the city but there are no passenger flights in and out of the Cuernavaca airport at present. The smartest way to get here from Mexico City is to buy a taxi ticket at the airport to take you to the *Terminal Sur de Autobuses* (South Bus Terminal).

The taxi ride should cost you about twelve dollars, though even the regulated prices seem to be escalating sharply. When you reach the bus station, buy a ticket for *Servicio de Lujo* or *Servicio de Primera* to Cuernavaca. The fifty mile ride to Cuernavaca, in an excellent bus, will cost only about four dollars. If you want to choose the *Ejecutivo Dorado* bus, the price will be around seven dollars. After a beautiful ride through mountains that look a lot like the foothills in Colorado, you will arrive either at the Selva station or downtown, depending on which destination you choose. Taxis abound and rates are much more reasonable than in Mexico City but it is wise to agree on a price before you get into a cab.

If you have already arranged to study Spanish at one of the language schools, housing will have been arranged for you. It is strongly recommended that you live with a Mexican family so you will be forced to practice your new second language daily. This is also a good way to cut your living expenses because you will also eat your meals with the family, all at a minimal cost. Hotel prices vary widely as do the amenities they offer. All the schools offer a list of very reasonably priced hotels, if you choose not to stay with a family.

As a tourist, whether you hire a guide or plan your own itinerary, there are many sights you shouldn't miss. Cuernavaca is so rich in history and culture, you should be sure to allow yourself enough time to enjoy everything it has to offer.

The list should include the gorgeous 16th century Cathedral close to the center of town; Jardín Borda, Maximilian's summer home when he was emperor of Mexico, now a cultural center; the Brady Museum (near the Cathedral) which houses the collection of Robert Brady, his gift to the people of Morelos, and my favorite museum.

The *Palacio de Cortés* (Palace of Cortés), close to the Zócalo, also is a museum now. Once it was Cortes's administrative headquarters. It is also famed because it boasts a mural painted by Diego Rivera in 1929-30, commissioned by Dwight Morrow when he was ambassador to Mexico.

You will probably want to visit Taxco, the silver capital of Mexico, while you are here. It is only about 50 miles away and you can hire a taxi, take a bus, or seek out fellow tourists to hire a van.

You won't want to miss Sumiya Restaurant and new hotel, originally brought from Japan as a home for one of Barbara Hutton's many husbands. A trip to Lake Tesquitengo, for water skiing or boating, is a popular outing and there are very good hotels overlooking the lake if you care to stay overnight. You also may want to visit the village of Tepotzlan, learn about its Indian heritage and enjoy its lovely mountain vistas.

If you have passed the tourist stage and have decided you want to retire in Cuernavaca, I would strongly recommend that you rent an apartment while getting acquainted with the city. You will soon find that this is not the cheapest place to live in Mexico, primarily because it is such a popular place to live in or visit and is close to Mexico City. There are many beautiful homes in Cuernavaca but most of then are hidden behind high stone walls with a beauty all their own. Many of the walls are completly covered with vines and gorgeous flowers. Tabachines and bougainvilleas, tulipans and lush green shrubbery abound.

When we had explored the city quite thoroughly, we bought a "horizontal condominium" in a complex of ten small homes, most of which are only used on weekends by visiting Chilangos. After we paid a hefty *escritura* (deed, including taxes, etc.), and installed our satellite dish (cable television is not available where we live, though it is inside Cuernavaca), the three bedroom house still cost only about $60,000 - a real bargain. The complex has lovely gardens and a heated swimming pool as well as an indoor squash facility. Monthly maintenance fees fluctuate somewhat but generally are about $200. Yearly property taxes are about than $30.00.

When we retired, we thought our everyday activities and hobbies, especially golf, would keep us busy, and they very well could have. Life is different in Mexico and it does take longer to accomplish some routine business. For example, you have to pay your phone and electric bills at a bank or at the utility offices, or pay someone to do it for you. No one would think of mailing in a check. The mail simply is not that reliable and you could lose your service or incur a late charge.

Despite our lifestyle changes, we still found that we had extra time on our hands. To keep busy, we started a small monthly newsletter, "Cuernavaca Calling", which is mailed to subscribers in seventeen states, Canada, Cuernavaca and Mexico City. We try to keep up on national and international news by reading *The Mexico City News* faithfully, in addition to watching the news on television. There are some excellent Mexico City newspapers, in Spanish, but the State of Morelos doesn't seem to have any outstanding newspapers of its own.

152

These activities, plus an active social life, make for a fulfilling, sometimes exciting, "retirement." We think we've found the perfect place for it. Springtime in the Rockies is wonderful but we like the City of Eternal Springtime even more.

(For subscription information about "Cuernavaca Calling", write to: Apdo. 4-587, Cuernavaca, Morelos, CP 62431, Mexico.)

Visit San Miguel de Allende

by Barbara Thompson

San Miguel de Allende, in the state of Guanajuato, is a charming, delightful, lively and stimulating old colonial town 257 miles (428 km) northwest of Mexico City, 50 miles (83 km) north of Querétaro, and 550 miles (917 km) to the U.S. border (a ten hour drive). There is one train a day from Mexico City, which takes four and one half hours. By car or bus on the excellent, divided highway from Mexico City, it takes three to four hours. The closest airport from San Miguel is a one-and-a-half hour drive (75 miles or 125 km) to León, which flies to Mexico City, Monterrey, San Antonio, Houston, Los Angeles and Tijuana.

San Miguel is a little bustling town with an altitude of 6,100 ft. (1879 meters) and has a population of 110,000 residents.

San Miguel de Allende sits on the side of a steep hillside into a very large valley. The town has quaint, steep, narrow cobblestone streets and narrow sidewalks, many with not room enough for two people to walk together side by side. The most famous view of the town is when you arrive from the south, and it is breathtaking. It is a painter's dream; many movies and postcards have portrayed this view.

San Miguel de Allende has been declared an official national monument. The old stone walls to the homes cannot be torn down or changed, and the rules are strictly enforced. When you walk by an open door, peek in. You just might see beautiful gardens, fountains, other buildings and other assorted gorgeous sites. But Mexico is the "land of gates and walls"; next door to that beautiful entrance and lovely home may be a rather broken-down door, and inside, a dirt-floored, dark room where a family of eight or ten live with chickens and pigs wandering in their small garden.

The main plaza, called the *"Jardín"* (garden) by most people, is where you will probably see someone you know. You pick up *The News* newspaper from Mexico City, published in English, or the weekly local English newspaper *ATENCION*, and sit on a Jardín bench and try to read, but the people-watching is even more fun and better. Around the Jardín are the colonial city hall, eating establishments, the police station, many stores, and the beautiful main Franciscan Cathedral, with its Gothic towers, called the *Parroquía*, designed and constructed by an Indian mason, Zaferino Gutierrez, in the last 19th century. It is said he used as his guides picture postcards and etchings of French Gothic cathedrals. For miles around you can see this landmark of a church because of its huge size and beauty. There are so many gorgeous churches in San Miguel, including St. Paul's Episcopal Church, near the

Instituto, with services in English. A day's walking tour around San Miguel, visiting many sites, would be very interesting. No matter where you are in San Miguel, I am pretty sure that the early morning (hopefully not before 8 a.m.) will greet you with many churches clanging their bells to wake you up. You **do** get used to the sound. This **is** Mexico. Nearly everything is within easy walking distance of the Jardín, but you do need very good walking shoes for the uneven, jagged, cobbled stones of every size and shape. It is a good ankle-twisting town.

The city was founded by a Franciscan monk, Juan de San Miguel, in 1542, and "Allende" was added later to honor Don Ignacio Allende, one of the initiators of the 1810 Independence movement. His magnificent, partly baroque mansion stands today as a museum to the left of the Parroquía, where you will also see his statue at the corner of the building.

There are more than 1,500 permanent residents in San Miguel de Allende from the United States and Canada, many financially successful. Of course, the number of people from these two countries swells in both the summer and winter months. The town's foreign colony is also made up of artists, writers, artisans, teachers, students, sculptors, drifters, "searchers", etc., which make a good blend of many different types of people. It is an old Mexican town, yet cosmopolitan, with good hotels, shopping, entertainment, education and culture. Also, many foreigners come to San Miguel for its art institutes, and to receive excellent instruction in the Spanish language from its many language schools.

The most renowned is the Instituto Allende, Calzada Ancha de San Antonio 20, San Miguel Allende, Guanajuato 37770, which offers many art courses and instruction in all levels of Spanish. Stirling Dickinson and other prominent residents founded the Institute in the late 1930's, and it has progressed as an important accredited arts and crafts school. It is housed amid the arches and fountains of a former palace built by the Conde de la Canal. The school is now part of the University of Guanajuato. Another art school is the Nigromante Cultural Center, locally known as Bellas Artes, at Dr. Hernández Macias 75. It is a branch of the famous National Institute of Fine Arts (Instituto Nacional de Bellas Artes) in Mexico City. Built in 1734, it was the Convent of La Concepción. There are also many other fine art and excellent language instruction schools. If you plan to study, come with a Tourist Visa, **not** a Student Visa, the latter being more complicated. Many storekeepers and others speak English in San Miguel.

San Miguel de Allende **loves** a fiesta, and there are many, perhaps forty of them. The year begins with the day of Three Kings, when Mexican children traditionally receive their Christmas gifts. There is a pre-Lenten carnival, Easter celebrations lasting two weeks, and Corpus Christi in June. "El Grito", September 15th, followed by Independence Day on the 16th, are full of speeches and fireworks. The third weekend of September, for three days, is the fiesta of San Miguel, honoring the patron saint, with bullfights, Conchero dancers, parades and fireworks. November 1st is All Saints Day, when you may buy candy figurines in the forms of skeletons, skulls, and other foods to take to the cemeteries the following day, November 2nd, Day of the Dead, in honor of all deceased family members. Christmas time is very festive, with many *posadas* from December 16th to the 24th.

Your stay in San Miguel **must** include a Sunday tour, so that you can view some of the gorgeous mansions and homes, which is sponsored by San Miguel's Public Library (*Biblioteca Pública*). The library is three blocks from the Jardín on Calle Insurgentes 25. The lending library, which was founded by United States and Canadian residents, has the second largest collection of English and Spanish books in Mexico. The House and Garden Tour, in English for a small fee, begins **most** Sundays at noon, and leaves from the library. The library is a gathering place for the large foreign community as many activities are held there.

There is always something going on in San Miguel, and you can keep as busy as you want. There are groups playing bridge, golf, tennis, folk dancing, horse riding, basketball, aerobics and live theater, and there are many concerts and other cultural and educational programs. San Miguel has successfully combined colonial charm with 20th Century culture. There are a few excellent hot thermal spas for your aches and pains not far out of town. Buses are available. There are also a couple of good trailer parks.

San Miguel is blessed with year-round perfect weather. The temperature averages out to be 72°F (23°C), with not many days reaching 90°F (32°C). It is a dry heat because of the arid surroundings and high altitude, so you do not feel the heat as much. Most nights you need a *rebozo* (stole) or sweater. For those chilly winter evenings and early mornings, you will like a nice fireplace fire that most homes have, and a wool sweater. The rainy season is from June through September, with heavy, late afternoon or evening showers.

There are laundromats, or perhaps you prefer the public washing basins, with spring water running through, at the end of Calle Recreo, where the less fortunate of the population go daily to do their wash. This is worth a trip to see. It is near the *Parque Juárez*. San Miguel is a photographer's dream!

In San Miguel there is a hospital, a car rental agency, an English bookstore, movie theater, at least two English-speaking television channels, and a lively, good market which is always a meeting place. Supermarkets around the Jardín are expensive. What to buy in San Miguel? Silver, gold, pottery, brassware, heavy wool rugs, lanterns, rebozos, woven sarapes, paper mache, masks, cotton cloth, and tinware, without forgetting the colonial furniture, among the finest in Mexico.

San Miguel de Allende has a varied selection of many excellent and fine hotels and restaurants. Two of the best hotels, with delicious restaurants (and perhaps the most expensive) are La Sierra Nevada, Hospicio 35, with good French cooking, and Villa Jacarandas, Aldama 53. A less expensive, quaint, colonial hotel, with the best location in town, is the Posada de San Francisco, directly across the Jardín from the Parroquía. The Mesón de San Antonio, Mesones 80, is a small renovated mansion, and is quiet, clean and friendly. The best value is the Hotel Quinta Loreto, Loreto 13, with clean, large rooms and excellent, inexpensive food. The Bugambilia Restaurant, Hidalgo 22, has very good traditional Mexican food.

Short day trips from San Miguel worth taking would be the nine mile (15 km) trip to Antonilco where there's a magnificent church built about 1740 or, a 17 mile (28 km) ride to Dolores Hidalgo, known as the "Cradle of National Independence", where Father Hidalgo's home was when he gave the announcement to begin the eleven-year Mexican Independence War. Or, if you're willing to go a little farther, an overnight trip to the silver city of Guanajuato, founded in 1548, could water your palate. Guanajuato, only a two hour bus trip from San Miguel, is the unique and beautiful capital of Guanajuato State, and a University city which also has been declared a national monument like San Miguel de Allende.

Negative aspects of living in San Miguel de Allende? It is growing rapidly and rents are climbing like everywhere in Mexico. Food and other products are more costly than when living in Guadalajara. There is no airport and air travel involves a trip to Mexico City and León. Because of the high altitude heat may be required in the winter months.

A Look At Guanajuato

Guanajuato, the capital of the state of Guanajuato, is located in the heart of the Mexican republic. The city nestles in a narrow valley and around the hillsides of the Sierra Madre mountains.

With a population of approximately 55,000 (including very few North Americans), Guanajuato is very European in atmosphere, rich in colonial charm, and an interesting city to explore.

Guanajuato is reported to have been settled as early as 1552, due to the discovery of its rich mineral deposits by Juan de Jaso. Five years later it was officially founded as *Santa Fe y Real de Minas de Guanajuato*, which means "Hill of the Frogs" in the Tarascan language. The later discovery of the *Veta Madre de Plata* (Silver Mother Lode) brought prosperity to many who consequently built magnificent homes, churches and other beautiful buildings representing the best in Mexican baroque architecture.

Guanajuato was declared a national monument by the government of Mexico in 1973; all restorations or new construction must conform to the old style architecture, therefore retaining its colonial appearance. Another similar recognition was bestowed when, in 1988, the United Nations named the city a World Heritage Zone. Although small, very conservative, and to some not considered to be a lively city , it offers much in the way of history and cultural entertainment.

For tourists or visitors to Guanajuato, who are without car or other vehicle, there are convenient flights in and out of the El Bajío Airport in León, about 25 miles away, plus several bus lines, including the super-first class "ETN" line (24 passengers per bus). For those visitors who are driving, it is advisable to park your vehicle at the hotel and put on comfortable walking shoes in order to fully appreciate and admire the beauty of the city's colorful buildings made from cantera stone (not to mention the almost impossible task of finding a parking space in the downtown area).

Driving in Guanajuato is tricky to say the least, since the city's freeway (Padre Belauzaran St.) is a mixture of tunnels running under the entire area and exiting into narrow, winding streets with such picturesque names as Nosegay, Monkey Jump, Deer, Angles, Holy Child and the most famous one, "Kiss Alley", which according to the natives was so named because two ill-fated lovers who lived on opposite sides of the narrow street were still able to share a kiss or two!

Easy to find and a good landmark is the **Jardín de la Unión**. Although small, this is Guanajuato's center square and offers an excellent place to sit and relax while enjoying band concerts. It is also a good place to begin your tour of the interesting places to see. We have listed some of the most interesting, for example: the **Teatro Juárez,** a beautiful and very ornate building, named after Mexico's most famous president, Benito Juárez, is an interesting mixture of several styles of architecture and is still used for special events. Also of interest is the **Templo de San Diego**, a Franciscan church built in 1663, and rebuilt after suffering severe flood damage in the 18th century. The San Diego Church is recognized by its very impressive ornate doorway. The **Templo de la Compañía** (Church of the Company, referring to the Company or Society of Jesus) is probably recognized as the grandest church in Guanajuato. This beautiful church of the 17th century has an impressive dome and pink stone façade. It definitely should be seen and appreciated.

La Basílica Menor de Nuestra Señora de Guanajuato (Minor Basilica of Our Lady of Guanajuato) boasts the oldest piece of Christian art in Mexico, "Our Lady of the Holy Faith of Guanajuato", a medieval wooden image mounted on a base of local silver, which was a gift from Spain's King Philip II. This splendid building sports a coral and gold façade.

The largest building constructed entirely of stone is the **Alhóndiga de Granaditas,** also known as "Corn Palace." It was once a grain warehouse and later used as a fortress by Spanish defenders during the War of Independence, the 1810 invasion led by Miguel Hidalgo. It is now a delightful museum, displaying paintings by Hermenegildo Busto, murals by Chávez Morado, and a collection of colonial pottery.

Another museum is the **Museo Diego Rivera**, birthplace of Diego Rivera, the great muralist, displaying his work. Also, the **Museo Iconográfico Cervantino**, which exhibits popular art inspired by Cervantes.

The **Teatro Principal**, located next to the University on Calle Cantarranos, is very popular for all cultural events and fine performances can be enjoyed for a very small fee.

Of interest to tourists and natives alike is the huge two-story market constructed from iron and glass. Here one can find anything from handmade clothing and crafts, to fresh vegetables and fruits. It is open every day.

Since Guanajuato has been recognized for its history of silver mining, it is a must for tourists to visit **La Valenciana**. This very beautiful church, with its hand carved altar and pulpit styled after a Chinese pagoda, perches atop the Valenciana silver mine, which is still active. Here, one may buy fascinating geodes and quartz crystals.

In Guanajuato many students attend the University, built by the Jesuits in 1732. There are special summer programs designed to offer different subjects of interest. The University is a definite focal point for ongoing cultural events.

Although not a favorite of mine, the **Mummy Museum** is considered by many to be a tourist attraction. It is located at the entrance to the **Panteón** (Municipal Cemetery). Here, in glass cases along the wall, one will see bodies displayed which are perhaps hundreds of years old. It is thought that the bodies have been preserved due to the dry mountain air and the mineral salts in the cemetery soil.

To plan your trip to Guanajuato, take in consideration the time of year and what you can expect weatherwise. With an altitude of 6,700 feet, the average temperature hovers in the mid 60's, making it necessary for sweaters or jackets in the evening. Also, if you go during late summer through early fall, you will be in the rainy season, so rain gear will be necessary. The mode of dress is casual, and above all, comfortable shoes are a must.

Hotels and restaurants offer a wide variety of accommodations and meals, limited only by one's taste and budget.

Guanajuato is definitely a place to visit so plan and see a little more of what Mexico has to offer.

Morelia, A City to Explore!

The city of Morelia, founded in 1541, is located approximately mid-way between Guadalajara and Mexico City, with actual driving time around five or six hours from either city. At an elevation of 6,300 feet, the air is clear, cool and crisp, and the climate is pleasant year round. There is much of historical interest in Morelia, which is the capitol of the state of Michoacan, and the city is full of beautiful Spanish colonial architecture, making it a delight to explore. The city is named for José María Morelos, a priest who was a leader in the war to liberate Mexico from Spain in the early 1800's.

In spite of Morelia's many attractions, the city is a little out of the way for North American retirees. Although the population has expanded greatly in the recent years, it is largely due to Mexicans relocating after the disastrous earthquake in Mexico City in 1985. With a population reaching over a million at this writing, there are reportedly only around 100 North Americans who have chosen to retire there. Many live in the Santa María area of the city.

Some think the main reason for the scarcity of North American retirees could be the slower rate of development such as air service and fewer modern conveniences than offered in other cities. This is gradually improving with the new large, modern shopping plazas, four star hotels and restaurants offering comfort and excellent dining facilities. Also, familiar names are appearing such as Kentucky Fried Chicken, Sears, Sanborns, and large supermarkets such as Aurrera and Gigante. Transportation around Morelia is also more satisfactory, with taxi and bus service available. These improvements are significant, and will in time help focus more and more interest on the city as a retirement location. Tourists will will be attracted to Morelia to appreciate its beauty and the wide selection of arts and crafts from the small villages nearby which make the state of Michoacan the largest producer of the beautiful pottery, wall hangings, straw placemats, lovely handmade clothing and linens along with outstandingly beautiful lacquer ware, copper items and many other delightful choices typical of the area. A wide selection of arts and crafts may be seen and purchased in the Casa de las Artesanías, located under the arcades near Plaza de los Mártires.

In the center of Morelia is beautiful Plaza de los Mártires, and on one side is the impressive Cathedral which has been called the most beautiful in the country. Constructed from pink stone, the Cathedral commands attention with its regal splendor topped with a 200 foot tower. Truly magnificent! One should walk around the city to really explore other samples of the architecture such as the Government Palace, built in 1723 and formerly used as a seminary.

It has fascinating historical murals by artist Alfredo Zalce of Santa Rosa on Santigo Tapia, as well as the second oldest educational institution, the College of San Nicolas. There are many fine museums, such as the Museum of Michoacan, located off Allende and Abasolo, which features pre-Colombian art. Of interest to history buffs is the famous stone aqueduct, constructed in the late 1780's and boasting more than 250 arches which stretch over a mile east of the city. The aqueduct was built to carry water from various springs into the city. Other sites of interest are the home of Morelos, on Morelos Sur and Aldama, plus just two blocks away is the original birthplace of Morelos, on Corregidora, where one will find many personal articles of interest belonging to this famous man.

Morelia is known as one of Mexico's most cultured cities, and now has one of the first modern Performing Arts Centers where many dance and musical events are held. Other recent additions to the city are several multiple cinemas, and for the more athletic, there are tennis courts available at Club Britannia along with golf facilities at the Club Campestre. Morelia is a college town and thus offers frequent concerts, plays and traditional folk entertainment, which could be another drawing card to the area.

It is almost certain that with the recent modernization Morelia is undergoing, plus the pride shown in retaining its history and tradition, the city will attract more and more visitors and those who will recognize the potential of a delightful retirement location.

Not To Be Overlooked - Zacatecas!

The city of Zacatecas is not well known to tourists or retirees and remains very Mexican in tradition and atmosphere. It is, however, a delightful city to explore ad offers a variety of attractions.

Zacatecas, founded in 1546, boasts a population of approximately 200,000, with very few North Americans mixed in. It is located at an altitude of 8,200 feet and built on hills of different levels, making it cool and windy.

Because of the chilly temperatures during the winter months, which range between 40° to 60° at midday, North Americans find it less desirable than other parts of Mexico for retirement, no do they enjoy the rapidly cooling night time summer temperatures. Zacatecas is only a 430 mile drive from the Texas border, and 200 miles north of Guadalajara, or a four and one half hour drive.

Along with Taxco and Guanajuato, Zacatecas is known for its silver, and now ranks first as the producer of silver in Mexico. It is also a large agricultural and wine producing area and is drawing a number of *maquiladora* factories. Silver mines are numerous in and around the area of Zacatecas, and anyone visiting should take the opportunity to explore them.

La Mina Edén is one of the oldest silver mines, and was opened in the 18th century as the *Mina de San Eligio*. Located directly under several of the city's subdivisions, and actually crossing under the Cathedral, it was forced to close over 20 years ago (its veins are still rich with copper and silver) due to severe flooding problems, plus the fact that there was too much construction above the mine. Now open to the public as a tourist attraction, one enters the mine by train through the principal entrance, and exits through the other end on foot. The mine was worked exclusively by hand labor, and the various chambers and shoots are an impressive sight. Through one of the shoots, the completely flooded lower levels can be observed. The water, because of its incredibly high mineral and salt content, is considered toxic (Zacatecans suffer from yellowed teeth due to the high mineral content of their well water so bottled water is a MUST here). Several small shops are located in the middle of the mine, which sell a variety of local craft work and semi-precious stones. On weekend nights, one of the chambers is converted into a disco.

Above ground level, visitors to Zacatecas will be drawn to the beautifully preserved 18th century colonial buildings which line the narrow twisted streets. The buildings are constructed from quarried stone slabs that have a pink luster and delightfully rich texture, making a very picturesque effect. Many have black wrought iron balconies, adding to the beauty.

The are several excellent museums in Zacatecas which should be seen and appreciated. The **Museo Francisco Goitia**, the former governor's mansion, is located across from the **Parque Sierra de Alicia**. The *Museo* houses many paintings and sculptures. Works of Mexico's finest artists can be viewed there, such as Pedro Coronel, Salvador Dali, and of course, Francisco Goitia. The **Museo Pedro Coronel** is also well known, and was formerly a Jesuit seminary. Here on exhibit are thousands of Mexican masks plus a marvelous collection of marionettes from the Rosita Arandas Theater, a popular traveling group that put on plays throughout towns and villages using delightful marionettes. Also on display is an outstanding collection of African masks, beautiful Japanese and Chinese screens and urns, pieces from ancient Greece, plus Hispanic artifacts and art. The museum is located in Plaza Santo Domingo and should not be missed.

One of the most beautiful and most famous buildings in the city is the **Cathedral** with its twin towers. Located in the **Plaza de Armas**, it was constructed between 1730 and the late 1750's, as a parish church, and was remodeled in the 1800's to become the Cathedral. The alterations to the façade are obvious. The arches located around the edifice also show signs of remodeling (nobody knows by whom and when these changes were ordered). This lovely old building is very ornate, Mexican Barroque style, and the life-size sculptures carved in the ocher stone are outstanding in detail. Inside the Cathedral, the ambiance is more Gothic, and several religious paintings and art treasures are displayed. Near the Cathedral is the city's **Plaza**, an excellent place to relax and "people-watch."

The **Government Palace** is another very interesting building in Zacatecas. Here, depicted in a fascinating mural, is the history of Zacatecas, and it deserves the attention of all visitors to the city.

The **González Ortega Market**, formally the central market, was fully remodeled to become a modern mall, respecting the old architecture. Shoppers will find it difficult to pass by the beautifully crafted silver pieces and a wide variety of intricately embroidered tablecloths and other hand made items.

A visit to Zacatecas should certainly include a ride on the **Teleférico** (cable car), which operates between the *Cerro del Grillo* to the *Cerro de la Bufa*, where one can enjoy the spectacular view of the area. It is here where many come to pay homage to the Virgin with miraculous healing powers in the Chapel of our Lady of the Zacatecans. Since the Edén Mine exit is located on the Cerro del Grillo, one can accomplish a "quickie" day tour of Zacatecas by beginning at the mine, then hopping on the cable car at its exit, seeing the Cerro de la Bufa, and then taking a taxi or bus for a spectacular ride down the mountain to the downtown to see the rest of the sites.

About thirty miles south of Zacatecas, just a mile east of Highway 54 to Guadalajara, are the **Chicomostoc Ruins**, also known as *La Quemada*. These were constructed by the Aztec Indians after 1170 and had been abandoned when the Spanish discovered this place in 1535. Located on a hillside overlooking a beautiful wide valley, this archeological site has been partially restored and includes a temple, building foundations and streets. It is certainly worth paying the small admissions charge to see.

This article has attempted to focus on the main attractions of Zacatecas, but the people themselves are also a great asset with their warm smiles and helpful attitudes. Visitors to the city will be delighted in many ways.

Visit Oaxaca

Since our retirement in Guadalajara, we have heard of many interesting cities and villages to visit, and among the most popular seems to be Oaxaca (pronounced Wa-ha-ca), which lies in the mountains about 340 miles southeast of Mexico City. Often we have heard of the similarities between the Oaxaca of today and Guadalajara thirty to forty years ago. Naturally this made us even more anxious to see for ourselves this much-talked-of city. After making plans several times to go and having to cancel them, recently we were finally able to follow through and make the trip. I'm happy to say we found it just as delightful as we had anticipated.

Oaxaca, with a population of about 450,000, is very Indian in its feeling and atmosphere. The people there seemed to us to be somewhat darker and shorter with facial features true to their Zapotec ancestry. It was quite impressive to watch the women and girls in their colorful skirts, aprons and ribbons braided into long plaits as they balance on their heads huge baskets, pails and bags filled with everything from bread and grain to flowers or anything else which needs to be transported.

Tourists who visit Oaxaca are offered much to see and do during their stay, and most is within walking distance of the large main square called the *zócalo*. The square is a delightful place to sit and "people-watch" while listening to the band concerts frequently held there. Eventually also, while sitting amid the trees, flowers and strollers, you will recognize another tourist you have met or seen around, and soon a conversation begins as you compare notes of interest. One such conversation with another couple, also "people-watching", revealed that they were from our home state and that they vacationed in Oaxaca several weeks for many years! Across from the square are several sidewalk cafés where one can order a meal, a snack or just a refreshing drink. Sidewalk vendors add local color as they parade by the tables selling their wares; everything from beads, carved book marks, candies, hand-loomed rugs and wall hangings, to baskets, and many, many other items. We found that they can be very persuasive!

Other things to see and do include a walk to the **Cathedral,** which is located at one end of the square. This impressive building was begun in the 16th century and finished one hundred years later. It is noted for its large wooden clock with bas-relief.

Also within walking distance from the square is the very beautiful **Church of Santo Domingo,** considered one of the finest baroque churches in the western world. Alongside of this lovely church is the **State Museum,** which is filled with relics excavated at nearby archeological sites. Another interesting museum worth seeing is the **Tamayo Museum of Hispanic Art,** about four blocks from the *zócalo.*

The **Mercado de Artesanías** is open every day and overflows with the well-known Oaxaca wall hangings and rugs, along with the popular black pottery in every size and shape. The Saturday *tianguis* or open market on the west side of the city gives one the opportunity to see and buy the wide variety of beautiful hand-made products available, which reflect the Indian influence of the surrounding small villages. If you are one who likes haggling over prices, you will enjoy the challenge presented here with the many vendors!

A trip to Oaxaca definitely should include the tours which are available to take you to the ruins located in nearby villages, such as the archeological zones of **Monte Albán** and **Mitla.** The tour buses cost very little and provide a guide who will explain and answer any questions. Each trip takes from three to four hours, so there is plenty of time left for resting and shopping, which in itself is a real treat. Many of the streets are lined with small shops where local art and handicrafts are displayed for sale.

In addition to the tours offered, we suggest that you rent a car, or if you have your own car, drive to some of the small villages surrounding Oaxaca in the various hills and valleys nearby; there are also local buses available if one is more adventuresome. To the south, **San Bartolo Coyotepec** is where the famous black ceramic pottery is made. This beautiful pottery is formed by hand using ancient techniques and is exported throughout the world. In **Santo Tomás Jalietza** you will see back-strap loom weavers, weaving bags, sashes, shoulder capes and a variety of other items. The Friday tianguis at **Ocotán** is quite large and offers a good selection of hand-embroidered blouses and dresses along with many other handicrafts. To the east of the village of **Teotitlán de Valle** the famous woolen Oaxaca rugs are woven. These rugs and wall hangings are very decorative and unique, and are woven on ancient foot looms using natural colors. Close by is the **Dainzú archeological site,** which dates back to 780 A.D. This site contains an interesting ball court with bas-relief representing complete human-like figures dressed and decorated as ball players. Also in the area is the **Lambityeco archeological complex,** and **Tlacolula,** the center for mezcal production (a very strong alcoholic drink made from mezcal plants). Each village has its own special market day and a visit to the Department of Tourism office will provide you with the dates of

165

each tianguis and ideas of even more interesting things to see and do while you are there.

Oaxaca has special festivals during Holy Week (*Semana Santa*) at Easter time, and also during the last two weeks in December. (Incidentally, these periods are when the majority of Mexican families take their vacations to the beaches and other tourist spots, so reservations of any sort should be made far in advance.) Of special significance is the **Fiesta Guelaguetza** starting in late July. Special performances of native dances and music are held on Mondays at the **Cerro del Fortín Amphitheater** (Hill of the Small Fort). Performers participating in this fiesta come in costumes from the various regions of Oaxaca and it is very colorful.

Although we feel that Guadalajara/Chapala is the best "starter" place for retirement in Mexico, Oaxaca is a city to be considered. The climate and altitude are much the same as Guadalajara, but perhaps somewhat drier. Oaxaca has a much smaller year around North American resident group, estimated at about 200 people, with a few hundred more during the winter months. As a consequence there are less English language cultural events and social activities. A person interested in study and research of the Oaxaca area archeology, anthropology and arts and crafts would find a gold mine of interests and activities. We feel that one would need a greater sense of adventure, independence, patience and adaptability to adjust to the greater cultural differences and isolation. A knowledge of the Spanish language would be of greater importance in Oaxaca, however, you may find that through the necessity to communicate you will learn the language more rapidly.

Oaxaca is a three or four day drive from the Texas border, as opposed to a one to one-and-a-half day drive from the Guadalajara/Chapala area. Many North Americans who live year around in Oaxaca drive to Guatemala every six months to renew their tourist visas. Oaxaca has a modern airport with frequent flights to Mexico City, where connecting flights may be made to the United States, Canada or elsewhere.

Should you have the time we recommend that you spend a few days relaxing at one of the resort beaches in the state of Oaxaca. The main areas are **Puerto Escondido, Puerto Angel** and **Bahías** (Bays) **de Hualtulco**. For reservations to Oaxaca we suggest that you contact a travel agency.

In Oaxaca, the **English Language Library** at Alcalá 305, just a few blocks from the zócalo, seems to be the center for communications and activities for North Americans. During our visit, we found the librarian very helpful and also were able to talk to several North Americans, both permanent and part-time residents, who seemed very pleased with their decision to live in Oaxaca. There are English speaking doctors, and a good hospital. There are no English language publications in Oaxaca, however, the *Mexico City News* may be purchased daily.

166

An area referred to as **San Felipe Neri**, located in the hills adjacent to Oaxaca, was described as a popular area for North American residents. However, many are scattered throughout the city. The United States government has a Consulate Agency at Crespo #209. The telephone number is (951) 6-0654. The **Universidad Autónoma "Benito Juárez" de Oaxaca** offers Spanish language courses year around from beginning through advanced levels. For more information write to Apdo. Postal #3519, C.P. 6800, Oacaxa, Oaxaca, Mexico.

In Oaxaca there are hotels and restaurants to suit every preference and wallet. We happened to stay at the Hotel Mesón del Rey at Trujano #212, just a block and a half from the zócalo. It is a small family hotel and was clean and comfortable, with modest prices (Tel. (951) 6-0033/0181/0199). A little more expensive and very popular with tourists is the Hotel Marqués del Valle, located at Portal de Clavena S/N on the zócalo (Tel. (951) 6-3677/3295/3474). A more elegant hotel, offering a view of the Oaxaca valley, is the Hotel Victoria, which is on the outskirts of town, just off the Pan American Highway. Write Apdo. Postal 248 (Tel. (951) 5-2633).

During our stay in Oaxaca we found many fine restaurants, including El Vitral at Guerrero #220, a small French restaurant called Las Chalotes at Fiallo #116, and our favorite, the Catedral, located about three blocks north of the zócalo.

(For more information on hotels and restaurants in Oaxaca, you may wish to refer to a recent Mexican travel guide book, or dial 1-800-262-8900 in the United States for other sources of information about the State of Oaxaca. For more complete information on Oaxaca, the book "Oaxaca - Crafts and Sightseeing" may be obtained from Editorial Minutiae Mexicana, S.A. de C.V., Insurgentes Centro 114-210, C.P. 06030, México, D.F., México.)

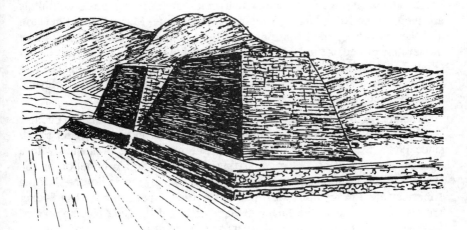

Thoughts on Mexico City for Retirement

by Jane Brown

If one has thoughts about retiring to Mexico City - think again as the city is plagued with overcrowding, pollution and traffic woes. However, on the plus side, it still maintains its cosmopolitan charm and way of life.

It is estimated that 20 million persons reside in the metropolitan area and suburbs of Mexico City. The city is divided into *colonias*, representing business and residential zones. Surrounded by mountains, Mexico City is 7,349 feet high.

Mexico City is international and offers many cultural, historical, educational and social advantages, including important established business opportunities. The city boasts various foreign communities, with the largest groups being American and Spanish. While Spanish is the native language, many Mexicans in the city speak a second language with English the most predominate.

Within Mexico City are 68 foreign embassies representing their country's diplomatic relations with Mexico, as well as consulates.

The city is also the home of the Mexican stock market (*Bolsa*) which is located in a very modern edifice on the main avenue of Reforma, often referred to as Mexico's *Champs Élysées*. The metropolitan area of the city has many hotels ranging in price from expensive to moderate. Among the deluxe hotels are the Camino Real, Nikko, Stouffer El Presidente, María Isabel Sheraton and the recently opened Marquis Reforma. A longtime favorite, and more moderately priced, is the Hotel Geneve located in the heart of the *Zona Rosa* (Pink Zone), a famed shopping and restaurant area. Others among the less expensive include the María Cristina, Bristel, Emporium, Regente, Reforma, Vasco de Quiroga and Crystal.

Theater in Mexico City is in Spanish with the exception of Theater Workshop, which has been presenting plays, musicals and readings in English since 1968. Many of the Broadway and London hits are presented with a Spanish cast but using the same settings, costumes and production as the Broadway and London shows. The city also has many movie houses showing American and foreign films with Spanish subtitles. Opera, concerts and ballet are also performed in the famed Bellas Artes and the Sala Netzhualcoyotl featuring local and international artists and musicians.

For archeological buffs, Mexico City and surroundings have an abundance of interesting and exciting sites to explore. Three of the best known are the Anthropology Museum, which is within walking distance from most of the main hotels; The Templo Mayor in the Zócalo and the Pyramids of Teotihuacan, about a half hour drive from the center of the city. There is also a wide selection of art galleries.

Most of the Americans live in Lomas, Polcanco, Anzures, San Angel and Coyoacan colonias; but some who want to be in the heart of city life prefer colonias Cuauhtemoc or Juárez.

Housing in Mexico City is very expensive and rents continue to climb. If renting, be sure the place has a telephone as it takes a long time to get one if possible at all. In most rentals the light, water, telephone and maintenance are separate from the rent. Make sure your get receipts that show they are currently paid up or you might suddenly find yourself without light or your water and telephone cut off. There are many reliable rental agencies and the newspapers also run ads.

Mexico City has many attractions in its surrounding areas for day trips and weekends. Cuernavaca, which can brag of beautiful sunshine almost every day of the year, is only an hour and a half drive. Other interesting Mexican towns close by include Toluca; Puebla, which is noted for its Talavera ware; Tepoztlan, Metapec, Istapan de la Sal and Oaxtepec.

Mexico City has restaurants to please everyone's taste and price range. However, the international restaurants, which represent many ethnic types, are expensive. A good source of information on restaurants in the city is the *Mexico City Restaurant Guide*, published by Publicaciones Pirámide, S.A. de C.V.

There are many golf and tennis clubs within the city or environs. However, they are private so one must have a member invite you, or some temporary arangement must be made to gain access. For sports activities it takes adjusting to the altitude if one comes from sea level. Even walking or climbing stairs can find one huffing and puffing. Bowling, baseball, polo, soccer and jai alai events are also available, as well as bull fighting, if one considers that a sport.

Shopping in the city is a delight. The three main department stores, which have several branches, are El Palacio de Hierro, El Puerto de Liverpool and Sears Roebuck. Markets are favorites and four that carry a variety of Mexican handicrafts include the Ciudadela, also known as the Balderas market, the Londres market, Sonora and San Juan. The Ciudadela and San Juan are close. The Londres market is in the Zona Rosa. Many new shopping malls have also become convenient and popular.

For persons interested in retiring in Mexico City, the Newcomers' Club is a pleasant way to get to know Mexico and its people. The Newcomers' Club consists mostly of wives of executives or retired persons from various countries. All meetings, organized trips and social events are conducted in English. Another is the American Society of Mexico which organizes seminars, trips and social events. The Society's membership is made up mostly of families.

The U.S. Embassy is located at Reforma 105 and is the largest foreign embassy in Mexico. A part of the Embassy is the U.S. Trade Center and the Benjamin Franklin Library.

For racing fans there is the Hipódromo de las Américas which also has the private swank Jockey Club. Racing in the city boasts a long yearly season and races are held Thursday, Saturday and Sunday.

In case of illness or accident, most Americans go to the American British Cowdray (ABC) Hospital where the latest medical equipment is available. It should be stressed for persons thinking of retiring to Mexico that Medicare is not available in Mexico. The person must return to the States for treatment in order to be paid by Medicare. Another bit of advice is to check your medical and health policies to see if they cover Mexico.

There are several schools where Spanish is taught. The most popular for Americans is the Mexican Northamerican Cultural Institute at Hamburgo 115 in the Zona Rosa. There are also many private teachers who advertise in *The News*, the English language newspaper.

Chapultepec Park, in the heart of the city, is divided into sections and is visited by millions of people per year. It also houses the zoo which has 2,750 animals representing 235 species - including the prolific Panda bears. The park also has two restaurants, Chapultepec Castle, The Museum of Anthropology, The Rufino Tamayo Museum, The Museum of Modern Art, and borders on the President of Mexico's official residence, Los Pinos.

The list of organizations one may belong to is too extensive to mention them all, but here are a few, besides Newcomers and The American Society of Mexico: if you have children the PTA, Boy Scouts, Girl Guides; Panhellenic, American Legion, Alumni clubs of various universities and colleges, Rotary, Lions, Navy League, Foreign Correspondent's Club, Friendship Club, Flower Arrangement Club, Mexico City Garden Club, Embroiders' Guild, DAR, Shriners, Womens Auxiliary of the ABC Hospital (Pink Ladies), Fondo Unido (United Way), etc., etc.

Churches offering services in English include St. Patrick's Catholic, Union Church, Christ Church Episcopal, the Lutheran Church of the Good Sheppard, the Mormon Church, Capital City Baptist, Christian Science and Beth Israel Community Center.

The International Airport, which is a twenty minute ride to the center of town, traffic permitting, has flights on most of the American carriers and foreign carriers such as KLM, Air France, Aeroflot, Lufthansa, Iberia as well as flights from Central and South America.

Mexico City is not an inexpensive place to live although services such as plumbing, electrical, painting, carpentry and maids are less than in the United States. For those on a fixed income and with the inflation, the best way before making the final move is to come to Mexico City and stay for about three months to see if your budget will cover big city living.

Happiness in a Small Mexican Pueblo

by Paul Katz

My wife and I were born and raised in Brooklyn and Long Island, New York, living there during the 40s and 50s. Those were the days when the family was very closely knit. Well, it's the 1990s, and in this small laid-back community where we live, things have not changed too much. As I write, the children in the elementary school, which is directly in back of us, are singing and enjoying another day of learning. The old school spirit still thrives in our little town as they prepare for a very important soccer game to be played this Saturday. Along with the children, you can hear the blackbirds singing, see flowers in bloom, and enjoy the fresh breezes that are so common in the area where we live. My wife is playing with our little dog that we brought with us from California and enjoying every minute of it. We live in a lovely home with every convenience at an extremely affordable rent (140.00 dollars per month).

Our typical day starts at 6:00 a.m. We start the day by walking our dog for about an hour and even though it's dark outside, we feel totally secure. We don't worry for a minute about being mugged or molested. In all the years that we have been living in Mexico, not once has there been an incident to make us feel insecure in our daily living. As we walk the dog the women are cleaning their sidewalks and watering down the street. Yes, there are sidewalks and paved streets in Mexico. After this little bit of exercise we are ready for our *desayuno* (breakfast).

We automatically turn on our satellite TV and watch the *Morning News* and *Business Report* (CNN). After breakfast we rest awhile and then head for the "*Mercado*", an indoor-outdoor market where there are twelve butchers (fresh beef, pork and chicken daily). Yes, the chicken is still warm, as it was freshly killed in the morning. The fish stall is full of the clear-eyed catch of the day, along with a superb selection of shrimp, oysters and clams. The produce is incredibly fresh; there's always something in season in Mexico. There are restaurants, candy stores, health food stands, flower shops, bakeries, deli's, fruit drink stands and just about anything you would need to stock your home for a week, a month or longer. Truthfully, one of the best aspects of this market is that you know all the merchants and they are always smiling and trying to help you in every way. I must tell you, my wife and I speak a little Spanish, enough to get by, but even if we didn't the Mexican people are so kind and understanding, they would help us get along. In our town the majority of the residents speak a little English. There is always someone from their family living and working in the United States.

We have finally (after about an hour) finished our shopping and head home, a ten minute walk or a three minute drive. We put our groceries away and wait for the maid to come. We really don't have to wait as she has had the keys to the house from the day we hired her, almost a year ago. At this time we can get in the car and visit some friends in other small towns in our area or hang around and try to stay out of her way. Today we relax in our backyard while my wife piddles around in the garden I turn on the stereo and listen to the great jazz musicians of past and present.

Every day varies because we are not set in our ways. One day we take a bus ride (we have a bus terminal in our town) to a different "*pueblo*" and see what this town may have to offer. We have found that each town is different, with its own characteristics and architecture. We always settle down in their "*Zócalo*" (town square), enjoying a few tacos or tamales and some fresh fruit. Before it gets dark we start for home and try to have a little catnap before our main meal.

In our pueblo there are always dances with live bands on weekends. We also have our own bullring and every few months the circus comes to town. Sundays are very special as we and most of the people in town go to the square around 8:00 in the evening and just hang around and "people-watch". This is the night the young men and women walk around the square in different directions trying to catch the eye of the opposite sex. It's really something to see and has been a Mexican tradition for many, many years.

Naturally, I could go on and on relating things that come up on a daily basis. Summing up living in a small pueblo, it boils down to this; we live in total peace and tranquility, love our neighbors and our Mexican friends, and hope to live here the remaining years of our lives.

172

VIII

Popular Coastal Areas

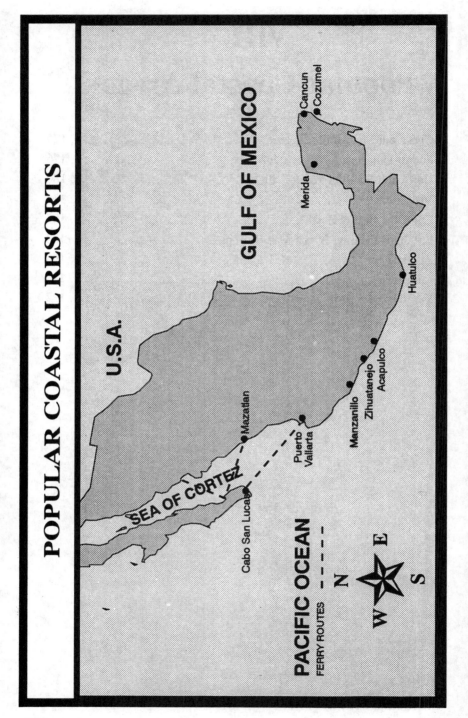

POPULAR COASTAL RESORTS

Check out Manzanillo!

Manzanillo, while once just an isolated seaport on Mexico's Pacific coast, has emerged as one of the most popular tourist spots, along with coming into its own as a attractive retirement location for winter "snowbirds." The high humidity in the summer months has discouraged most year around North American retirees except for a few of the heartier ones who do not mind the extreme heat.

Beautiful beaches along this part of the "Mexican Riviera" are the primary attraction for tourists as well its reputation as a "fisherman's heaven" which brings thousands of sun and fun seekers each year, especially during the months of November through February when the national and international sailfish competitions are held.

Manzanillo, pronounced *mahn-zah-NEE-yo*, is the home of the Mexican Navy, and with the easy availability of rail connections, is a major port transporting products all over Mexico and to the United States border. Recently a toll road was completed which enables one to go from Guadalajara in a pleasant four hour driving time. Also adding to the easy access is a coastal highway going north to Puerto Vallarta.

Popular beaches to visit are the "La Audiencia", which is the site of the beautiful Hotel Sierra Manzanillo, a five star hotel, Playa Miramar, Playa El Tesoro, Playa Las Brisas and Playa Azul. For those who wish to explore a little and are without a car, it is a simple matter to rent a car and seek out smaller more secluded beaches such as beautiful Playa de Oro or the bays north of Barra de Navidad and Melaque Bay. In these smaller villages there are some good hotels and restaurants, friendly people, good fishing and, of course, the lovely beaches offering breath taking views - a special treat for camera buffs!

The most famous beach resort is lovely Las Hadas. Quite luxurious, Las Hadas was developed by a Bolivian billionaire named Antenor Patiño in 1974, also called the "Tin King" by many due to his huge accumulation of wealth from tin mines. From its early conception Las Hadas has been a delightful fairyland drawing a constant stream of the famous and wealthy from all over. For a special romantic outing, check out the Puerto Las Hadas for a tour of the bay on a trimaran that leaves each afternoon returning at sunset.

Manzanillo offers much in the way of entertainment besides the beaches. There is great fishing for dorado, sailfish, marlin, tuna and red snapper, you can dine in quaint thatched roofed palapas, as well as at the newer elegant restaurants. You can watch the activity around the docks where you may hear fascinating tales about the interesting old seaport and its growth into what it is today. Shopping is probably not a main attraction, although there are a variety of Mexican crafts to be found in front of the main downtown plaza, as

175

well as many boutiques and small shops which offer a good selection of jewelry, clothing, paintings and sculpture. Golfing is also available at resorts such as Las Hadas and Club Santiago for those who wish it.

In the past three years many new hotels and time share developments have been constructed. However, our favorite place is Vida del Mar. This beautiful two hundred condominium development located ten minutes north of Club Santiago, built about twenty years ago, is located on cliffs overlooking the bay in a beautifully landscaped park-like setting. There is a small private beach and snorkeling is great with coral beds and beautiful fish. It is the sort of tranquil place where residents may lock the door when they leave in the spring and return the following season to find everything just the same. A good restaurant is located on the grounds. Prices of condominiums that are for resale appear reasonable when available.

This is a part of Mexico not to be overlooked, and for beach lovers it's simply a must!

Puerto Vallarta - A Tropical Jewel

Puerto Vallarta, in the state of Jalisco, is no longer a typical sleepy fishing village, but in fact has become one of the most popular beach resorts in Mexico. Puerto Vallarta has a rapidly expanding population of approximately 300,000 inhabitants, including many people from other countries, and thousands of sun-loving visitors each year.

Named after a state governor, Ignacio Luis Vallarta, in 1918, Puerto Vallarta is located on Banderas Bay (the largest bay in Mexico), with its back towards the Sierra Madre mountains, on Mexico's Pacific coast.

From Guadalajara one can drive the 225 miles in around five hours, or take an easy half-hour flight. There are several U.S. airlines serving Puerto Vallarta with regular flights from all major United States cities, making it easily accessible.

In spite of the rapid growth and development, Puerto Vallarta has managed to retain much of its original beauty and charm. Its cobblestone streets are lined with quaint whitewashed houses and their red tiled roofs, thanks to the strict enforcement of building codes which specify the traditional "Puerto Vallarta" architectural guidelines, and prohibit the construction of high rise buildings that could possibly block the spectacular beach views.

Running through the middle of the downtown area is the *Río Cuale* (Cuale River), which divides the city into two distinct sections. The northern section consists mostly of older hotels and businesses, while the southern end consists primarily of new modern hotels and private residences.

In the middle of the river sits the "Isla del Río Cuale", a delightful five acre island full of small shops, restaurants, a small museum, small botanical garden and a popular facility where art classes are given. Also near the island is the city's largest market, where local art and handicrafts are on display for sale.

Little was known of Puerto Vallarta until it was discovered by film director John Huston, who thought it would be the perfect setting for his film *"Night of the Iguana,"* starring the popular actor Richard Burton in 1964. The actual spot used for the filming was Mismaloya, about seven miles south of town. The publicity given to this was the beginning of Puerto Vallarta's recognition, and there has been a steady flow of tourists ever since, making it the popular resort it is today.

Mismaloya is still a favorite for sightseers, especially those interested in exploring the lagoon from canoes, by scuba diving or by hiking. There are jeeps or cars to rent for those who wish to see more of this relatively unspoiled sector.

The first five-star hotel, Posada Vallarta (now the Krystal Vallarta), was built in 1960, and soon followed by many others, heralding the opening of an international airport receiving early tourists from all over.

As the publicity grew so did Puerto Vallarta, and consequently more and more shops, hotels, restaurants, plus all the modern conveniences that are an added attraction to those seeking beauty and relaxation along with sun and fun.

The strip of beaches is, of course, the main attraction. All are beautiful, most have thatched roof stands or small restaurants where one can freshen up with a cool drink and a quick snack; some offer sail boats or canoes for rent, or the more adventurous may decide to try out the exciting sport of parasailing or surfing.

Here are a few of the best known beaches:

Playa de Oro - stretching from the Krystal Vallarta hotel to near the airport, quite popular but not overcrowded.

Olas Altas or *Los Muertos* (Dead Man's Beach) - offering much activity, water sports, beach games and snack stands. It is approximately six miles south of town. Sheltered in a natural cove and surrounded by high cliffs, this is considered by many to be one of the most beautiful beaches.

Playa Las Estacas - running in front of the Camino Real Hotel, this beach offers fishing gear, water skis and boats to rent.

Las Amapas - located near Playa de Oro, Las Amapas has an excellent view of the beautiful homes built along the cliffside.

Besides the delightful beaches, everyone enjoys taking a leisurely stroll on

177

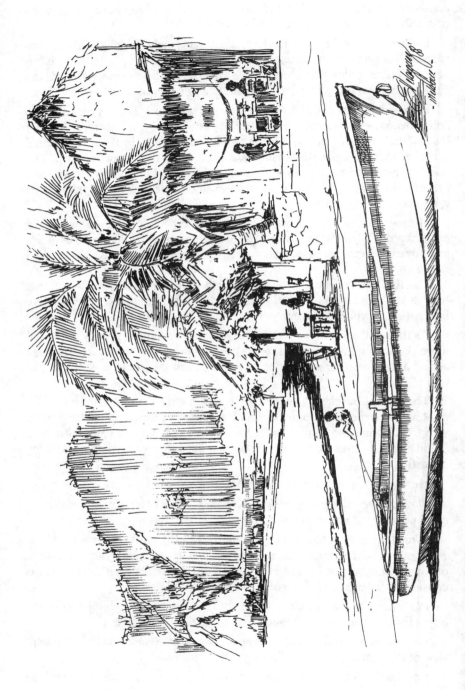

the *Malecón* (seawall or "promenade") which goes north and south along the bay. The Malecón is dotted with shops and restaurants, and is a lovely place to watch the beautiful sunsets, a nice way to end a delightful day, or to catch your breath before taking on some of the lively discos or restaurants where one can enjoy a delicious meal as well as entertainment.

While in Puerto Vallarta you should not miss the small fishing village of Yelapa. This rustic community can be reached by boat only, and there are daily scheduled trips costing just a small fee. Excursions to Yelapa usually leave the town by 8 a.m. and return around 4 p.m. There are small open-air restaurants and very rustic accommodations. Within a twenty minute walk you will find a spectacular 150 foot waterfall and an Indian village to explore and admire. Take your camera!

In direct contrast to the rustic village of Yelapa is the new and modern Marina Vallarta subdivision. It is home for the largest marina in Mexico, said to have a 300 vessel capacity. Covering one and a half miles of beach front, the subdivision boasts an eighteen-hole golf course, tennis courts, spas and club house, as well as ultra modern hotels on the beach, shopping center and lovely homes, villas, condos and time share accommodations.

Puerto Vallarta has a few year around North American retirees. However, the high humidity makes it uncomfortable for most people from May to October. Many North Americans rent houses or apartments during the winter months.

Puerto Vallarta seems to have it all, both the old Mexican charm and the new modern conveniences which are so much a part of our life. Let's hope the new doesn't crowd out the old!

North and South of Puerto Vallarta
by Wendy A. Luft

In a land where tourism mega-projects are the vogue, the beach highways north and south of Puerto Vallarta are a welcome relief. Most of them still haven't been discovered as tourist destinations, and all are within easy reach of Puerto Vallarta and can be seen in a series of one-day trips.

Travelers who choose to overnight will find accommodations ranging from luxuriuos hotels designed for unwinding in understated elegance to pleasant low-budget hostelries, all set far apart on miles of unpopulated beach, with tranquil waters, and incredibly fresh seafood at simple beachfront restaurants.

North and South of Puerto Vallarta

by Wendy A. Luft

The coastal highways north and south of Puerto Vallarta are a welcome relief in a land where tourism mega-projects are the vogue. They lead to places that still haven't been discovered as tourist destinations, and all are within easy reach of Puerto Vallarta and can be seen in a series of one-day trips.

Travelers who choose to overnight will find accommodations ranging from luxurious hotels designed for unwinding in understated elegance to pleasant low-budget hostelries, all set far apart on miles of unpopulated beach, with tranquil waters, and incredibly fresh seafood at simple beachfront restaurants. What travelers won't find are chic restaurants, golf courses, great shopping or a spirited nightlife. Indeed, nightlife may be limited to dancing to your own music on the beach, under more stars than you have ever seen.

Heading South

On the road south to Barra de Navidad there are widely spaced, self-contained resorts hidden in a series of delightful coves. Route 15 follows the coast until it reaches Boca de Tomatlán where it turns inland and begins its climb up the mountains until it reaches Tuito. There it descends once again and continues on to Chamela, Barra de Navidad and Manzanillo, sticking fairly close to the sea.

Accommodations on this stretch range from trailer parks and tent-type dwellings to several luxury hotels, all widely spaced and tucked into almost private coves—the kind of place that become a part of the setting without overpowering it.

Chamela, approximately 50 miles south of Tuito, is another world. Here, choice in accommodations is limited to camp sites and "concrete tents" for two at Villa Polinesia, or large spaces with full hookups at the Chamela Trailer Park. The seemingly endless beach is one of the most beautiful in Mexico; even Queen Elizabeth visited Chamela during her Pacific cruise in the early 80s. The waters are calm, there are no crowds, and rates are super-budget.

About 12 miles south of Chamela, Costa Careyes, or Turtle Coast, is one of the most breathtakingly beautiful coves in all of Mexico. It was so named because thousands of giant sea turtles return here every year, leaving the crystalline waters filled with brilliantly hued tropical fish to nest and lay their eggs on the soft cream-colored sands. Costa Careyes is the site of a Club Med and the exclusive Costa Careyes Hotel, that even has a polo field and a string of

30 polo ponies. The two hotels are almost side by side, but not within sight of each other.

A delightful spot a few miles further south is El Tecuan, a small hotel with only 36 rooms, a long stretch of beach, its own lagoon and two private airstrips, at surprisingly reasonable prices. This is a relaxed, get-away-from-it-all kind of place, but probably not for long: development plans include a golf club, marina and additional hotels.

Just south of El Tecuan is Tenancatita, a Lilliputian village on yet another gorgeous beach. It is the site of the all-inclusive Blue Bay resort. Along this stretch of road you will find other beautiful beaches such as La Manzanilla.

The next stops on Route 200 are San Patricio Melaque and Barra de Navidad. Facing each another over the same bay, they both look somewhat abandoned. These are the last, and least, attractive beach resorts on this route before you reach Manzanillo. Both towns were hard-hit by the 1985 earthquake and tidal wave. Many hotels are still closed, their owners undecided whether to demolish or restructure the very damaged buildings.

Prior to the opening of a new super-highway that cuts driving time between Guadalajara and Manzanillo to about three hours, Barra de Navidad was a popular vacation destination for *tapatios* (the name used to describe people from Guadalajara). Back in 1564, the Spanish built galleons here to be used for their expeditions to the Philippines. *Navidad*, which is the Spanish word for Christmas, refers to the date the Spanish arrived here to begin their voyage. *Barra* refers to the large sandbar that divides the sea from the lagoon.

Heading North

Towards the north from Puerto Vallarta, Route 200 winds through low mountain ranges and plateaus of farmland. It sticks fairly close to the coast, but the mountain terrain allows only a few glimpses of the sea. When it reaches Rincon de Guayabitos, it turns inland until it joins Route 15 at Compostela.

Nuevo (New) Vallarta is our first stop. It is just across the Ameca River, which divides the state of Jalisco from Nayarit, about 10 miles north of Puerto Vallarta. Considered at this moment to be the "boomtown" area of Vallarta, Nuevo Vallarta has 3 miles of cream-colored sand, a network of waterways, a marina, and a state-run beach club. Several new beach-front luxury hotels have been completed in the last few years,

Still able to avoid the giant construction fever that seems to be overtaking the area is the town of Bucerías. There are a few luxurious homes, a number of very modest hotels, long stretches of beach, and some of the most delicious oysters you have ever tasted. The turnoff to the Punta Mita is a few miles north of Bucerías. This road is 13.5 miles long, zigzagging through the hills, and passing some of the most beautiful and unpopulated beaches on Banderas Bay. Cruz de Huanacaxtle is the first beach, with gentle waves and soft sand. Next is Destiladeras, with soft, marble-white sands, and long rolling waves perfect for boogie boards and body surfing. Punta Mita is the name of what was a small fishing town and also the northern point of Banderas Bay. This area is now the center of one of the most ambitious tourist developments being constructed in Mexico. It has been totally closed off to the public, and the fishermen that used to live there were given new homes a few miles outside of town. There are excellent snorkeling reefs off the point, but at this moment are inaccessible. There have been very polemic discussions as to this manuever of shutting off the beach and town, as the beaches of Mexico are federal property, and therefore by law have to be open to the public. The concept of private beaches is not contemplated by the law, and quite frankly, illegal. Unfortunately, the terrain around certain beaches has allowed certain land developers to shut them off and make them for their own exclusive use. (Careyes, Club Med, Las Hadas and El Tamarindo are other examples of this.) The government has turned a blind eye to this problem, thinking that the heavy investments done by these people justifies closing off the beaches...well, an interesting problem that will have to be solved in the coming years.

Continuing north 8.5 miles from the turnoff to Punta Mita, you come to Sayulita, a quiet beachfront village with nice beaches. No problem here about being able to use the beach. Next is Lo de Marcos, a pretty town with a great beach, a trailer park and some rooming houses, but no dining facilities.

The main road continues north through mountain ranges and plateaus of tobacco farms to Rincón de Guayabitos. This subdivision really never took off, but is still home to a number of Americans take up residence here during the winter months, parking their trailers in beachfront sites shaded by tall palms, or staying in the string of pleasant and economical, but somewhat run-down, hotels along the beach. At the northern end of the beach, the waves are good for boogie boards and body surfing. Swimmers share the calmer waters of the southern end with a pelican colony that resides on a large offshore rock.

Next in line are two towns; La Peñita, just next-door to Rincón de Guayabitos, and further along, Las Varas. These two towns can only be described as "slum paradises". The rooming houses are not fit to stay in, and food services are very, very iffy. La Peñita has a trailer park popular with the American and Canadian crowd.

San Blas, basically the last spot on this route, is a tranquil town with a population of about 25,000. The stone ruins of a fortress and ancient mission church built by the Spanish are the few testaments to San Blas's history as one of the most important ports and shipbuilding centers on the Pacific from the 15th to the 19th century. This was the point of departure for the Spanish conquest of the Californias and for expeditions led by Friar Junipero Sierra and Francisco Kino. Although hardly charming or picturesque, San Blas's good beach, great surfing, excellent deep-sea fishing, and laid-back atmosphere have a staunch following of tourists who return year after year.

One of the most popular activities in San Blas is the boat trips that go down the La Tovara river through natural tunnels formed by mangroves and jungles of banyan trees, ferns, palms, hibiscus and cypress. 400 species of tropical birds live here. During the summer rainy season, tiny gnats, called jejenes, come to feed on unsuspecting tourists (they don't seem to bother the locals). So, when visiting San Blas at this time of year it is imperative that you bring insect repellant - lots of it.

From San Blas, a bumpy road leads to the island village of Mexcaltitan, set in the waters of a lagoon. What is so unusual about this island is that during the rainy summer months the streets of the village are turned into canals and the island appears to float on the waters of the lagoon. The similarity of the shape of the island, its canals and its fauna to Aztec pictographs depicting the voyage of their forefathers from the lost land of Aztlán to Tenochtitlán, which later became Mexico City, have given rise to the theory that Mexcaltitan may have been their ancestral home. Mexcaltitan isn't tourism oriented, but there's always someone available to take visitors for a tour around the island through the estuary in a dugout canoe.

Inland

For a change of pace and scenery, you might consider visting a charming colonial town of San Sebastian, hidden in the Sierra Madre Mountains east of Puerto Vallarta. Now practically a ghost town of about 1,000 inhabitants, San Sebastian was once an important mining center. It is now a popular hiking and horseback destination. For the less adventurous, a local airline provides air service several times a week. San Sebastian is also accessible by car (a 4-wheel vehicle is best).

Another inland possibility is Tepic, the capital of the state of Nayarit. After leaving Rincón de Guayabitos, Route 15 continues north to Tepic. Founded by the Spanish in 1542, nothing much happened in Tepic until 1912, when the first locomotive chugged through, and not much has happened since. The city itself is not really tourism-oriented, but is worth visiting to see the 18th century Church of the Holy Cross, the Regional Museum, and the shops around the main plaza that carry handicrafts made by the Huichols and Coras, indigenous groups native to the area.

Nearby are the El Salto and Ingenio de Jala Falls, the latter appearing only during the rainy summer months. The Santa María del Oro lagoon, an impressive volcanic-crater lake located southeast of Tepic, is worth visiting.

Travelers who feel that no trip to Mexico can be complete without a visit to an archaeological site, can zigzag about 31 miles east of Tepic to Ixtlán del Rio. Although little of the site has been excavated, its Temple of Quetzalcoatl is considered to be one of the most striking examples of western pre-Hispanic architecture. Especially noteworthy are the crosses found on the railing surrounding the platform. They are thought to signify the pre-Hispanic concept of the universe in which the four corners of the universe intersect at its center.

Visit Mazatlán!

Mazatlán, sometimes referred to as "The Pearl of the Pacific", is perhaps not as well known as other beach resorts such as Acapulco and Cancún, but is a favorite with many who prefer a less commercialized atmosphere yet with a large variety of sport activities available, including lovely beaches and beautiful clear blue water, a surfer's delight.

Located in the state of Sinaloa, Mazatlán is about 200 miles north of Puerto Vallarta, and 325 miles northwest of Guadalajara, easily accessible with three direct international flights from Denver, Los Angeles and San Francisco, and national service from most major Mexican cities. There is also daily bus and train service from Nogales, Arizona.

Mazatlán was first used as a fort by the Spanish conquistadors in the early 1600's, but was not actually incorporated until 1837. The city developed into an important seaport in the northwest, and has the largest sport fishing fleet in Mexico. It is a haven for the fishing enthusiast. The name Mazatlán (Mah-saht-LAHN) originates from the Indian name meaning "place of the deer" referring to the abundance of game which is still found in the area.

Fishermen will find Mazatlán to be a place of their dreams! Tuna, shark, and swordfish are bountiful year around, marlin is plentiful from November to May and sailfish from May to November. Those interested will find many hunting and fishing expeditions readily accessible with excellent facilities and competent crews.

This beautiful resort is one of Mexico's largest Pacific seaports. It is also involved with international trade to the United States, Mexico's largest customer, and the far away Orient. Mazatlán boasts the largest shrimp fleet in Mexico and ships tons of frozen shrimp daily to various ports.

Tourists will find Mazatlán to be an easy city to walk around. However, there are open-sided cars and taxis available. It is easy also to find tour guides in the city who will point out interesting sights such as **El Faro**, the lighthouse, which stands over 500 feet above sea level, and is the second highest in the world, offering a spectacular view. Also of interest are **The Anthropology Museum**, located in Olas Altas, with its collection of art and pre-Hispanic artifacts, **The Mazatlán Art Gallery**, in the Three Isles Mall, displaying interesting exhibits of many artists. Beginning at Olas Altas, north of El Mirador, is the **Malecón**, or sea wall, where one will find excellent shops, restaurants and hotels, and is a great place for a leisurely stroll. The sea wall marks the point where the swimming beaches begin. A few of the more popular beaches are **Playa Norte, Avenida del Mar, Las Gaviotas** and **Camarón Sábalo**. Other places to visit are the Moorish-style **Cathedral** and **Acuario Mazatlán**, located at Av. de los Deportes. The aquarium is especially interesting to children who love to watch the many species of fish such as shark and eel, and to see the documentary films which are shown daily.

Mazatlán offers something for everyone, from beautiful sunsets, boat trips to the nearby islands, beach and water sports, historical points of interest and fine luxury hotels and restaurants to moderately priced family accommodations.

Mazatlán is not considered a popular year around retirement choice because of the high humidity during the months from May to November. However, there seem to be as many as 100 year around Americans. Apparently there are no American organizations and Americans are scattered throughout the city.

To find out for yourself just what Mexico is all about, consider a trip to Mazatlán where you will find natural beauty, history and culture, and warm, friendly people.

Enjoy the Best of the BAJA!

In recent years people who love the sun, beautiful beaches and the challenge of fishing and other water sports have been flocking to the Baja California peninsula. The peninsula is an elongated strip stretching down from the State of California-Mexico border. Measuring 800 miles long, this rugged terrain is approximately 140 miles at its widest point, and 40 miles at the narrowest part.

Baja (meaning low or lower) *California* is divided in two separate states: *Baja California Norte* (North), whose capital is the small pleasant town of Mexicali, and the southern section, or *Baja California Sur* (South), whose capital is La Paz. The Pacific Ocean laps the western shore of the Baja peninsula (nothing pacific about it), and the eastern shore faces the Sea of Cortez.

Baja California is noted for some of the best fishing in the world. It is estimated that over 800 species of fish can be found, and from December to March one can see the California Gray Whale migration from the shoreline. Quite a sight and a delight for nature enthusiasts!

Midway down the peninsula, continuing south, is the small and somewhat underdeveloped village of Loreto. This part of the peninsula offers a particular beauty of its own, with beautiful beaches plus the spectacular Sierra del Gigante mountains in the background.

Loreto was settled in 1697 by the Jesuits who built the first successful mission, which has been fully restored and now houses many artifacts documenting the region's history. One can spend hours exploring cave paintings, (going back around 1,000 years), visiting the Anthropology and Historical Museums, as well as taking advantage of deep sea fishing and many other sports.

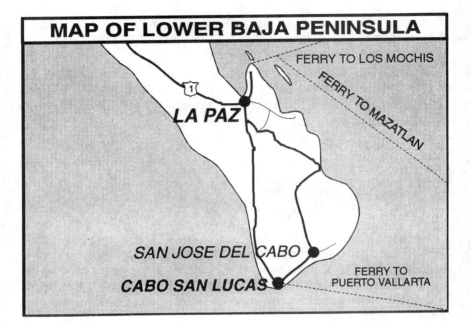

MAP OF LOWER BAJA PENINSULA

FERRY TO LOS MOCHIS

FERRY TO MAZATLAN

LA PAZ

SAN JOSE DEL CABO

CABO SAN LUCAS

FERRY TO PUERTO VALLARTA

Farther south is the capital of Baja California Sur, La Paz (meaning peace). La Paz was named by Padre Eusbia Kino in 1683 when the Spanish first settled there. La Paz is the busy center of government and commercial business. It is said that years ago pirates were lured to this area because of the oyster beds where rare black pearls could be found. The city of La Paz is an important resort known for beautiful beaches, great shopping, tours of the city monuments, and of course fishing. It is said that the city has the highest per capita income in Mexico.

Los Cabos (the Capes) are two rapidly developing resorts located at the very tip of the peninsula and separated by a twenty mile seaside highway, Transpeninsular #1. The largest of these towns is San José del Cabo, around 250 years old, with a population near 30,000. San José del Cabo is only 8 miles from the airport, and offers much in the way of entertainment. Along with the

186

water sports, one can take tours to the Santiago Zoo, the bird sanctuary, where there are reportedly two hundred species of birds. Here one can also explore the museum, the Iglesia de la San Jose (church), the 18th century Jesuit Mission Viejo, plus take a walking tour on the Paseo Mijares (walkway) to admire the old stone arches and quaint white cottages.

The second town, Cabo San Lucas, said to be the livier of the two, is a charming resort presently booming with construction of new hotels and businesses. Cabo San Lucas claims to have the safest and most beautiful beaches in the entire Baja area. The most popular are Playa del Amor, Playa Palmella, Playa el Medano, the Bay of Cabo San Lucas, Santa Maria and Chileno Bay. One should not miss the boat trip to Los Arcos (the Arches), where the Sea of Cortez meets the Pacific (the official geographical separation point between these two bodies of water). There you can watch seals, dolphins and sea lions sunning themselves on the spectacular rock formation forming the arches.

When you plan a trip to the Baja take into consideration the time of year. Although the year round temperature is around 75°F, during the months of May through September it can become extremely hot. The winter months are pleasant, requiring only a light jacket or sweater at night.

One should bring only clothing worn for casual resort wear - bathing suit, lots of sunscreen, gear for water sports, camera and binoculars for the beautiful scenery and anything else you would ordinarily take on vacation.

For those interested in fishing, the following chart might help to decide on the best months to try your luck for your favorite catch:

- Grouper - All year
- Swordfish - January to March
- Yellowfin Tuna - May to Dec.
- Wahoo - November to April
- Sailfish - March to November

- Cabrilla (Bass) - May to October
- Snapper - All year
- Marlin - All year
- Dorado - March to December

Good Fishing - and enjoy a delightful trip!

For Sportfishing, Ixtapa May Be Tops

by Susan Kaye

Three years ago, a Mexican-registered fishing ship anchored in the bay at Zihuatanejo, the neighboring town to Ixtapa. To make amends for having fished offshore, the crew donated several large tunas to the community.

"Since then, I haven't seen any fleets near Ixtapa - not Mexican, Japanese, or Korean," says Juan Barnard, a marine Biologist who has lived in Zihuatanejo - on the Pacific coast north of Acapulco - for eleven years.

As a result, people who've fished the world claim Ixtapa has the best deep-sea billfishing anywhere, including Hawaii, Baja Mexico, and Costa Rica. Ken Stewart, president of Sportsman's Tours & Travel in San Diego, says, "It's a place where there's an 80 percent probability you'll come back with a sailfish."

The annual Sailfish Tournament draws up to 200 entrants in early May, and the annual Ixtapa/Zihuatanejo Billfish Classic is held in Jaunuary.

Tuna, dorado and red snapper are abundant as well. With the exception of large prawns brought from Guaymas, virtually all restaurants serve only local seafood. Even homegrown oysters are considered safe for consumption, since three water treatment plants in Zihuatanejo and two in Ixtapa provide complete assurannce of no sewage runoff into the bays.

Zihuatanejo is one of the few resorts where some 200 fishermen still practice their trade, casting nets about 20 miles out through the night and pulling their boats at dawn on a beach fronting the plaza. But that hardly qualifies it as the "quaint fishing village" that most guidebooks mention in their Zihuatanejo write-ups. With a regional population swelling to 60,000, "burgeoning" is a better description.

For sport fishermen with their own boats, the 430-acre Marina Ixtapa, northwest of the hotel zone, is nearly complete. Three piers, waterways and 622 slips are operational, as is the nautical center and club house. Before winter's end, the yacht marina and Ixtapa's second 18-hole gold course should be ready.

As for scuba diving, there's incredibly rich sea life, water that warms to nearly 90 degrees, and visibility past 100 feet in the summer. The confluence of the Humboldt and Equatorial Counter brings in just about all Pacific varieties of coral reef fish and species common to the Sea of Cortez; seahorses and 20-foot manta rays abound. The plankton-rich water is a draw for big fish: humpback whales spout year-round.

188

Twenty-eight dive sites from shallow coral to 100-foot-deep canyons. A recently discovered two-square-acre coral garden teems with marine life 30 feet under the surface. Forty-five minutes south, submarine caverns tunnel to a dome that rises high above the water.

Biologist Barnard claims that Mexico's healthiest coral reefs are found off Ixtapa/Zihuatanejo. "There's a cultural revolution today," he says. "Fewer anchors are being dropped on coral reefs and damaged reefs are being repaired with implants fixed in concrete. Beaches are noticeably cleaner. Even sea turtles, which used to be killed on sight, are being reported so their incubation sites can be fenced off."

It's not an environmental paradise, not yet. Two sea lions, rarely seen in the region, were killed this past year by fishermen. But their rash acts raised loud and angry protests from locals who hope to increasingly protect and enhance their rich marine treasures.

More information

Dates for the 1994 Billfish Tournament are January 20 through 22. Information and Reservations for American registrants is handled by John Doughty, Balboa Island, CA: 714/723-0883.

Deep-sea fishing boats range from 24-foot outboards that hold two angles plus crew to 38-foot sportfishers; $120 to $250 daily. Make arrangements on the Zihuatanejo pier with the boat co-op; phone 42-056.

The Zihuatanejo Scuba Center offers NAUI Certification courses with check-out dives. A week-long certification course is $350; the abbreviated two-day final ocean check-out, $160. Zihuatanejo Scuba Center, FAX: 011-52-753-44-468. For packages, including air travel, accommodations and diving, call Destination Consultants in San Francisco: 415/781-5588.

For more information, contact your regional Mexican Government Tourist Office.

Zihuatanejo - Hard to Pronounce, Easy to Enjoy

by Susan Kaye

The ying and yang of Mexico's beach resorts - Ixtapa and Zihuatanejo.

Spiffy Ixtapa, built in the last two decades, languidly stretches alongside a flawless beach. Its eight stylish hotels are interwoven with golf courses, enormous pools bisected with volleyball nets, and forests of sun umbrellas.

Four-and-a-half miles south, Zihuatanejo squeezes tightly around a crescent bay and fans out far into the hills. There's no master plan here, but plenty of common sense: locals claim all the prime beachfront real estate.

Fishermen store pastel-painted boats and wooden lockers on one side of the town beach. At the ocean end of main street, practically tickling the beach, the cement-plain municipal plaza is the boisterous home court for sunset basketball games. The homespun archeological museum rates another stellar beach location, as does the kitschy sea shell market.

Lapped by tepid waves, Zihuatanejo basks like an iguana in the tropical sun. It's the kind of place where market vendors debate the merits of red vs. yellow papaya (red wins: it's much sweeter); where herbalists promote tlanchalagua tea for weight loss; and where city hall secretaries stick firmly by their two- hour lunch breaks.

In other words, it's the perfect retreat for a laid-back vacation in the sun.

Unlike Ixtapa, Zihuatanejo lodging comes in all varieties and price ranges. There's nothing fancy at Hotel Avila but it's the only in-town hotel directly on the beach (phone 4^2- 0210). (Note: to call Ixtapa or Zihuatanejo from the United States, the prefix is 011-52-753.) A fifteen-minute walk from town, with sweeping ocean views and private terraces large enough to host 30 friends, Bunglalows Pacificos' six villas come with airy bedrooms, private baths, and well-equipped kitchen (phone/fax: 42-212). There are many other bargains, including rooms at the Little Grass Shack on the La Ropa beach 15 minutes from town that go for $200 a week.

But Zihuatanejo doesn't just have bargain basement rates. It also cradles pearls: three small hotels and one B&B that are among the most exquisite you'll find anywhere on the Pacific coast.

The *Hotel Villa del Sol* enhances relaxed but genteel beach vacationing at its best. Five steps from the open-air dining room or bar and you're smack in the middle of La Ropa beach, a mile or so of perfection. All 36 rooms have muslin-canopied beds and hammocks on the terrace. High season, (Nov. 15 - Apr. 30). Box 84, Zihuatanejo, Gro., 40880 Mexico. USA: 1-800-223-6510.

A few rocky steps above La Ropa beach, the *Villa de la Roca* B&B is perfect for morning beach strolls and leisurely afternoons with a good book by the small, cascading pool. Each of the five rooms has a king size bed, a sitting room with 12-foot couch, and private terrace. Full breakfasts and an open bar. USA TEl. 801-277-2535 or 801-262-2577.

The 18 suites of ultra-romantic *La Casa que Canta* hotel spill down the cliffs above La Ropa beach. A spectacular pool overhangs the bay; there's no beachfront, but a small salt-water pool perches just above the waves. Bar and restaurant. Camino Escenico, Playa la Ropa, Zihuatanejo, Gro., 40880 Mexico. 800-525-4800 or, direct to the hotel, 800-432-6075.

Across the bay in its own rocky enclave, *Puerto Mio* is an ambitious development that in a couple of years will have 100 units. Only 26 of those are complete, but it's already an oasis of peach tones and pools, with head-on views of crashing surf. There's a marina and a soothing open-air nightclub which favors romance over rock. Paseo del Morro, Playa del Almacen, Box 294, Zihuatanejo, Gro., 40880 Mexico. Tel: in Mexico, 753-427-48. Fax: 420-48.

Cancun

Cancun is a carefully planned resort, started in the early 70s and located on the east coast of the Yucatan peninsula.

It is an island 14 miles long and 1/4 mile wide and it is often described as an outsized sandbar.

Easily accessible by air, Cancun is approximately 1 1/2 hours from Mexico City and 1 1/4 hours from Miami, Florida. Many airlines have direct flights to Cancun from major cities all over the United States.

Often compared to its neighbor resort, Cozumel, Cancun reportedly has a bit more glamour and lively atmosphere rather than the quieter and more peaceful pace set in Cozumel. The main attraction, of course, is the superb beauty of Cancun's beaches. Each year over a million tourists come to enjoy the activities of deep-sea fishing, sailing, snorkeling, diving and exploring the coral reefs, home for a wide variety of colorful fish.

The beaches are especially spectacular with the white powdery sand which is nearly 100 percent limestone. Its porous quality makes the sand cool and pleasant for walking or sunbathing.

Looking beyond the breathtaking white beaches, tourists are always impressed by the clear water whose color ranges from deep blue to lovely turquoise in the more shallow areas. Exceptional beauty!

Swimmers should be aware of the sometimes strong undertow on the east side and should check the posted warning signs. The rough surf is excellent for water surfing, but swimming is safer in the calmer water along the north shore.

Apart from the lure of water sports, there is much to please any visitor to Cancun.

The city offers bullfights, ballet, sightseeing, excursions to the nearby Mayan ruins of Chichén Itza and cruises to the small island **Isla Mujeres**, where one can take a glass bottom boat trip to glimpse the underwater gardens and interesting caves.

Cancun, like any other beach resort, has a variety of hotels, restaurants and night clubs where entertainment is excellent and tourists come away with a feeling of relaxation and a brief taste of Mexican flavor.

Merida - A Pleasure to Visit!

This fascinating inland city of approximately 700,000 people is the capital of the state of Yucatán. The city itself is full of charm with the colorful horse-drawn carriages or *calandrias*, which take you through narrow streets (all with numbers instead of names!) for a leisurely view of many interesting places that you will want to explore more fully.

You will be treated warmly by the friendly, handsome people of Merida who often bear the features typical of their Mayan ancestry (easily recognizable by their almond shaped eyes, high cheek bones and very straight hair).

While your are in Merida you should be sure to spend time in the *Zócalo* (main square), called the *Plaza de la Independencia*. There you will be treated to folk dancing, lively musical performances, vendors selling a variety of beautiful native crafts, and of course, it is always a pleasure to "people-watch."

Merida has several museums worth seeing. One is the **Museum of Popular Art** where examples of Yucatecan art are exhibited. **The Cantón Place** (or **Museum of Anthropology and History**) is also of interest, as well as the **Home Museum of Instruments** which displays original musical instruments of the pre-Hispanic era along with popular present day instruments. Your sightseeing should also include the **Cathedral**, a stately twin-towered church

192

located east of the plaza, and the **Casa de Montejo** and the **Government Palace**, all of which have historical and architectural significance.

Tourists are encouraged to take a carriage ride through beautiful **Paseo de Montejo**, a boulevard lined with trees where you will see a variety of architecture represented in the lovely mansions of French, Italian and Spanish-Moorish design.

These beautiful homes were built by the 19th century settlers who became vastly wealthy by making use of the hardy fibrous plants (henequen) which they harvested and used for making rope. Later these plants were also used for many other items such as door mats and hammocks.

While riding through **Paseo de Montejo** you will come to the **Monumento de la Patria**, sometimes referred to as the **Monument to the Flag**. This is a large semi-circle sculpture made of rose colored stone and depicting the history of Mexico. Take time to appreciate this interesting piece of art.

Many people are attracted to Merida because of its easy accessibility to such famous Mayan ruins as **Chichen Itza**, **Dzibilchaltun** and **Uxmal**, which are around 80 miles east of Merida. Also nearby are the **Balankanchin Caves** where there is an altar containing carved stone offerings left by the Mayans 800 years ago.

As you will discover, Merida has much to offer. You can spend days exploring this intriguing city, thus gaining another fascinating insight into the history of Mexico.

IX

Vacations Within Mexico

Take a Vacation in the State of Michoacán

Even in retirement one occasionally needs a vacation, and one of our favorite vacation trips is to the State of Michoacán, with principal destinations being the cities of Pátzcuaro and Uruapan. This area is rich in natural beauty much like that of mountainous areas of the eastern United States, such as the Blue Ridge and Appalachian Mountains. In addition, one will see many volcanoes for which central Mexico is noted. We usually allow four to seven days for this trip.

From Guadalajara or Lakeside Chapala we recommend going on the south side of the lake for the shortest route and best scenery, following Route 15 and the signs to Sahuayo, Jiquilpan and Zamora. When approaching Zamora from the west we usually take the new by-pass around town. Our first stop is at Lake Camécuaro Park. It is located about ten miles after leaving the Zamora by-pass on a side road to the right before passing the village of Tangancicuaro. This is a small, crystal clear, spring-fed lake with beautiful old cypress trees. It is a good place to relax and have a picnic. There is a small admission charge.

We then proceed to nearby Carapan Junction and follow the signs toward Morelia. The next stop is the town of Quiroga. We have found this small village a good place to shop for leather items, clothes, furniture, etc., with

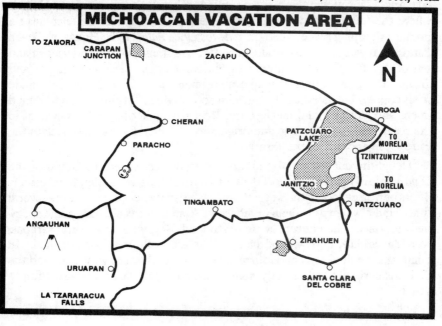

MICHOACAN VACATION AREA

197

prices *más baratas* (cheaper). Most stores close between two and four, so if you are interested in shopping, plan to arrive before or after *siesta* time. As you approach Quiroga, you are at the north end of the *Lago de Pátzcuaro* (Pátzcuaro Lake).

At Quiroga we usually leave Route 15 and drive south to the village of Tzintzuntzan, which is noted for its fine selection of straw products. Just outside of town make a left turn to the top of the hill to the pre-Columbian Tzintzuntzan Pyramids of the Tarascan Indians. You may see some of the pyramids from the road, but it is worth the extra time to drive up and walk around.

Next to Patzcuaro. It is among the oldest cities in the State of Michoacán, reportedly settled as early as the mid 1300's, and was officially proclaimed as capital of the State in 1544. Visitors to the area are impressed with the quiet, serene atmosphere of this quaint Indian city. Even with a population of nearly seventy thousand, it remains much like a small village. Most towns have a *Zócalo*, or main plaza. Patzuaro has two, one is near the market and a larger one that covers two blocks. The latter is surrounded by old ash trees and has a statue of Don Vasco de Quiroga, a priest who founded hospitals for the Tarascans in the mid 1500's. Vendors are not permitted in this plaza, nor are the restaurants and other businesses allowed to show flashing neon signs which would disturb the wonderful quiet tranquility. This plaza is one of the prettiest we have found.

Pátzcuaro is really divided into two distinct sections; downtown and the lake area. Downtown there are many shops, hotels and restaurants. Here is where the huge Friday open market takes place. You'll also encounter a popular shopping place called *Casa de los Once Patios* (The House of Eleven Patios) that was once a convent. Here, one can spend hours wandering in and out of the many shops scattered on different levels. The shopping in and around Pátzcuaro offers a unique assortment of local crafts, articles made from copper, lacquerware, beautiful wood carvings, furniture, hand-loomed linens and clothing, and much more. The artistic heritage that is evident in the color, design, technique and originality of the craftwork goes back to the Purépecha ancestry of the Tarascos.

Delightful dances are also an ancient tradition; especially famous is the *Danza de los Viejitos* (Dance of the Old Men). A local restaurant/hotel usually offers performances of this special treat. We have watched the dancers several times, and always enjoy them immensely. Appearing as old men, some seemingly toothless, the dancers come in stooped over, wearing colorful sarapes, wooden sandals, be-ribboned hats, and masks with gray hair attached. In contrast to their elderly and infirm appeaancene, they are very agile, and the dance is sprightly and cleverly done. Unique to the area, it is great fun to watch.

198

A walk or drive around the city is recommended so you can see the attractive white-washed adobe houses with their red-tiled roofs and bright red doors. The air is clean, and at an altitude of 7,200 feet, it is always crisp and cool even during the hottest months.

The lake area should definitely not be overlooked by tourists. Here there are small shops and open restaurants which feature freshly caught white fish for which Lake Pátzcuaro is famous. Here you will find the boat dock with motor launches available to take passengers to the Island of Janitzio (about a thirty minute trip each way).

Janitzio is a hill now covered with houses and shops, and dominated by a huge statue of General Morelos perched at the summit. It is said that the size of the statue is comparable to the Statue of Liberty in New York. Inside the statue are interesting murals depicting the life of Morelos. Stairs are available if one wishes to climb to the top. The Island of Janitzio is also known for the "Day of the Dead" observance on November second. Thousands of people come for this special day to pay tribute to loved ones who have departed, by spending the night eating, drinking and sharing memories.

About twelve miles south of Pátzcuaro is Santa Clara del Cobre, a former copper mining town, famous for a large variety of copper items at reasonable prices. Every store is full of copper, but not much else, and it is fascinating to watch the craftsmen at work pounding and molding a large piece of copper into a work of art. Each year, about the middle of August, the village holds a large fair that attracts coppersmiths, as well as tourists from all over. Be sure to walk through the *Museo del Cobre* (Museum of Copper) while you are in town to see the displays of antique copper art along with current designs.

When we are in the Pátzcuaro area, we usually stay at the Hotel Mesón del Gallo. We eat many meals at the El Patio restaurant located on the main Plaza. The hotel is convenient to shopping and the main patio and is clean and reasonable priced.

There is a small community of twenty-five to fifty *Americanos del Norte* who reside in Pátzcuaro, particularly artists, who find this to be a desirable place to locate.

While in Pátzcuaro you might wish to visit the state capital of Morelia, about thirty-five miles away.

Traveling west toward Uruapan, twenty miles or so from Pátzcuaro, is the Pyramid of Tingambato. To see this interesting structure, you watch for a pyramid sign and go left for a mile.

The main highway, continuing west, will take you to Uruapan (altitude 5,500 ft.). Uruapan was founded in 1533 and is one of the largest agricultural producers in the Republic, known especially for the abundance of avocados that are shipped all over the world.

There are several good hotels and restaurants in Uruapan. We often stay at the Motel Pie de la Sierra located about 1.5 miles north of town on the Carapan road. The motel sits on a hill overlooking the city, and has a heated pool, beautiful gardens and grounds, plus secure parking. The food at the motel restaurant is good and prices are moderate. Upon arrival in Uruapan, we usually take the by-pass around the city and go directly to the hotel. The city of Uruapan is a busy commercial center, appears congested, and in our opinion does not have the charm of typical colonial Mexican cities. For us, Uruapan's main attrations are the *Parque Barranca del Cupatitzio* (also referred to as the *Parque Nacional Eduardo Ruíz*), the nearby Paricutín Volcano, the La Tzaráracua Waterfall, and the relaxing atmosphere of the motel.

To visit Parque Barranca del Cupatitzio go back downhill toward Uruapan and continue straight at the Pemex station. Shortly you will see a sign pointing to Hotel Mansion del Cupatitzio where you make a right turn to the parking lot and the upper entrance to the park. Here you will follow a wooded trail downhill (it is easier for us older folks to walk downhill) and see the headwaters of the Cupatitzio River develop into a raging stream with hundreds of springs feeding into the main stream of water. The path is very picturesque with lush tropical vegetation, flowering plants, fountains, stone bridges, small falls and the crystal clear unpolluted water. The walk, about a mile in length, is one you will never forget. We always exit at the main entrance to the park and take a taxi back to the car at the upper entrance.

Seven or eight miles north of the Motel Pie de la Sierra on the Carapan road and to the left is the road to the Paricutín Volcano, a distance of about eighteen miles on a typical country road. On February 20, 1943 this volcano started forming in a cornfield and during a period of eight years inundated the town, except for the church spire, and also covered several other villages. It is a beautiful drive through forests and fields to an Indian village named Angahuán, with its small unpainted wooden houses. From here you can go to a viewing point (*mirador*) to see the volcano, the blackened countryside and the San Juan de las Colchas Church spire. Horses and a tour guide may be employed to ride to the top of the volcano, a trip taking several hours. For those wishing to enjoy a little exercise there are walking trails leading to the church, a forty-five minute excursion.

For a visit to the La Tzaráracua Waterfall follow the Playa Azul highway south out of Uruapan for about seven miles and then to the right to the parking area. These beautiful falls from the Cupatitzio river are accessible by walking, or taking a horseback trip to the bottom of the canyon, a distance of little more than a half-mile. The over one-hundred foot falls and numerous springs gushing out of the mountains are beautiful and one should make a point to see them.

Returning to the Carapan junction you may want to stop at the town of Paracho, especially if you're interested in violins or guitars. Paracho specializes in making these instruments, and there are shops all over town. At some you can see them being made. The quality will compare favorably with those made anywhere and the prices vary, but are quite reasonable.

For a change of scenery, and restful diversion, a trip to the State of Michoacán should be on everyone's list!

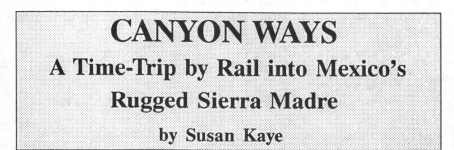

CANYON WAYS
A Time-Trip by Rail into Mexico's Rugged Sierra Madre
by Susan Kaye

The rugged Copper Canyon, only 400 miles south of the border from El Paso, Texas, is nevertheless the ends of the earth.

This dramatically immense gorge — guesstimated at three to four times larger than the Grand Canyon — qualifies unreservedly for national park and a World Heritage Site status. But it is neither, so goat herders and developers alike can and do build huts and hotels just feet from the rim, claiming as their own a vast panorama bounded only by a violet-shadowed horizon.

But even without protection, no more than a dozen modest lodges peek through the canopy of pines along the edge of the spectacle in northwestern Mexico, and the shadowy abyss of the canyon itself remains the exclusive preserve of a few prospectors and the Tarahumara Indians.

This reclusive tribe, some 40,000 of whom live in the canyon, lead a near-subsistence life, burrowing their homes into rocks and recesses, and farming minuscule plots that teeter on sloped valleys.

Most of the men have adopted western wear, but the woman stand out like tropical flowers, with sweeping hand-stitched calico skirts, high-necked calico blouses, and head bandannas in yet another print.

Although their colorful dresses would delight the most exuberant of gypsies, the Tarahumarans themselves are as shy as hesitant children, ducking their heads as they whisper the prices of the simple wares they sell and shaking hands with a touch as insubstantial as the flutter of a butterfly wing in the palm.

Just to observe them — quietly riding on the train with their families or purposefully walking along up the canyon burdened by a bundle slung across their backs — is to sense life's immutable rhythms.

The women bring in much of the families' cash by selling hand- made drums, roughly carved dolls, meticulously crafted pine needle baskets, and larger baskets woven out of *sotol*, a thorny leaf. Most items cost $1-$5 U.S.: bargaining doesn't seem to be in order.

Whereas Arizona's canyon is a dramatic geology lesson, Mexico's *Barranca del Cobre* (Copper Canyon) is a study in placid beauty. Vast distances diffuse the light into a milky haze and the vista ricochets with green: *piñón* pines blanket the upper reaches while banana, fig and orange groves thrive in the lower altitudes amidst bamboo. Interrupting this monochromatic kaleidoscope are raw swatches of fiery red soil.

The almost total lack of roads to this wilderness stronghold explains why, deep within the Sierra Madre Mountains, the last few centuries have almost slipped by unnoticed.

Only since 1961 has the Chihuahua al Pacífico rumbled through the canyon on its 400-mile, 12-hour journey between the homely town of Los Mochis and the agricultural center of Chihuahua. Last year, the line carried over a half-million passengers. Most were dozing commuters — the men in straw hats and jeans, and the Indian women in voluminous skirts — but thousands were tourists feeling as adventuresome as if they were on the first leg of discovering a brand new world.

The ride qualifies as one of the world's great train journeys. At times, the tracks are secured into sheer rock ledges and views stretch downward 1,000 feet. As the train climbs 7,200 feet to the Continental Divide, it crosses 37 bridges and enters 86 tunnels — at one point circling around itself within a mountain.

But the best part is the distance-defying canyon and its secretive inhabitants.

Four hours out of Los Mochis, the train pulls into Bahuichivo, no more than a clearing and a lean-to selling sodas and chips. Guests staying at La Misión Hotel disembark for a seven-mile van ride to the small town of Cerocahui. Rooms at La Misión, all of which open to a grassy courtyard patio, are heated by wood- burning stoves.

In this time-warped village overlooked by gray granite hills and surrounded by small farms, fresh produce often arrives at the town's three small stores via boys leading donkeys burdened with gunny sacks of onions and potatoes. For everyone, including inn guests, it's "lights out" at 10:30 when the generator is turned off. The wake-up call is just as sudden, as bells peel vigorously from the white-washed mission church.

Next door to the hotel, 50 Tarahumara girls study at a mission boarding school. "They also learn to cook and they do their own washing in the long concrete tubs," says Sister Juanita, a teacher.

Two hours further down the railway line is Divisadero, the half-way point of the journey and only a few steps from the rim of the gaping canyon. During the fifteen-minute layover, travelers dash for a peek at the canyon then cross the tracks to browse at the Tarahumaran outdoor craft market.

The nearby Posada Barrancas, with fireplaces in each of the 36 rooms and family-style dining by a roaring fire, is reminiscent of a well-run, rustic lodge in Americas's National Parks. As in the La Misión Inn, the food is hearty and delicious and the water purified. Every morning, the hotel's flowery courtyard erupts into an informal market where the Indian vendors tend babies and weave baskets.

Breathtaking vistas of the layered canyon are just around a hillside. Using the hotel's telescope, guests scan the canyon. One man focused far, far across the canyon on a minuscule plateau, and spotted a Tarahumara household: horses grazed on emerald meadows, vividly colored clothes were spread to dry, and a man chopped wood by an already large pile.

Without the telescope, the distant plateau on which these isolated Indians live out their lives was no more than a speck. It was if, just for a moment, he'd tiptoed through a veil of clouds and glimpsed Shangri-La.

IF YOU GO:

WEATHER. The high season for the Copper Canyon trip is October through April. Most North Americans, however, make the trip in summer, when, despite the heat in Los Mochis, canyon temperatures remain comfortable.

TRAIN SERVICE, first-class, runs about $25 U.S. each way. Tickets may be bought at the station or reserved ahead. The first class train generally carries a dining car and a smoking car. Windows are smeared and dust-streaked and reading lights function haphazardly. But, the seats recline, the dining car drinks are cold and it's easy to find fellow travelers to swap tales with.

The best one-way direction for the trip is from Los Mochis to Chihuahua, as the most scenic portions will be during daylight. To maximize the scenery and limit train-time, go from Los Mochis to Divisadero or Creel, spend the night, and return.

HOTELS. The Misión and Posada Barrancas lodges run about $115 U.S./day for 2 people, including 3 hearty meals served with purified water. Simple, comfortable rooms are heated by fireplaces or pot-bellied stoves.

It is necessary to stay overnight in Los Mochis (best choice is the Santa Anita Hotel) to catch the 6 a.m. first-class train. Any extra days are best spent along the route rather than on the day-long tour from Los Mochis to the coastal town of Topolobampo.

(Editors Note: Tony Burton, director of Odisea Mexico, A.C., arranges a limited number of "ecotourist" trips to the Copper Canyon each year. Write: Apdo. 79, Jocotepec, Jalisco, Mexico. Telephone: (376) 3-01-64. FAX: (376) 5-25-59.)

The Fascinating Scenery of Western Mexico's "Volcanic Belt"

by Tony Burton

A broad belt of high relief, the so-called "Volcanic Axis", which is far more easily accessible than virtually any comparable area in the world, runs across Mexico from the west coast to the east, forming one of the major "ecotourism" areas in the country. Within it lie all of Mexico's important volcanoes from the smallest, only a few yards high, on the outskirts of Puebla, to the largest, the 18,865 foot Pico de Orizaba, located between Mexico City and Veracruz.

Wherever volcanoes occur people have marveled at their power, unpredictability and sheer elegant beauty. Nowhere is this more true than in Mexico. Thousands of years ago, long before even the Aztecs appeared on the scene, the Olmec tribe fashioned a mound of earth into a crude pyramid exactly resembling a volcanic cone, modeling it from Mother Nature. The Volcanic Axis has an even longer history, going back millions of years.

Travelers in Western Mexico often glimpse the attractive twin volcanic peaks of the 13,911 ft. *Nevado de Colima* ("Colima Snowtop", its name always a heated point of discussion as it is located in the State of Jalisco) and its near neighbor, the still active 12,533 ft. *Volcán del Fuego* ("Volcano of Fire"). Thousands of tourists pass close to these mountains each year on their way from Guadalajara, Mexico's charming and cosmopolitan second city, to the popular Pacific coast resorts centered on Manzanillo. As a matter of fact, these volcanoes are in view for over ninety miles along the new 190 mile express way connecting Guadalajara with the Pacific Coast at Manzanillo. They are both difficult to climb since access is via rough forestry roads and steep trails.

The unusually high precipitation and low temperatures during this past winter (the worst in thirty years) has caused a tragic death toll, due to the freezing temperatures and snow avalanches. Although the Forestry Department extends multiple warnings every year about the dangers of exploring these snowtops, and even cuts off road accesses, the foolishly brave (unfortunately mostly teenagers) get around these barriers for the thrill of seeing and touching real snow, and ill-equipped to face these circumstances, perish under weather conditions they never thought could exist.

Luckily, many other dramatic and interesting parts of the Volcanic Axis are more readily accessible to the tourist, needing only an ordinary car (and car rental in Mexico is easy) and little if any walking. These "drive-in" routes cross some of the most difficult and arduous terrain imaginable, providing access to shortwave communications posts. They represent tremendous engineering feats: triumphs of man over nature in environments which would have otherwise to be regarded as total victories for nature!

Close to Guadalajara, the 9,580 ft. Tequila volcano forms the backdrop to the typical Jaliscan town of Tequila, home of the world famous beverage. A pleasant day out can be had by combining a tour of one of the tequila factories in the town with a drive to the top of the volcano. The eleven mile cobbled road to the shortwave post on the crater rim passes the plaza in the center of Tequila and the small railroad station on Av. Hidalgo. On the climb towards the summit there are many delightful picnic spots, some with a magnificent view over the entire valley which lies spread out far below. At the end of the road, a short, pleasant walk takes you to the very brink of the crater itself. Without question the most arresting thing about the view is not the crater, tree-lined and green though it is, but a giant monolith with almost vertical sides rising perpendicularly from the middle of the crater floor. This spine represents the hardened lava which cooled in the central vent of the volcano and which, at a later date, solid and unyielding, was pushed upwards by a subsequent eruption of tremendous force. Few such good examples exist anywhere in the world. Looking across the crater on a day when clouds drift overhead and temporarily obscure the view is like watching a modern day video equivalent of ancient Chinese landscape drawings.

Further west on Highway 15, relatively close to Ixtlán del Río, in the state of Nayarit, is the 7,100 ft. Ceboruco volcano, which also has a cobblestone road to the top. It starts from the old and pretty village of Jala, five miles off the main highway. There are several small hotels in Ixtlán, with double rooms for about twenty dollars, enabling visitors to see not only the Ceboruco but also an intriguing post-classic archaeological site two and one-half miles east of the town and to climb the "thousand steps" of the *Cerro del Cristo* ("Christ Hill") for a spectacular panoramic view. The lava field that surrounds this volcano crater is literally "out of this world," as it looks like a science fiction movie set, with brick red/black pumice spread as far as the eye can see. It has to be the most heart-stopping scenery in Mexico.

The road up the Ceboruco is a geologist's or biologist's dream come true, a slowly unfolding series of volcanic forms and different types of vegetation with abundant surprises even for the scientifically expert. Small wonder that the great German explorer, Baron von Humboldt, was so impressed when he visited the Ceboruco.

Near the top are several short but interesting walks, some in shady, thickly vegetated valleys hidden between towering walls of blocky lava, some along the many overlapping rims of the various old craters, which together make this complex peak. Wherever you choose to walk, a veritable profusion of multi-colored flowers and butterflies will greet your eyes. On the south side of an attractive grassy valley at kilometer sixteen, fumaroles send hot gasses and steam high into the air in the volcano's final death throes.

A few miles further along Highway 15, the Guadalajara-Tepic highway, at kilometer 194, a short, perfectly paved road branches off to the north, passing first through the former mining town of Santa María del Oro and then, rising slightly, affording an absolutely splendid view of a beautiful slate-blue crater lake, set in the middle of a ring of verdant hills. Several scientific expeditions have tried to determine the depth of this lake, with no success. This idyllic spot, scarcely developed at present, must surely become a major vacation spot in the future. For now it is an undiscovered oasis of beauty and tranquility and is, in reality, a drive-in volcanic crater! Around the lake are several small restaurants highly recommended for their fresh fish. A meal for two at one of these lakeside restaurants should cost only about fifteen dollars. The only tourist accommodation is at the Koala bungalows and trailer park, run by Chris French, a world-traveled Englishman, his Mexican wife and their four children. A more restful or peaceful place from which to contemplate the calm, serene waters of the lake and the outstanding natural beauty of this area is difficult to imagine. Geese flying in formation across the crystal-clear, ripple-free lake at sunset are but one variety of the numerous birds to grace the scene. An expert ornithologist can identify dozens of species.

There are many attractive walks in the vicinity; a particularly pleasant and satisfying one is around the lake which so far has no encircling road, only a path. At an easy pace, this takes about an hour and a half and provides a wonderful range of lake and mountain views. Alternatively, a short climb to an abandoned gold mine offers a glimpse into the area's past and an opportunity to strike it rich! Or how about swimming or hiring a rowboat to venture out onto the lake?

The peaceful crater lake of Santa María del Oro and the more rugged attractions of Ceboruco can easily be combined into a single, memorable "volcanic" weekend. Either can provide a novel and unusual overnight stay for motorists driving from Guadalajara to Puerto Vallarta or Mazatlán.

(Note: Another interesting volcano is Paricutín, near Uruapan in the State of Michoacán. This was mentioned in our chapter "Take a Vacation in the State of Michoacán!")

Snowbirds and Butterflies

by Tony Burton

Every winter two large groups of escapees from the northern cold fly to Mexico. Many thousands of so-called "snowbirds," American and Canadian Tourists who come to enjoy the warm Mexican sunshine and hospitality, form the first group.

The second group is numerically much greater, but also comes from the U.S. and Canada. They, too, have flown south to avoid freezing weather but, unlike the average tourist, they arrive unencumbered by suitcases or documents, and are, believe it or not, small, defenseless insects - the fabulous Monarch butterflies.

The snowbirds congregate on the semi-tropical coast and nearby Guadalajara and Lake Chapala - the Monarchs form their tightly- knit communities in about a dozen localities high in the fir forest of the state of Michoacán. Reluctant to travel by night, anxious to avoid delay, both species fly the 1900 miles each way, though the butterflies' average speed of 15 mph compares poorly with that of a Boeing 747!

Scientists are still unable to explain all the details of the Monarch's enigmatic annual migration, a migration without parallel in the butterfly world. How is it, for example, that those returning in November to Mexico, four or five generations down the line from those who flew north in April, manage to find exactly the same groves of trees as their ancestors, high in the Sierra Madre?

That their numbers are not decimated by predatory birds and animals during their somnolescent dormancy on Michoacan's oyamel fir trees is a surprise, but the butterflies' favorite food is the milkweed plant. This, while poisonous to most wildlife, is nevertheless digested by the Monarch (*Danaus plexippus*) rendering is sufficiently venomous to deter would-be predators after their first mouthful.

The Monarchs are one of the most amazing natural spectacles to be seen anywhere on Earth. Several million orange butterflies with black and white-spotted wings flying overhead, or clinging to gray-green trees in such profusion that the trees appear to be in blossom, are an absolutely unforgettable sight. Their sheer weight of numbers can be sufficient to break the very branches supporting them!

February and March are the best months to see them. As early spring sunlight penetrates the forest floor, the butterflies, having successfully overwintered the worst weather, unfurl their solar-panel wings and flutter in search of food and water.

207

Tourists arriving at this time of year to the El Rosario Reserve, located between Morelia and Mexico City, are rarely disappointed. Rain during these months is unusual, and mid-day temperatures are usually of the "no sweater" variety. A short walk along well-made and shaded paths (though the altitude of nearly 10,000 feet may make you feel it's a lot longer!) and you reach the main congregation of Monarchs, literally tens of millions of them.

The Reserve is well-policed by local *campesino* (farmer) guides, under the control of the Federal Environmental Protection Agency. There is a modest fee (currently US $2.00 per person) and an instructive display about the butterflies and their life styles at the entrance. There is ample, supervised parking and several small stands selling soft drinks and home-cooked, absolutely delectable "blue corn" tortillas. If you've never experienced this culinary delight of Mexico, then try one sometime, you won't regret it!

Obviously the chance to see this miracle of Mother Nature is not one to be missed. Sadly, habitat destruction in both Mexico and the U.S., and the use of herbicides to destroy the patches of milkweed essential for migrating Monarchs, are now threatening the continued annual "tourist traffic" of these colorful insects.

Before taking a Monarch tour, check carefully that the tour will be accompanied by a qualified naturist (it makes it so much more interesting), and ask to speak with people who have been on the tour before; not all companies now offering trips to see the butterflies can be recommended.

X
Important Mexican Holidays and Customs

Mexican Holidays...
Take Note!

The holidays celebrated each year in the U.S.A., plus the religious and national holidays observed in Mexico, add up to quite a list and often leave North Americans bewildered. Therefore we obtained a complete list of Mexican holidays when one may expect to find the American Consulate and Mexican banks, businesses and government offices closed for that particular day.

It is well to be aware of these special days and to mark them on your calendar. Be prepared for the probable absence of your maids or other workers who take full advantage of each official holiday (marked with an asterisk in the list below), and many of the non-official ones, too!

Mexican holidays are as follows:

Jan 1*	New Year's Day	May 10	Mother's Day
Feb 5*	Mexican Constitution Anniversary	Sep 16*	Independence Day
		Oct 12	Día de la Raza
Mar 21*	Benito Juarez's Birthday	Nov 2	Día de los Muertos
variable*	Holy Thursday		(All Souls Day)
variable*	Holy Friday	Nov 20*	Mexican Revolution
variable*	Easter Sunday		Anniversary
May 1*	Labor Day	Dec 12	Virgin of Guadalupe Day
May 5*	Anniversary - Battle of Puebla	Dec 25*	Christmas Day
		Dec 31	New Year's Eve

The "observance" day of holidays is never changed in Mexico, as in the U.S., to create long weekends, but Mexicans are famous for creating their own *puentes* ("bridges"). If a holiday falls on Tuesday or Thursday, many people will take the preceeding Monday or following Friday off. This type of activity is frowned upon by government and school authorities.

Taking into consideration all these "free" days, when practically everything comes to a complete stop, it is amazing that businesses are able to function with any efficiency. But they *do* manage for the most part, and then of course, there is always *mañana*!

Happy New Year
(Behind the Taco Curtain)
by June Summers

My maid, Perfecta, has been very helpful with my indoctrination into customs and traditions of Mexico. Last year I learned there was more to New Year's Eve festivities than *abrazos y besos* (hugs and kisses) and New Year resolutions. Perfecta told me about the twelve grapes.

You don't peel them...you eat them. One grape at a time, on each stroke of midnight, the grapes are consumed. You make a wish for each month of the coming year. I took care of that Mexican custom by making a list of 12 wishes in advance.

Now, I asked Perfecta, is that all there is to it...to have a 100% Mexican New Year? Not by the hair on your chinny-chin-chin, she told me. Having mastered the twelve grape routine last year, Perfecta feels I can go on to bigger and better (and definitely more Mexican) civilities.

Perfecta then gave me a list of activities to be performed within seven minutes preceding midnight, Perfecta for aspirants to a 100% successful New Year's Eve. Furthermore, one would be well-advised to have all props and preparations made in advance and the procedure rehearsed for timing and efficiency:

- First, light twelve candles to illuminate each month of 1993.

- NEXT, throw a bucket of water out of the window to rid yourself of sorrow and tears.

- THEN, get rid of evil spirits by sweeping the doorstep and throwing salt over your left shoulder.

- IF YOUR PALMS ITCH, and you want money, put a coin in your shoe.

- ROMANCE IS A BURNING THING, wear red underpants.

- YOU WANT TO TRAVEL, pack your suitcase and run around the house as many times as you want trips.

- FINALLY, if you want lots of company, assemble a cage full of birds and turn them loose in your house. Lots of birds brings lots of company, so saith Perfecta.

- AND ONE LAST THING! Just to clinch the ritual, eat those twelve grapes if it kills you, before the last stroke of midnight.

212

Should you wish to personalize your performance with specific desires, Perfecta says to incorporate these in with other rites - but they must be done within the same seven minutes. For example: I plan to execute a war dance around my computer in order to enrich and increase my 1993 journalistic output.

VIVA New Year, MEXICAN STYLE!

Easter Behind The Taco Curtain

by June Summers

Semana Santa (Holy Week): The most traditional and important celebration on Mexico's festive and ritual calender.

Fiesta Time: "Every day is fiesta time, somewhere in Mexico. A little fiesta may last for a day only, a big fiesta for as long as two weeks. If the fiesta is an important one, like the one before Lent, the whole town or village is decorated with colorful paper streamers, and people from the hills or nearby villages start coming into town several days in advance. Some stay with friends or relatives, but the greater number simply sleep in the main plaza or along the side streets. They may cook their meals on braziers, or buy tortillas and chili from itinerant vendors. At night, they sleep rolled up in their *serapes* or on some straw mats called *petates*, oblivious to any discomfort. After all, the joy of the fiesta is ahead." *(Octavio Paz)*

* * *

Holy Week in Mexico is a blend of the ethnic traditions of the Spanish, who brought Christianity to the New World, and of the native Indian cultures. Spanish Padres used to teach the Indians Christianity. Ritual dances and the colorful costumes of the Indians, used in the worship of their gods, were blended with plays and pageants, depicting the story of Christ, to form the New World's Christian religious ceremonies.

Semana Santa Calender

Palm Sunday (a week before Easter Sunday) celebrates Jesus' entry into Jerusalem, when people threw branches of palms in his path, only a few days before his trail and execution.

People gather in plazas and weave palm fronds into artistic shapes. The priest blesses the palms and then leads his palm- bearing parishioners into the church where a mass is held. Afterwards, palm fronds may be fixed to door

213

fronts to ward away evil spirits, or burning fronds are held in the winds so that prayers will be carried to heaven on the palm's smoke.

Wednesday Night of Holy Week: The LAST SUPPER is reenacted.

Maundy Thursday (first of two mourning days): Horse hooves are bound in cloth, church aisles are covered with olive leaves, and church bells are replaced with *matracas* (wooden clappers) to muffle sounds. The devout visit seven churches in memory of Christ's last seven words. Mass is not held.

Good Friday Passion Plays unfold depicting the sentencing of Jesus, and the procession of the "three falls", dramatizing the walk to the hill of Golgotha, the crucifixion, and the descent from the cross. This day celebrates the crucifixion, sometimes with a living "Christ" actor. Again, no Mass is held.

Sábado de Gloria (Day of Glory) custom is to lift children by their ears, or to stand them on their heads, after Mass. It is supposed to make them grow. An old Spanish saying, if you are short..."*que te pongan de cabeza en el sábado de Gloria.*" (May they stand you on your head the Day of Glory.)

Tradition also has it that pulling on fruit trees on this day will make them bear more fruit.

Also on this day a Mass of Glory celebrates the anticipation of the resurrection. Church bells ring once more to signal the start of Mass. Preceding the Mass, pots of flowers are brought to the church and blessed by the priest, then used to decorate the church.

This day is also known as the **Day of Judas**, and children dress up as Judas, with long flowing robes and black beards, and chase each other. Many villages celebrate the Mass of Glory with the burning of huge paper maché figures representing Judas. (If you are traveling through small villages during this celebration, it is quite common to be stopped on the road, next to the Judas figure-in-creation, and be asked for a small donation to finish the Judas figure).

Easter Sunday Masses continue throughout the day. The pageantry which marked Easter Week is over. Mexico's celebration of Christ's resurrection has ended. The tortilla curtain comes down on Mexico's many-faceted cultural and ritual fiesta, for another year. *Feliz Semana Santa* (happy Easter week) *y que te pongan de cabeza en el sábado de Gloria.*

* * *

"The art of the fiesta has been debased almost everywhere else...but not in Mexico...There are few places in the world where it is possible to take part in a spectacle like our great religious fiestas...in all of these ceremonies the Mexican opens out...they all give him a chance to reveal himself and to converse with God, country, friends or relations...." *(Octavio Paz)*

Mother's Day
in Mexico

In Mexico, as everywhere, it really pays to be a mother. As in the United States, Mother's Day is very special. May 10th is invariably Mother's Day, regardless of what day of the week it falls on, with the obvious working day disruptions.

The first Mother's Day for us in Mexico was quite an experience. We were awakened around 3:30 a.m. on May 10th by a group of Mariachi singers serenading a mother next door. We had not been aware of this custom, plus the fact it was not on Sunday, our traditional day to celebrate this special occasion. After jumping out of bed, bumping into each other to get to the window, and gradually realizing just what was happening, we settled back down in bed and enjoyed the lively and sentimental music which continued for most of what was left of the early hours. Personally, I have mixed emotions about being so *"treated"* that early, but, to "each his own." This is a very popular way to begin the Mother's Day celebration in Mexico, and the recipient is greatly honored. Mothers are later taken to a special Mass, then out to dinner and also are given gifts much as mothers are in the United States. (Don't attempt an impromptu dinner at a restaurant on this day, because reservations are made weeks in advance. Also avoid shopping, as stores will sell almost as much merchandise on Mother's Day as at Christmas.) I understand one traditional gift for the occasion is a set of six glasses decorated with a floral design, perhaps a white carnation or *nardo* which is the most popular flower and usually a favorite for arrangements on Mother's Day.

It is a nice custom in Mexico that the maids of well-run households who are mothers are also given special gifts, usually a piece of material for a dress, a favorite cake or a plant to express the family's thanks for her faithful service.

Note: Fathers in Mexico also have a special day, just as in the United States. It is celebrated June 19th, when the head of the family is given gifts and perhaps a special cake. But the celebration in no way compares with the elaborate planning which is involved with honoring the mother of the family.

It is interesting to know that in Mexico there is a special day set aside for small children. On their day, April 30th, families plan parties with piñatas, cakes, games and gifts to celebrate the little ones.

The Virgin of Zapopan Comes Home

Our introduction to the Virgin of Zapopan celebration was very impressive and we suggest that all newcomers attend at least once. We had been in Guadalajara about five weeks when we were invited to go to the special procession, and we eagerly accepted.

Our friends explained that the procession, held annually on October 12th, celebrates the Virgin's homecoming to the Basilica in Zapopan after a lengthy visit to each of the churches in the Diocese. The little figure of the Virgin is made of straw, stands a mere 13 inches tall, and is housed in a small glass case. Each year she travels to surrounding villages to ensure enough rain for crops, and to offer her protection against storms and other disasters. Each village is blessed by her visit. When Lake Chapala suffered a terrible drought during the 1950's, the Virgin made a special trip to the Lake to pray for rain.

October 12th is designated for her return and calls for the colorful, much-celebrated procession. The Guadalajara Cathedral is the last stop on her yearly itinerary before her return home. The Virgin of Zapopan, protected by her glass case, travels in a carriage drawn by people pulling a long rope, led by men and boys. A long rope is also attached to the back of the carriage for braking when going downhill. Preceding and following her are native dancers and musicians, each dressed in the costume of his particular village or neighborhood, some decorated with feathers, some wearing masks, all delightful to watch. In the neighborhoods close to the Basilica, you will see young people practicing on the side streets during the evening for months before the big day. Each village is also represented by most of the families living there, who may have walked many miles to attend. Some arrive the night before and often camp along the streets.

We were told to expect a crowd, but even though our group arrived at the procession site around 6:00 a.m. there was barely room to move. Never had we seen so many people! The mention of the word *Romería* (procession) to the people who live on the route is enough to make them cringe - it was estimated that well over a million faithful followers were on hand to attend this very special event. We were fortunate to get a least a glimpse of the little figure, and the procession will always be an exciting and colorful memory.

The Fiestas de Octubre!

by Lupita Villaseñor, Director.

People often think of Mexico as a never ending party, because you can be sure that almost every day during the year in some city or little village there is a fiesta or party celebration.

It is especially true here in the atmosphere of a cosmopolitan city such as Guadalajara, modern and up-to-date, but also keeping the joy and colorful taste of Mexican traditions, where one of the largest of the festivities is held, which is known as "Las Fiestas de Octubre." The fame of this festival has spread throughout Latin America.

Las Fiestas de Octubre combines the characteristics of a large traditional festival with the importance of a huge commercial fair, where merchants and visitors from all over the continent gather to enjoy a magical and colorful *fiesta* with an international touch.

With this special combination of festivities and the constantly increasing number of events, a new concept of the *fiesta* has been established. The festival involves, over a specific period of time, a whole series of activities: artistic, cultural and sports. This offers a very diversified variety of things to do. Thanks to the success and growth each year, the Fiestas de Octubre is now a great event; the State of Jalisco opens its doors during the thirty-one days of October (and sometimes during the first week of November), offering approximately 260 different kinds of activities - something for everyone!

It has become a custom to open the "Fiestas" with a big parade, which normally takes place on the first Sunday in October. This parade is very popular, attracting around one million people who line the streets in anticipation.

Another annual tradition is the selection and crowning of a "Queen," who will represent the beauty and all the best attributes of the women of Jalisco. For this event three young girls compete in the metropolitan municipality in search of votes from friends as well as support from different companies; the candidate who obtains the most votes and support is declared the winner!

The main location of this festive extravaganza is the Benito Juárez Auditorium, where hundreds of displays surround the huge pavilion featuring arts and crafts, cultural developments and extensive entertainment shows.

Outside events include a number of competitive and entertainment sport attractions, such as cock fights, bull fights, charreadas, stock shows, horsemanship and bicycle races, all held at famous sites throughout the city.

In Guadalajara's colonial downtown, approximately one hundred booths are erected near the Plaza Tapatia, which is an important showcase for the visitors' displays.

Some of the attractions are of technical and cultural nature, including the fine folkloric displays provided by the participation of foreign embassies and governments, various states of Mexico and municipalities of Jalisco.

Approximately twenty countries participate in the festival displaying exhibits, folkloric dancing, food specialties and many other cultural activities, helping to increase good relations among countries through this international celebration. Popular music, open-air cafes, and the presentations of different artists make this a very pleasant setting.

Some of the top quality cultural events are opera, renaissance music, ballet and other excellent artistic performances, which are a special treat for the residents of Guadalajara, and vary from year to year.

There are three different contests for Mexican handicrafts; one contest is limestone sculpturing by the talented craftsmen who carve their designs at the main plaza for the competition at the end of the month. Another popular contest is the National Jewelry competition by artisans from all over the world where one will be delighted by the beautiful and unusual designs. Last, and as part of the closing ceremony of the Fiestas de Octubre, is the magnificent fireworks display competition put on by Mexico's most talented and skillful pyrotechnists. Examples of their skill are beautiful and colorful *castillos* (fireworks castles) and figures, which leave a fascinated and admiring crowd very impressed and eager for the next year's "Fiestas de Octubre."

Guadalajara and all its people, with their long-standing tradition of hospitality and friendship, welcomes the world with open arms. Excellent weather and a delightful atmosphere make Guadalajara the place to be during the month of October.

OCTOBER

Day of the Dead is National Holiday

by Susan Kaye

Once a year, Hilaria Sandoval waits beside her parents' graves to welcome back their souls in Mixquic, Mexico.

She kneels on the ground in the crowded, but eerily quiet village cemetery, her feet tucked under her cotton skirt and her shawl wrapped tightly against the coolness. Monitoring her nearby children and the flickering candles atop the flower-strewn plot, she will remain at her vigil until past midnight.

"It's something my mother did, and her mother, too. Now it's my turn," she says, her hand sifting through a mound of *cempazuchitl* petals.

For millions of Mexicans like Mrs. Sandoval, in thousands of pueblos like Mixquic, the Day of the Dead on November 2 is the most important day of the year. Incense, marigolds, and food all encourage visitors from the beyond to return to their family for a night of feasting and remembering.

The incompatible but accepted mix of Indian superstition with Christianity governs this uniquely Mexican custom. Aztecs set aside the ninth month of their year to honor dead children, the tenth month to honor deceased adults. This period has been compressed into two days that the rest of the Catholic world celebrates as All Saint's Day (Nov. 1) and All Soul's Day (Nov. 2).

In cities, the middle and upper classes either scoff at the tradition or give it no more than a nod with a simple home offering. But in outlying areas across the country, death is everywhere in the weeks before the holiday.

Street vendors sell amaranth seed skulls with raisin eyes and peanut teeth. Newspapers run ditties about death by local wags. Bakeries stack shelves with *pan de muerto*; these rounded loaves, topped with a design of crossed bones, show up on graves, in breakfast buffets at the Sheraton María Isabel, in humble home altars, and in bread baskets at chic San Angel Inn. Candy shops fashion ghost-white marzipan skulls by the thousands. Customers buy ones with their name written in frosting across the forehead. *Cempazuchitl*, large marigolds called by their Nahuatl name, are bought by the dozens; their petals often carpet altars.

Everywhere, the atmosphere is celebratory, not funereal. "Aztecs weren't afraid to die," explained Ivonne Pablo, an anthropologist with the Templo Mayor museum in downtown Mexico City, "but they needed supplies to take with them on their journey through the nine undergrounds. The offerings we make for the dead continue this belief."

219

Offerings - found in homes, shops, offices, and on graves - are usually simple ones such as the Pablo family prepares: candles and *cempazuchitl*. Others are elaborate, with plates of tamales, a bottle of the deceased's favorite beverage (anything from sodas to tequila), flowers, candles, bowls of oranges, *chayotes*, limes, bananas, and sugar cane, as well as *pan de muerto* and a scattering of marzipan skulls all surrounding a picture of the departed.

In Mexico City, several locations annually produce elaborate offerings. Lola Olmedo, director of the Diego Rivera Museum, arranges an intricate altar of food, drink, and candles that will be useful to souls navigating the subterranean rivers to Mictlan, the final resting place. Three of the best displays are within a block of one another: The Bazar del Sábado (open only on Saturdays), the Centro Cultural San Angel, and the Carmen Museum, where thousands of *cempazuchitl* petals are arranged in complex patterns, along with palm leaves, votives, skulls, candied fruit, and macabre pictures. An obligatory stop is to descend a level to view 12 mummified skeletons set amidst fabulous frescoed walls and tiled floors.

But the pace picks up considerably at Mixquic, a village at the southeastern tip of sprawling Mexico City still inhabited by ancestors of the original Indian settlement. At noon on November 1, Mixquicas gather in front an altar to mourn their dead. Then they head for the cemetery where for the next twelve hours they take turns sitting at their family's plot so that the spirits will not be alone, a ritual known as "the weeping." The chapel bell tolls at 4 p.m. to begin the town's Day of the Dead remembrance and again at midnight, when graveside rosaries are recited.

Families sweep the burial plots that surround the San Andres church before blanketing them with *cempazuchitl* petals. Wooden cross markers are flanked with several large bouquets: vases are large tin cans that still bear their Havoline or Quaker State labels. The penetrating fragrance of *copal* incense, along with the light from the two-foot-tall white candles that cluster on each grave, help the returning souls find their way back.

Thick columns of city folk - with no more than a handful of Americans among them - twist through the compact graveyard. Adding to the supernatural effect is a quartet playing homemade drums and flutes. While the families of those buried at Mixquic sit patiently by the graves, the crowds wind into the church to view a four-tiered offering that fills the elaborate chancel.

Outside the walled cemetery, Mixquic's dirt main street is filled to capacity and beyond as visitors take in the sights and bargains of a country fair: candy stands decorated with papier- mache skeletons draped with crepe paper; counters spread with appliances; copper pots piled high; rainbow-colored Chinese paper cut-outs hanging from wires. Food stands sell roasted corn cobs; homemade potato chips, grated and fried on the spot; enormous cauldrons of punch, thick with cubed fruits and rinds; and tortillas, tostadas, and tacos of every sort.

220

"This is a day of happiness, not sadness," says folklore dancer Lilia Rosas of Mexico City. "The dead haven't left but come back for the night to be with us."

Late that evening, on the long, dark route between Mixquic and Mexico City, many families light small fires outside their homes; costumed youths set up blockades and approach cars asking for money.

Funereal remembrances vary region to region. In Oaxaca, a path of flower petals may be scattered from the home to the cemetery where flowers and *copal* incense are arranged around a design of painted sand. In the village of Coatetelco, near Taxco, an harvest offering of corncobs and paper wreaths is made on the 28th of September so that the dead will help the gods ensure the following year's harvest. In that same village, a feast that includes bread, *mole verde* sauce, a jug of water, and chicken is placed out on November 1 (a distinction in this village is the belief that the dead will eat only hen, not roosters, and will partake of the meal only if the chicken belonged to the household flock).

The island town of Janitzio, in Michoacan, has one of the best-known remembrances. On November 1, men construct five-foot arches over the tombs, decorating them with flowers, fruit, bread, and sugar figurines. From midnight until dawn, the family watches the site, which is mounted with marigolds, candles, and food. The next day, the offerings are eaten in large family gatherings. "But," says a former resident Lourdes Mata, "the food is bland. The dead have taken its essence."

But where there's plenty of food, there's a fiesta. The Day of the Dead is a nationwide fiesta for both the living and the dead.

Christmas in Mexico

When you spend Christmas in Mexico you *might* miss the snow, ice and cold temperatures... or you *might not.* You will probably miss Bing Crosby's rendition of "White Christmas" or "Winter Wonderland," or possibly even the constant jingle-jangle of Salvation Army volunteers' bells, but believe me that is about all that will seem different from Christmas back home!

Christmas shoppers with their lists are the same everywhere, bargain-hunting or looking for the perfect gift. Decorations are out in full array. Streets are hung with colorful lights and draped with glittering tinsel. Santa's face greets all of those who pass, and Christmas music is very much in evidence - loud and clear!

Roman Catholic religious Christmas festivities begin with the Feast of the Immaculate Conception of the Virgin Mary on December 8, followed by the very important celebration on December 12 for the Virgin of Guadalupe, commemorating her appearance in 1521. Both are very impressive and well attended.

Other common Christmas celebrations include the *"pastorela"* or Christmas pageant, portraying Mary and Joseph's search for shelter in Bethlehem, the nativity, and the visit of the shepherds to the Christ child. All the while, the devil - a broadly comic character - tries to distract attention from the baby Jesus. Actors and actresses in full costume take part, along with lambs, goats, and other live farm animals, adding to the realism. As Mary and Joseph go from place to place on a live burro looking for a room, Christmas carols are sung softly in the background. Ending this very impressive performance is the invitation to enjoy tamales, *buñuelos* or Mexican Christmas cookies, and many other traditional delights, washed down with warm fruit punch - most probably with a little something "extra" added.

The *posada*, or traditional Christmas party, is somewhat similar. Often neighborhood events, guests stroll from house to house stopping at each door and singing a verse requesting "posada" or shelter. At each house the residents reply in song that there is no room, and then they also join the group. The posada ends at a designated house where all are invited in for refreshments and sometimes piñatas, as a special treat for children.

We have been fortunate to be invited to attend these pastorelas and posadas and look forward to them each year.

In Mexico, the traditional Christmas feast and exchange of gifts almost always takes place on the night of the 24th, and continues well into the wee hours of the morning. This is a very important family evening and dinner is served late, anywhere from 10:00 p.m. to midnight, and sometimes even later. Homes here are decorated much the same as those back home, with elaborate nativity scenes, the bright poinsettias which grow abundantly here, and Christmas trees - mostly artificial, since the live trees imported from Canada are very expensive.

Those who plan to spend the holidays in Mexico will find that by taking part in as many of the local customs and festivities as possible will add greatly to their appreciation and enjoyment of this special time of year.

In the traditional Mexican family Santa Claus is not the one who brings the childrens' gifts. A shoe is left outside the bedroom door on Christmas Eve, and sometime during the night the *Niño Dios* (Christ child), also affectionately called the *Niñito Dios*, leaves the goodies in or next to the shoe. Many North Americans are a bit bewildered when they get a vacant look upon asking a little boy or girl on Christmas Day what Santa brought them. Only children who have contact with U.S. culture know what they're referring to. (Many Mexican parents will deny in an almost venomous manner the existence of Santa in an effort to preserve their traditions; this battle is unfortunately being lost a little more every year because of mass media.)

Gifts are also given to the little ones on Epiphany *(Epifanía)* or Three Kings Day *(Día de los Reyes Magos)*. It's such a pleasure to see their open smiles and bright eyes on these occasions, as the simplest gift brings them so much happiness.

222

XI

Impressions of Mexico

Other Helpful Information and Impressions of Mexico

- Prices in Mexico are quoted in pesos. It's a good idea to obtain a two- or three-day supply before crossing the border. For this, go to a bank or a *casa de cambio* (currency exchange). Check the exchange rate in the Wall Street Journal or Mexico City *News*. The "free" rate of exchange will give you a guide as to what you should receive at the border.

- Mexican restrooms are labeled *Caballeros* or *Hombres* for **his**, and *Damas* or *Mujeres* for **hers**. When you travel on the highway, take your own supply of toilet tissue, bar soap and wash cloth.

- In bathrooms at hotels and motels you'll notice the letter **C** on one faucet (usually the one to the left) and the letter **F** on the other (again, usually the one to the right): **C** means **caliente** (hot) and **F** means **fría** (cold).

- The PB button on elevators means *planta baja* or ground (main) floor. When we arrived in Guadalajara the hotel clerk assigned us room 1237. We thought we'd be on the 12th floor, when actually we were on the 3rd floor. We still don't understand the logic of the numbering systems in public buildings.

- Guadalajara is at an altitude of over 5,200 feet (1500 meters) and many people feel fatigued for a day or two after arriving. If you're not used to the high altitudes, take it easy until you adjust.

- When taking a walk, pay attention to the sidewalk or roadway. There are occasionally uncovered utility manholes, broken or expanded concrete, cobblestones, and other hazards. Be extra careful at night.

- Rental cars are more expensive in Mexico than in the United States or Canada. Major U.S. rental agencies are represented here.

- Mexico has good public transportation in its cities and villages. In Guadalajara you can ride the bus for about twenty-five cents.

- Your United States or Canadian driver's license is good in Mexico.

- As a tourist (if you've been out of the country for 48 hours or more) you can import $400 worth of retail merchandise duty free into the U.S., but it must be for your personal use, or for gifts to friends, and can't be used for business purposes. You can import an additional $1000 worth of retail merchandise by paying a 10 percent duty ($100)

- Spanish last names are always double, with the first one being the last name of the person's father, and the second the last name of his or her mother.

For example, if you meet a person called José Hernández García, this means his father's name was Hérnandez and his mother's name García. You would ask for Sr. Hernández, or Sr. Hernández García, but never for Sr. García.

- A mistake we made when coming to Mexico was not bringing our automobile. After being here a few weeks we discovered that to enjoy Mexico we needed a car, so we bought a new VW Beetle. It's excellent for getting around town and fun to drive on the Mexican roads and mountains. We later brought our Oldsmobile sedan from the United States and use it mostly when going out with other couples. You may have a problem taking your Mexican car into the United States.

- If you've ever been skipper on a small sail boat you'll already know a lot about driving in Mexico, since you'll know to yield to anyone who gets in front of you. If someone heads you off in a traffic circle (*glorieta*), slow down and ride with the tide. Theoretically you have the right-of-way when you are already in a *glorieta*, but be alert - others may not know (or respect) this. It's usually more important to be aware of vehicles directly in front of you and those to your side than those to your rear.

- The only thing that hurries in Mexico are motorists and taxi drivers. Many Mexicans seem to undergo a personality change when they get behind the wheel of an automobile, becoming aggressive. Mexican young adults are very much like their counterparts in the United States or Canada, and have a heavy foot on the gas pedal.

- It's always wise to respect the laws of your host country. Mexican law derives from Spanish law and differs somewhat from United States and Canadian legal procedures, that descend from English Common Law. The "ground rules" are basically the same: in other words, don't do anything here you wouldn't do in your native land. Remember, you'll be a guest in Mexico and the culture will differ considerably from that to which you are accustomed. Go along with it - don't try to change it!

- The writer and his wife solved the problem of what to do with our "things" by sending a letter and a list of our furniture to each of our five children. We told then (they knew anyway) that we were planning to go to Mexico and that they should review the list and mark with #1 things they **really** wanted; #2 things they would like to have; #3 things they would take - and wouldn't throw away - and #4 things to take to the "dumpster." When the lists were returned, "things" were pretty evenly distributed except for the grandfather clock that everyone wanted. After three weeks of pondering and not wanting to buy four more clocks, we decided to give it to our second daughter who had recently purchased a new colonial home in South Carolina. Very little was dispatched to the dumpster. Some "things," like old clothes, were given to the Salvation Army. Incidentally, "Old Dad" paid for all of the moving expenses. We sent a few things to the Southwest for storage in case we later want to return to the United States. In determining what to do with your "things" basically one must decide: "Do I own my things or do my things own me?"

- When you arrive in Mexico your "things" will no longer be your status symbol, and you'll learn to be happy without them. Many people here drive old Mexican jalopies, and are happy with basic transportation. Many Mexicans admire our polished black 1980 Oldsmobile Cutlass with clean white sidewalls. At home, people might think we are about ready for Welfare. If you buy a Mexican car you'll have fewer problems obtaining parts and repairs, and never need to worry about driving it back to the border every six months. Cars are much more expensive than in the United States, however, they do not depreciate as quickly.

- Mexico has direct-dial telephones. To call the United States or Canada, dial 001, the area code, and the seven digit number. To dial Mexico from the United States or Canada, dial 011-52 (the country code), then the area code and the telephone number (3 for Guadalajara, plus the seven digit number; 376 for Chapala, plus the five digit number). Dial 01 for all long distance calls within Mexico, and then the area code and number.

- You won't be able to work legally in Mexico unless you're a writer or an artist, and your work is sold outside of the country. It's possible to get special visas to teach English or possibly specialized technical professions needed here, but we don't know what these are. Certain types of investors may also obtain visas. **Don't plan to work in Mexico** - you may be deported if you're working illegally. Just enjoy your stay.

- According to I.R.S. regulations you're required to pay U.S. Federal Income Taxes. The long arm of the I.R.S. follows you all over the world, the tax attorneys tell us.

- Attorneys tell us your will, drawn in the United States, is valid and may be probated in Mexico as well as in the United States. However, if you own Mexican real estate, a Mexican automobile, or other Mexican property, a separate will should be drawn specifically for your Mexican assets.

- The Memorial Society of the American Society of Jalisco assists in case of the death of one of its members. They provide for disposition of your remains according to your wishes, arrange for death certificates and notify the American Consulate. It's well worth the one-time charge. You may join at the American Society office or at the Lake Chapala Society, or phone or write the American Society about the service. You are encouraged to join even if you only spend a short time in the area.

- The telephone directory is often worthless since you'll probably never find the name or address of a friend located here. That's because when they buy or rent a house or apartment they don't bother to change the directory listing. The telephone may be listed in the name of a person who has not been there for many years.

- If you have telephone or other utility services, pay your bill upon receipt. If you haven't paid when due, your service might be cut off the next day. There have been times when we didn't get our bill until two days before it was due.

- Garbage is usually picked up daily (or at least three times a week) - much better service than in most United States cities. You're responsible for keeping your half of the street clean in front of your house.

- Mexicans are "family people" and show much affection toward each other, their children, parents and relatives. You'll enjoy seeing how well they dress their children, and the affection and consideration that children show toward each other. You'll often see three generations of families together.

- Should you come to Guadalajara, or consider retirement in the city, ask others about the mistakes they've made here. We all learn from our mistakes and profit from those of others.

- The smells of Mexico are different. You may smell beans cooking at 11:30 p.m.; the aromatic smells in the restaurant nearby; the bakeries; the fish market; smoke belching from a bus; or the brewery. And of course, the year-round fragrance of beautiful flowers.

- You may not believe this, but the attendant at the mail drop at the main post office will often **thank you**. Letters are still hand-postmarked. The postman will leave your mail in the yard if you have no box - even on a windy day. Most postmen **will** take your letters for mailing if they already have stamps (a special favor, which should be corresponded with a cash gift on "Postman's Day"). Collection boxes are rusty and hard to see, and are being slowly replaced with new, bright red mail boxes.

- You'll be amazed at the "intersection" enterprises. There are the Indian dancers, the fire eaters, the people selling maps, newspapers, figs, strawberries, peaches, sugar cane and flowers, and some surprisingly good ventriloquists. Here, almost everyone who's physically able hustles. They don't consider it demeaning to do whatever they can, however humble, to make a living. It's a point of pride as well as survival.

- The sounds of Mexico are different. In your neighborhood you may hear the morning street sweeper; the garbage truck with workers going ahead ringing a cow bell; the shrill whistle of the postman; the bottled water truck and with a man going ahead yelling *"agua"* (sounds like sheep when I was a boy on the farm); the microphone of the vegetable vendor (I first thought he was announcing an impending revolution); the multi- toned whistle of the knife sharpener; an occasional klipity-klop of a horse and wagon; children and the school bus; and occasionally the family argument in Spanish that you will **never** understand. You may also hear a mariachi band early in the morning. The neighborhood "roof-dog", the watchdog that is confined to prowl the flat roof, is for all to hear, especially when the chorus line begins in the moonlight.

- (Note to wives) If your husband goes with you for shopping to just half the places mentioned, we suggest you give him a medal. (Note to husbands) If your wife says she isn't feeling well some morning ask her if she'd like to go shopping. If she says no, she's really sick.

- Learning a few basic Spanish words before you come would certainly be helpful, such as *"¿Dónde está el baño?"* (Where is the bathroom?) My first attempt to use my limited knowledge of Spanish was the above phrase. When asking this question of a bus boy in a restaurant I was told in perfect English "Down the hall to the left." Another time after struggling with Spanish in a store to purchase a certain item the clerk said in perfectly clear English "Do you speak English?" I was so shocked and surprised that my answer was "Yes, a little!" You'll have many interesting and funny experiences as you learn your second language in Mexico. All you need is a sense of humor and a lot of patience.

- I stumble by without formal Spanish language education on the theory that "every old blind hog will occasionally find an acorn" and learn a new word or phrase once in a while. With the single challenge of trying to learn Spanish one should never become bored living in Mexico. You will be happier if you make a concentrated effort to learn the language since you will enjoy your Mexican neighbors and more efficiently handle the everyday chores of living without the constant frustrations. Your life will be enriched.

- Taxes appear to fall heavily on the poor. There is a ten percent value-added tax (*IVA - Impuesto al Valor Agregado*) that is tacked on to most items except very basic food goods. The price marked on an item in grocery and department stores, and prices in restaurants, already has **the tax included**, but not in many other less "formal" establishments with no marked prices. If you want an invoice (a necessary part of "paper- chasing" a guarantee, for example), you sometimes will suddenly find 10% added to the price quoted. Always ask if the tax is included if in doubt.

- We're impressed by the public transportation system of Guadalajara. It's cheap, covers the whole city and nearby villages, and passengers may be carrying their produce to market on rural routes.

- Taxi transportation is fairly inexpensive. Fares are even more reasonable when you hail a cruising cab than at a *"sitio"* (taxi stand). We learned early to agree on the fare before entering the cab, and have plenty of small bills and change when paying. Drivers often say they don't have change.

- If you're a history buff you'll enjoy studying Mexican history. When walking in downtown Guadalajara, founded in 1542, it's sometimes difficult to comprehend that Guadalajara has been here for over 450 years. In fact it was here for 250 years before our ancestors began cutting their way across the Appalachian mountains, of what is now West Virginia, about two hundred years ago. In downtown Guadalajara the Hotel Francés was founded ten years before the pilgrims landed at Plymouth Rock. The old buildings in downtown Guadalajara give you a different perspective of time, when compared to the history of the United States or Canada.

- For a country with such huge economic problems, we're impressed with the amount of new construction. The economy's depressed and many Mexicans are suffering, but it doesn't appear that way.

- Guadalajara's an ideal place for a music lover. It has an excellent symphony orchestra and several other classical music groups. October is a good time to come for musical events when the October Fiesta occurs. We've attended more operas, symphony performances, ballets, plays and piano concerts than we would in several years in the United States.

- To better understand living in the Guadalajara area we talked with Americans and Canadians who have retired here. You will find people eager to talk when you go to places such as church, the American Society or Lake Chapala Society office, the American Legion, etc. Another idea is to offer to take a couple to lunch or dinner - it's an inexpensive and relaxing way to get acquainted and also find answers to your questions about living here.

- In Mexico there are speed control bumps as you enter villages or certain residential areas. Usually a sign will be posted saying *Tope* or *Topes*, or the international "vibrator" sign will appear. You will never forget this Spanish word (or the symbol) after you hit one when driving at 50 mph. We have learned a lot of our Spanish this way!

- Friends and relatives in the States still write of their concerns for our safety here. I have never seen a bandido or a pickpocket nor have any of my friends. We seldom hear of any sort of violence. Violent crime is much less than in the United States.

The following is from **Mexico Travelog**, published by Sanborn's Mexico Insurance Service:

- For motorists the most important word in Spanish is the first letter of our alphabet - just plain simple, little old "a"...In Spanish it's pronounced "ah" like, "Ah, Sweet Mystery of Life"...And it means "to".

When you're driving in Mexico and aren't exactly sure where you're going or whether you're on the right road, just stop and ask any Mexican "Ah Monterrey?", or "Ah Motel Santa Fe?", or "A Mexico?" (That means Mexico City. Hardly anybody refers to Mexico City as Mexico City - they either call it just "México" or "La Capital".

When you use "ah" by all means there should be a couple of gestures, too. With your forefinger, sort of point ahead down the road. And at the same time nod your head in the general direction you're going.

230

- Many things in Mexico will remind you of teenage days forty to fifty years ago. Can you remember when quality of life, friends and people were more important than a dollar - and by contrast the rush that everyone is in today?

Things We Like and Dislike about Guadalajara

These are some of the things we like about living here: warm days, cool nights, the handsome people, beautiful babies, birds chirping in the morning, a walk in the park, swimming year-round in the thermal pools, flowering plants, the many low-cost cultural events, our new and interesting friends, lower medical and pharmacy expenses, fresh low-cost vegetables and fruits (there's something in season **every** season!), and the countless tourist attractions, including markets where beautiful native craftwork is sold, a shopper's delight!

It is interesting to explore the traditional Mexican villages nearby and watch the friendly people. Often there are entire families, with grandparents, aunts, uncles and children of all ages in colorful clothes, as they enjoy just being together in the town square, which is the focal point of every village - large or small. There is much history to be learned here concerning the beautiful churches, museums and other buildings.

We are aware of many strange and different sounds, such as the knife and scissor sharpener's pan pipes, the postman's whistle, the trash truck's jingling cowbell, the bottled water salesmen's sing-song of "A-g-u-a-a-a-a!", the swish-swish of sidewalk brooms each morning and the constant horns of the cars and buses.

There are a different variety of smells: the fragrance of ever- blooming roses all around, an exotic spicy aroma from sidewalk taco stands, the abundance of fruit trees giving off a tangy freshness and, of course, the usual presence of a pot of beans simmering somewhere.

It is a treat to eat in the excellent restaurants which feature European cuisine along with Mexican specialties. Prices are still lower for a first class dinner than usually found elsewhere. Even though there has been a definite increase on living costs during the years we have lived here, we feel it's still a good choice. This decision was confirmed again recently when we visited the U.S. and heard of the high utility bills, high taxes, expensive medical services, household help, etc.

Movie buffs will be pleased to know that there are many theaters, especially in the plazas, which show current films in English with Spanish subtitles for a fraction of the cost in the United States. The same films can be rented at the

231

multitude of video stores for a similar price, again with Spanish subtitles.

A complete list of the things we like about living in Guadalajara would be too long to write and would certainly outnumber the list of **not** so favorable things. But we must admit we have a few complaints, and we will mention them also to be completely above board; after all, no place is perfect!

For us, probably the most irritating thing is the much talked about *Mañana* attitude. No matter how often we tell ourselves not to expect differently, it is definitely a mistake to take it for granted that anything will be on schedule - whether a repairman call, a delivery service or other business appointments. Just because an appointment is made for ten o'clock the next day doesn't necessarily mean it will take place then. More likely it will be at least 10:30, 11:00 or possibly later! Time is not as important here as it was when we lived in the United States. "Patience" is the key word for living in Mexico, as we remind each other constantly.

Gringos here will often complain also, and with good reason, of the long lines and slow service at banks and other businesses. It seems that everything, even the simplest transaction, is done with triple paperwork, and occasionally a "friend" or "regular customer" will edge in front of you in line just as you reach the counter. This edging-in also occurs often in grocery store lines and, since I was taught to respect my elders, I used to let the little "older ladies" ahead of me to be checked out. However, I soon realized that these same little "older ladies" would practically run over me to get there first, so now my good manners have been put on "hold" in that situation. The computer age has hit Mexico with vengeance and things will probably speed up over a period of time - as soon as everybody learns how to submit to "electronic masochism," and get all the computers, scanners, etc. running efficiently.

We've found that asking Mexicans for directions can be very interesting. Rather than admit they don't know the answer, they'll come up with an answer anyway, and we have been led on some wild goose chases! If they really know the correct direction and it is nearby, they will often lead you directly to it, smiling all the way because they were able to help you! To distinguish the "knowledgeable" from the "un-knowledgeable," the hesitation interval between the question and answer is a good indicator. If you get a really fast answer, then usually they know what they're talking about.

The above situations might sound discouraging, but they are light-weight compared to the many pleasures of living in Guadalajara, and we feel that for every nuisance factor there are at least a dozen or so delightful pleasures! These and much more add up to a totally different way of living that we find exciting and interesting.

If you're on the right track, the Mexican will say "Sí" (Yes), and you say "Muchas gracias". If he says "No", then turn around, head the other way, and ask somebody else "Ah wherever-you're going?" Sooner or later someone will say "Sí".

I'm sure you'll have no difficulty getting around in Mexico if you'll just make excellent use of their very important little word "a" ("to") - with gestures.

- Recently we had the occasion to attend the funeral of a friend in Chapala. You have no doubt heard the expression about a person who is always tardy "would be late for his own funeral." The funeral was scheduled for 4:00 p.m. and the minister and a group of friends were assembled at the appointed time. There was no casket! At about 4:20 p.m. the minister announced that the "guest of honor" was obviously late, but encouraged the group to stay a little longer. Finally at about 4:30 p.m. the hearse with the casket arrived and the service began. Despite the fact that the deceased was a person noted for his promptness this is one of those things that happens "Only in Mexico." Otherwise it was a fine service.

- As in the United States, pay phones are frequently out of order. The cost of a local call can vary considerably, from three to thirty cents (U.S.), depending if the phone has been recalibrated lately. A disproportionally large percentage of new pay phones work only with "Ladatel" cards, which can be purchased at many locations, including supermarkets, and are available in different denominations, good for several calls. These cards are good for long distance calls, also.

- We're pleased with the friends we've made since we arrived here. Local retired people are more active and venturesome here than many of those back home. To make a friend - be a friend!

- In the United States we saved for years to have all the electrical conveniences. Now that we're in Mexico we don't even miss them. Housewives don't have many of the appliances they had in the United States or Canada, but on the other hand most housewives don't have maids in the United States and Canada. There is no garbage compactor, or garbage disposal. I'm back to being the garbage man.

- We've always heard there wasn't much night life in Guadalajara until our single son visited. He met some nice señoritas and with several nights of partying disproved this thought - probably the same activities as in the United States - just different young people doing them. As in the States, there are discos, night clubs, and piano bars, as well as restaurants with mariachis and folkloric dance entertainers. Mexicans don't start to swing until ten or eleven at night, and often watch the sun come up through a glass of tequila (usually accompanied by their favorite anti-hangover remedy - a pungent plate of *menudo* (tripe)!

233

Things We Have Noticed about Mexican People

- We have found that most Mexicans will constantly apologize for their English even though it is quite good (We are the ones who should apologize for our Spanish).

- We have learned to ask for the check in a restaurant when we are served dessert to speed things up. (It is impolite to present a check until it is requested.)

- We have observed that Mexican families are very close and their "family values" are given top priority.

- We find that no matter how limited your Spanish is, the effort to try to communicate in their native language, plus a smile, is greatly appreciated.

- It seems to us that Mexicans with less money for material things are more courteous, more concerned about each other and happier in general than those with high incomes. (Perhaps this is true in the United States also.)

- We are impressed by the neatness of even the poorest Mexican in contrast to the sometimes sloppy, unkept appearance of Americans both in Mexico and in the U.S.

- We are impressed with the way older children often watch and take care of younger ones, a seemingly second sense of inborn responsibility.

- We are amused at a particular restaurant, where we go for entertainment, when the waiter will caution us at great length that our serving plate is *"muy caliente," very hot, which it usually is, but at the same time the food on the plate may be "muy frío," stone cold!*

- We find that sometimes Mexicans take care of a problem entirely differently than we would. For instance, during a dinner conversation recently, my husband was waving his hands to make a point and managed to topple over a tall glass of water all over the table. We all tried to soak it up with our napkins while waiting for a waiter to come. The waiter took in the situation and did what he thought was needed. He brought another equally tall glass of water.

- Going to a Catholic Church can also solve the problem of where to eat afterward. Usually outside the church one will find taco or tamale stands, fruit or soft drinks to buy, potato chips, cotton candy and other sweets, plus even crepes to take away the hunger pains!

- We have learned to double-check, even triple-check any directions we ask for in Mexico. It is considered impolite not to help foreigners, so rather than admit that they don't know, you might find yourself on a wild goose chase and completely lost.

- We think that Mexican children, with their easy smiles, lovely dark eyes, the whitest white teeth and lovely black hair, are truly beautiful. (We have been told that all babies have their head shaved three times during their first year to ensure thick hair.)

- We are constantly amazed at the imagination and entrepreneurship of the Mexican people to earn money. At street lights you will see children turning cartwheels, juggling fruit or balls, wanting to wash car windshields or, as the older men and women do, selling such diverse items as shoe racks, seat covers, newspapers, flowers and edibles of all kinds. Anything to earn a honest peso.

- We have discovered than even the poorest villages will have a lovely, well kept church and park area and clean streets.

Mexican Food - Give it a Try!

If Mexico is on your travel agenda you might want to familiarize yourself with what you will see on a typical Mexican restaurant menu. Don't panic! There are also plenty of restaurants where you will be able to order selections just as you find in the United States, and they are delicious, but every visitor should try the authentic Mexican dishes at least once. Believe me, "Taco Bell" doesn't really fill the bill for real Mexican food!

On a typical Mexican restaurant menu you will find for *desayuno* (breakfast), *huevos* (eggs), and you can order them *revueltos* (scrambled), *fritos* (fried), *estrellados* (sunny-side up), or an omelette, with *tocino* (bacon), *jamón* (ham) or *queso* (cheese). Also if you want to try the really typical Mexican breakfast, order *huevos rancheros*, which are eggs lightly fried and served on *tortillas* with a hot chili sauce. Another big favorite with Mexicans are *chilaquiles*, which are pieces of browned tortillas added to a green or red tomato sauce, flavored with chili and other spices, topped with melted cheese, chopped onion, and a sunny- side up egg or cooked chicken.

By the way, don't hesitate to order hot cakes (same name in Spanish); they are served just as in the United States, with syrup, honey or strawberry jam, and are very good. A fresh fruit plate (*plato de frutas*), or juice (*jugo*) are also delicious in Mexico.

If breakfast is a success, you will certainly want to sample dishes offered for the midday meal or *comida*, the traditional "heavy" meal of the day. Usually the *sopa* (soup) is a good choice for people not accustomed to eating their principal meal at this hour, and we have seldom been unhappy with this selection. There is a wide variety of *sopas*, most of which are excellent.

235

If you want to go all the way with *comida*, you will be sure to see *carne asada*, which is a thin beef fillet cooked over an open fire and served with *tortillas*, refried beans and *cebollitas* (grilled small green onions). *Carnitas* are small pieces of pork, deep fried and served with refried beans, *guacamole* and *tortillas*. You may have noticed that *tortillas* or *bolillos* (hard rolls) are used instead of the usual bread or hot rolls served in the United States. *Tortillas* are also used to make soft *tacos*, filled with chopped meat or chicken (*pollo*), cheese, or any combination you can think of. They could be considered the Mexican "sandwich."

Deep fried tacos are referred to as *flautas* or *tacos dorados*, and are topped with sauce, grated cheese, sliced radishes and lettuce or cabbage. If the tortilla is covered with a special hot sauce, and then lightly fried before being filled, it is referred to as a *enchilada*.

Chicken appears on just about any menu in Mexico, and can be fried *(frito)*, grilled *(asado)*, or prepared in a variety of sauces, one of the favorites being *mole*, made with a variety of spices and chocolate.

A word to the wise about sauces: we generally ask for the *salsa* to be served *aparte* (aside) or *por separado* (separately), so that we may add as much or as little as we want. Although the sauces are all excellent, and considered in Mexico the "make-or-break" part of a meal, sometimes they are extremely *picante* (hot). Even if you see a child "digging" into a sauce, don't take for granted that it won't be overpowering; better to try it first.

Pescado (fish) is plentiful in Mexico, and is usually a very good choice for the seafood enthusiast. You will find it prepared *a la plancha*, (broiled or grilled), *al mojo de ajo* (sauteed in butter and garlic) or *empanizado* (breaded and fried).

Be sure to leave room for the wonderful *postres* such as *flan* (caramel-topped custard), *pay* (pie), *pastel* (cake) or *helado* (ice cream). You might be offered a selection of regional candies, the most famous being from Puebla.

All of this with a glass of *vino* (wine), *café* (coffee), a *refresco* (soft drink) or *cerveza* (beer) makes for a delightful taste of Mexico!

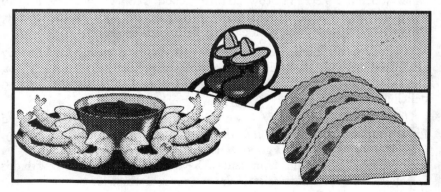

Pandemonium at the Gas Station

Filling your gas tank can be quite an experience, sometimes entertaining but sometimes irritating.

The Pemex gas stations are owned by the Mexican Government. In small rural communities they are the center of individual entrepreneurial commercial activity. Children and adults greet the car before it stops, selling everything from fruit, candy, machetes, brass bells and more, or offering to wash your windshield (which will be good and "buggy after a few hours on the highway), check the tires, change dollars to pesos or, in a few cases, even offering to buy your car! It takes a firm "no" to discourage them if you are not interested.

When we stop at a Pemex, our sole purpose is to buy gasoline and possibly use restroom facilities (which in the majority of cases do not have soap, paper towels or toilet tissue: if there is running water, you're doing well!) The restrooms on toll roads are always well kept up, though. One learns early to travel prepared. When the attendant comes to the car you should say *"lleno, por favor"* (YEH-no, por fah-VOR) if you wish to fill the tank. Make sure the pump is cleared and doesn't have the previous charge on it. We always ask for a receipt which is called a *nota* or *recibo*, in order to direct the attendant's full attention to the correct amount. Upon receiving the receipt, we have the currency ready in hand for a little more than the correct amount and proceed to pay the amount owed. **Don't** let the attendant walk off with the bill you've paid with in order to make change - it's the oldest trick in the book - he then claims you gave him a lower denomination than you really did. Make him go for the change, and **then** give him your large bill. Obviously, count your change. We have been shortchanged many times, and whether on purpose or simply due to the fact that the attendant had a problem making correct change is a good question. At any rate, it is wise to be alert.

If the attendant checks your oil, water or tires, or washes your windshield, it is customary to tip him (two or three pesos for a complete job) - this is above and beyond his regular duties.

To Stop or Not to Stop?
To Buy or Not to Buy?

A red traffic stop light always means stop, yes? Perhaps in most cities the answer would be a simple, unquestionable "yes" but in Guadalajara occasionally drivers don't agree, so watch for them!

Since moving to Guadalajara we have found that a red light is often totally disregarded. Other times a red light causes a slight hesitation, which brings about the old game of "go-chicken-go" with on-coming traffic. Further complicating this situation are the pedestrians who live dangerously, and don't mind taking a running chance to cross a street no matter what the cars are doing or what color the traffic light happens to be!

Naturally, there is always a chance you'll find yourself in a lane when the traffic really has stopped. In this case, while you wait you'll find much to see and many decisions to make as you watch the young - and sometimes not-so-young - entrepreneurs making their sales pitch for "bargains" that are not absolutely necessary. Common items are windshield wiper blades, toys, candy, fruit, nuts, newspapers, flowers, the ever-present Chiclets and much more. Along with the street vendors are the colorfully dressed Indian dancers, jugglers, clowns, ventriloquists, clever mimes and fire-eaters performing for your entertainment. Of course you are expected to show appreciation by putting pesos in the basket or hand of the performer's helper. We find it difficult to resist such enterprising people, especially the children doing acrobatics or the Indian women carrying tiny babies in their shawls. While stopped for a red light it is also easy to get your windshield washed (sometimes very necessary after a rain or dust storm) - if you are not bothered by a greasy rag or a possibly bent wiper blade.

Needless to say, with all of this activity going on there's no time to worry about the fellow in the next lane trying to edge you out, or the five cars behind you blowing their horns hoping to start some action.

At any rate driving in Mexico is **never** dull! Should you come by car you will soon learn the unwritten rules of the road, and in short order be driving like a native!

Retire to Mexico - Were We Crazy?

In one of the early issues of the Guadalajara/Chapala Update we published an article with much the same title as above relating the general reaction of friends and relatives to our decision to retire in Mexico. Well, it has been many years since we made that decision and our actual move to Mexico. So now at this point we ask ourselves the familiar question and feel certain that it definitely was a good step, and one we certainly would make again. With this in mind, we answer the question once and for all, "No, we were not crazy," nor are the thirty-five to forty thousand North Americans who are here in the Guadalajara area and those with plans to come.

We are not naive and we certainly can feel the crunch of inflation which has hit Mexico in the past few years, especially in rentals and real estate, representing the largest single impact on a retiree's budget. Other living expenses have also been affected. However, on our trips to the United States we see much the same thing happening there, causing us to get our "balance scale" out in order to determine exactly the benefits of a Mexico retirement. Here are a few of our conclusions:

First, most of us were drawn to Mexico for the beautiful climate where we do not need air-conditioning or much in the way of heating, therefore eliminating the huge utility bills we had in the United States. The mild year around weather also lessens our chances of bad colds, flu, or "heaven forbid," complications which would make it necessary to be hospitalized. We are aware of the outrageous medical costs prevalent in the United States that could possibly wipe out one's life savings. Medical care cost in Mexico remains reasonable and medical care is excellent. A definite plus to be considered!

One's budget determines one's life style wherever we choose to retire, but we feel our life is fuller and that we are able to enjoy the variety of entertainment offered at a more modest cost in Mexico than in the United States. (A ticket for a new movie in Mexico is still only $2.60 and in some cases senior citizens are admitted free of charge.)

There are many events such as musical and dancing performances that are without charge for those who seek them out.

During our retirement in Mexico, we have met more interesting and congenial people than in any period of our lives. These are people who want to do something with their "golden years," people who are interested in experiencing new customs, learning about a different culture, while at the same time enjoying a perfect climate for travel, golf or any of the other activities they looked forward to during their work years.

Even though Mexico is not the bargain paradise it used to be, it still is a beautiful country where we feel one can enjoy a far better quality of life no matter how large or small one's income is.

Many other things tip the scale in Mexico's favor, such as very low taxes, cost of personal services, utility bills, excellent and reasonable health care, and new friends with whom to explore a new and interesting country. Add to these factors the ever increasing modern conveniences available, the beautiful plazas (malls), and the fine restaurants and supermarketsn that add to our comfort and adjustment.

Would we consider moving back to the United States? Our first thought would have to be, "**Where** could we possibly live as well as we do here with our modest, fixed income?" So far we have not come up with an answer, and do not expect to!

XII

Appendix

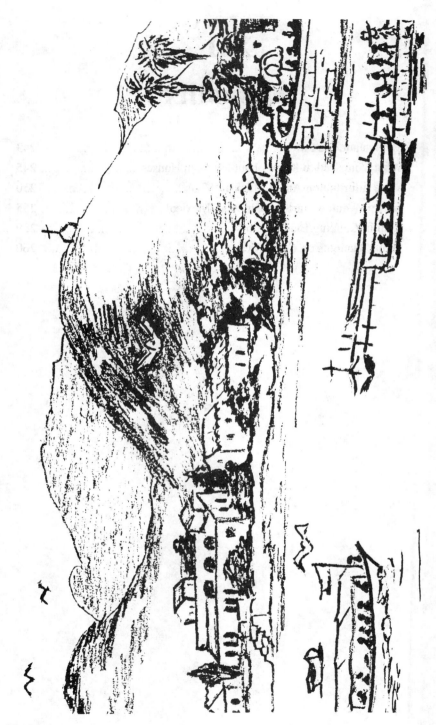

Mexico and The Law

There has been much confusion among people from the United States and Canada about the laws of Mexico. These laws give visitors and foreigners the same rights as those enjoyed under the Mexican Constitution by the general resident population of Mexico, and they include the right to liberty and freedom to travel throughout the country. These laws may not be restricted by any civil or military authority. As a visitor or foreigner you should abide by the laws of your host country. Should you ever be arrested there are procedures for obtaining your release. When in Mexico you are cautioned and urged not to become involved in any way with narcotics and drugs. Mexico considers these offenses more serious than do legal authorities in the United States and the penalties are much more severe!

In order that tourists and foreigners have an acquaintance with some of the procedures related to legal circumstances in Guadalajara and the State of Jalisco, a booklet entitled *"Guide of Protection of the Rights of Liberty for Tourists"* has been prepared. A copy of this may be obtained at the Guadalajara Department of Tourism Office in the Arch at Av. Vallarta and Av. Los Arcs near Minerva Circle. It also contains addresses and telephone numbers of important government offices and is very helpful.

Some of the important points outlined in this booklet are as follows:

- Should you be accused of a crime and are arrested, you should be released immediately if there are no witnesses or other evidence.

- You should be given a receipt for any objects taken from you at the time of arrest, and a copy of this receipt must be added to the bill of indictment.

- During detention in no case will you be held incommunicado. A telephone will be made available for your use.

- During detention you should not be subjected to mistreatment, violence or intimidation.

- You should not pay any money to authorities.

- Should you be a minor the Public Prosecutor should place you immediately to the Tutelary Council or turn you over to your parents or guardian, or the consular representative of your country.

- No tourist may be held in prison for civil debts.

- A person may be detained only under the following circumstances: (1) by order of a judge, (2) when caught committing a crime, (3) after prosecution procedures when a crime is committed and (4) when there are fears that

243

the suspect may escape and there are no judicial authorities present because of time or distance.

- When a person is arrested he should be brought before a judge without delay, (maximum 72 hours) and the date, time and place should be recorded and an inquiry should be made.

- A person detained should be informed of the accused crime and the elements that constitute the crime-like circumstances, how it was committed, and the time and place.

- A tourist or visitor under arrest may be put on probation before the Department of the Public Prosecutor, requesting bail, as long as he is dealing with negligence in driving, arms handling, etc., and provided that he is not intoxicated, and assures the payment or redress of the damages that have been causes, if any.

- The person detained should be given all the facts he needs for his defense and the results of the inquiry.

- The declaration of the person detained should not be held behind closed doors, except when it is a moral attack.

- A public defender will be appointed if requested.

- You may abstain from making a statement, and you may offer proof needed for your defense.

- A person detained who is injured or sick must be taken to a hospital.

- Petitions made in writing to the Public Prosecutor or Judicial Police will always be answered in writing.

- Should you no speak Spanish you will be assigned a translator. You have the right to submit your statement in your native language for translation.

- You have the right to present personal details about yourself for proper correct identification so that you will not be confused with someone else.

- All foreign tourists should present their immigration documents that prove they are in Mexico legally when doing any legal procedures with Federal, State and Municipal authorities.

You will notice that most of the procedures outlined above are similar to legal procedures practiced in the United States. There have been so many rumors and much misinformation about legal procedure in Mexico, and hopefully this will clarify some of the confusion.

(Should you be detained, or need an attorney for other reasons, we strongly urge you to check with the United States Consulate to determine that any attorney you use is on their recommended list.)

What you Need to Know about Mexican Houses, Public Utilities, Landlords, Rental Contracts, Condo regulations, "Package Deals", etc.

Mexican houses and their services, landlords, rental contracts, condo regulations and "package deals" are completely different from anything the typical person of U.S. or Canadian origin has ever confronted. This article is dedicated to those poor souls who assumed things functioned like "north-of-the- border" and were in for a **big** shock. Don't misunderstand us: it's not bad, only **different**. When you are in doubt about something, **ASK!** Mexicans and foreigners who have lived here for years will accept many things as normal; someone just taking up residence could find some details very frustrating, a frustration due to pure ignorance.

Mexican Houses, their Internal Function, and Public Services

The typical kitchen usually will have a sink and built-in cabinets. The refrigerator and stove **may or may not** be included; find out beforehand. Dishwashers, garbage compactors, washers and dryers do not exist except in brand-new, luxury rental properties.

The property's water equipment should include the following permanent fixtures: hot water heater, underground cistern, roof tank and the water pump. The water system in a typical house works as follows; due to the fact that street water pressure in Mexico tends to be low, the water trickles into an underground cistern, called an *aljibe*, then is pumped up to a roof tank, called a *tinaco*, and finally gravity provides the water pressure for the property's faucets, toilets, etc. Many times the city water pressure is enough to allow the water to make it up to the *tinaco* without the boost from the pump, but towards the end of the "dry season", March through June, water pressure tends to be extremely low, or may trickle into the underground cistern only a couple of hours a day. An underground cistern and a working water pump are absolute MUSTS, and never accept a rental house or apartment that doesn't include one, no matter how good the owner claims the water pressure is. One never knows 1) when the water supply might be temporarily cut off, a very common event in Mexico, which could be for days, or even weeks and 2) simply how

245

good the water pressure is going to be tomorrow, even if it was good today. Save yourself some major headaches (nobody likes going without water) and always check out the existence of these articles (I would compare it to checking out the existence of a furnace in the far north).

The same articles must exist for apartment houses, and, by law, they should have a primary pump **and** a back-up pump for emergencies (principally for when the primary pump burns out, a common event). **MAKE** the landlord show you the two pumps - and check that they work - or you might be carrying water in buckets. Be extra careful about this when the landlord doesn't live on the premises - if he or she is there all the time, the water situation is probably well under control. Remember, it's no skin off a landlord's back when YOU don't have water. Many a time in the history of my own rentals I've been confronted with a broken pump, and been informed that if the tenants want water, they can fix the pump themselves (an expensive repair). A second pump is not necessary in a house; the roof tank contains enough water to get you through a repair job, if you are careful and don't waste it. Modern, larger apartment houses have a central pressure and pumping system, and the concierge will usually take care of any problems.

Another question you should ask: who picks up and pays the "general" electric power bill (exterior and hall lighting, etc.) and water works bill in an apartment building? The water pump runs on electricity, and even if you pay your own apartment's light bill, you could feasibly find the water supply cut off for lack of a running pump. Obviously, if the water bill isn't paid, the water will be cut off. Don't think Mexican authorities are as lenient as up north about unpaid utility bills. Telephone service is usually cut the NEXT day after a bill is overdue, and the power company and water works are EXTREMELY fast about cutting off service (a period of days, maximum a few weeks); there is NO mercy. These "general services" could be picked up and paid by for the owner, or the responsibility of paying and the cost shared by the tenants - FIND OUT.

If by chance you pay a water or power bill late, for any reason, your fault or not, get a photostatic copy and stick it next to the power meter or water meter, and have the original on hand. If they arrive to cut you off, the copy of the paid bill MIGHT be enough to stall them, and they'll only leave you the order to disconnect - take this order and your paid bill (original) immediately to the competent authority to have the cut-off order canceled. This tactic is useless with the telephone company - they cut you off right at the central exchange. A reconnection charge will **always** appear on your next utilities bill, whether they actually cut you off or not.

All cooking and water heating is done by butane gas. Gas is supplied two ways: in portable cylinders, which are considered personal furnishings, and rarely will be included in a rental, or by a big stationary gas tank, usually located on the roof, which is seen as part of a property. The portable tanks are ordered by phone and delivered the next day (very hard to do when you don't have a phone and you don't speak Spanish, plus you have to wait at home to receive the delivery), and will last a typical couple anywhere from two weeks to a month; the stationary tank is filled regularly by contract with the gas works, the bill being paid at the bank or their offices located in several locations around town, and will last at least two to three months in the case of two people. The later arrangement is obviously a better choice. Sometimes apartment houses have a giant common gas tank, with individual lines to each apartment, also saving you a big hassle. This type service sometimes has meters in each apartment, or maybe the gas will be included in the rent, or perhaps the cost of the gas is shared equally between tenants. Sharing the cost with other people is sometimes not so desirable. I was confronted with a $20 U.S. monthly gas bill (my share of a $100 U.S. bill between five apartments, each one with two occupants) for a two-bedroom apartment; nobody had a washer, dryer or dishwasher. Now that I own my own large three-bedroom home, with a washer, dryer, dishwasher, and two children to boot, my gas bill is still only a maximum of $25 U.S. a month. Something was very wrong at that apartment house, and an extra $20 was a real strain on my personal finances, an expense that should have been no more than $5 a month. The gas companies, when it comes to overdue bills, are really the most decent of the lot; they will actually call you and let you know that they filled the tank, and haven't received payment (the bill is left under the door or in your driveway if nobody is home). They will ask you, after giving you the invoice number and amount due, to pay in their offices. Failure to pay will cause immediate cancellation of your gas contract. Again, FIND OUT! Direct underground gas lines exist in other parts of Mexico, but not in Guadalajara.

Properties will have a complete electrical system, although the number of outlets will be less than what you are used to: the voltage and cycles are the same as in the U.S. or Canada, so you will never have any problems with appliances you bring down. Electricity is rarely included in the rent, and you might have to draw up a contract with the power company. Light fixtures are considered personal furnishings, and most of the time you will find bare light bulbs, except in very modern buildings, which have built-in, recessed light fixtures. Be careful as to the number a lights and appliances you turn on at once in a new place: the circuit breakers and fuses in older homes and apartments were designed long before the arrival of modern electrical appliances, and can't take the strain of a microwave oven functioning the same time as the fridge and toaster oven.

A general rule you can count on when you rent an unfurnished property is if a given article or fixture can be carried away without damaging the property, you rarely will find it included!

Your relationship with your landlord: Mexican landlords are notorious for turning over a property for rent in poor condition, and insisting when the contract is up that everything be ship- shape before they return your deposit. **Check everything carefully before you accept a property in rental!** This includes painting, as a favorite trick is to not return your deposit because the walls are dirty, and need to be painted, even if it was in that condition when you took it over. Sometimes a personal recommendation about the landlord of a certain apartment building is the best idea: the person already living there can give you a good idea about what the landlord is like.

To sign a typical rent contract you will need to pay the first month's rent in advance, and put down a two-month damage deposit.

If there is a telephone, a larger deposit may be demanded. You will need to save all your utility bills you have paid over the course of a lease, as the landlord will probably insist that paid utility bills be turned over to them with each months rent. I see no problem in this, as he or she is quite justified in requesting this to avoid being stuck with a series of expensive utility bills, but, as always, it a good idea to have a photostatic copy made of paid bills before you turn them over. You should NOT turn over the telephone bill if you purchased the telephone from somebody besides the owner, or had it installed yourself. If the landlord is in possession (and vice versa, if you are in possession of) two years worth of paid telephone bills, the name (and ownership) of the telephone can be changed. If the telephone is yours, keep the receipts: maybe when the lease is up, you can make some arrangement to sell the telephone to the landlord, although in some cases they will not want the telephone, and they will tell you to pass it along to the next tenant, or maybe another neighbor. The moment the telephone is "sold" is when to give the purchaser the old bills.

Even if you don't have to settle with landlords, etc., **always keep a file of your utility bills - the telephone and power company are notorious for demanding proof of payment of old bills (even months or years ago), and if YOU can't prove you've paid, you're stuck with the bill (that is, if you wish to have electricity or a functioning phone).**

Condo regulations: sometimes you will find yourself in the position of renting somebody's condominium, short- or long-term. A number of "horizontal condominiums" also exist in Mexico, in other words, groups of houses on a communal property. Condo regulations also apply in these cases. Find out if 1) the owner is allowed to rent the condo according to the condo regulations, and 2) who is going to pay the maintenance fees to the condo association.   Parking can be a big, big problem in certain condos. Parkingáspaces can be individually owned (bought with the condo), or, again, communal property to be shared on a first come, first served basis. Condo regulations **can** be enforced by a court order (a long a difficult process), but since few owners are willing to put up the money for a legal fight, their enforcement will be due principally to everybody's good faith, rather than somebody policing the property.

The *"package deal"*: this is a tenant's furnishings that is sold for one price to the new renter. This type deal is very common, almost completely substituting furnishings "included in the rent", and purchasing the "package deal" allows you to take over the lease on a choice apartment or house.

If you purchase a package, always make sure the lease is in order with the landlord or lady, and speak to him or her directly - you might find yourself sub-letting without realizing what's happening - maybe a desirable situation given your personal circumstances, but under most leases - which in this case you didn't even sign - sub-letting is not permitted. The majority of tenants selling are looking to recover their original investment (many times they bought the "package deal" from the previous renter), so the price can sometimes be a bit on the high side - but if you take into account the rental price, the extras that come with the property, the hassle to furbish a home, etc., many times the price is well worth it, and you can pass the "package deal" on to the next person, when and if you move. Many of these packages include linen, dishes, kitchen ware, TV's and appliances, and a **telephone** (the telephone having been installed by the tenant, not the owner) - you literally move in. Old hands here in Guadalajara sometimes will take over a "package deal" without even seeing it just to get the right to rent a certain apartment or house, even if they already own furniture. They sell it off holding a garage sale or by advertising, maybe keeping a few things they like, and swallow a small loss for the privilege getting a better rental.

Never pay for a "package deal" (a small deposit is acceptable to formalize the transaction) until you are given physical possession of the property - many a "lightning" garage sale has been held, and, lo and behold, no furnishings when you open the door for the first time.

La Casa de Joan

More Information About Mexican Visas

The FM-3

The FM-3 holder is referred to as a *"no inmigrante visitante"*. This visa allows a tourist to stay in Mexico for a period of five years, entering and exiting the country as desired, with no time restrictions, and with or without a vehicle. With much perseverance and patience, application for an FM-3 visa may be made without assistance from an immigration specialist. The FM-3 visa is relatively easy to obtain if all paperwork is in order. We have found that most immigration specialists are better informed about procedures than attorneys, and are less expensive.

The *"no inmigrante visitante"* is given a book in which each border crossing is recorded. It is necessary to prove an income of a certain minimum level. There is an application fee and an annual renewal fee, at which time proof of income is again required. Husband and wife may apply together, or if both have sufficient independent income, they may apply separately.

Income requirements, application fees and renewal fees are changed frequently by the Mexican government. Should this document be lost and the bearer wants to leave the country, an exit visa will be issued, and the lost book replaced, both for a fee. The FM-3 status is renewable at the end of the five-year period. An FM-3 *"no inmigrante visitante"* visa may be obtained in Guadalajara at the office of the "Delegación de Servicios Migratorios", located ont he third floor of the *Palacio Federal* (Federal Palace), Av. Alcalde #520, between Hospital and Juan Alvarez streets (telephones 614-9749 and 614-5874)..

The following documents are required to obtain an FM-3 visa:

- Letter of request. This will be prepared free of charge at the Delegación de Servicios Migratorios office.
- A letter in Spanish signed by two persons stating that they know the applicants and verifying their present domicile. The format for this letter may also be obtained at the same office.
- Original and one copy of the FM-T tourist visa. Copy of passport notarized by a Mexican Notary Public. In Mexico, the government bestows notorial powers upon certain attorneys.
- Proof of income. If the applicant receives a government pension check, a letter stating so may be obtained from the U.S. or Canadian Consulate. Also proof must be given that the last three monthly checks were deposited in a Mexican bank account. Should income be received from Mexican bank deposits, a letter from the bank will be required, along with a copy of

the certificate of deposit or other investment instrument. Three monthly deposit tickets and two monthly statements indicating U.S. dollars changed into pesos in a Mexican financial institution is ordinarily sufficient.

Certificate of marriage, translated and certified, if application is made by husband and wife.

The translation and certification process is always demanded in the case of any document that originates in a foreign country. The translation is done by an "official" translator, whose work is recognized by the Mexican Judicial System, or other official agency.

United States citizens should be married in the United States in order to simplify certification and document processing by Mexican immigration officials.

The Mexican Embassy in Washington, D.C. or Ottawa, Canada can provide a list of locations of Mexican Consulates General and fees charged (subject to change). The address is Mexican Embassy Consular Section, 1019 19th Street NW, Suite 7020, Washington, D.C. 20036, Telephone (203) 393-1711. The U.S. Consulate General in Guadalajara also has a list of Mexican Consulates.

After approval of the application, several black and white photographs will be required. At this time, any fees must be paid and the applicant will be fingerprinted before the book is issued.

FM-3 and FM-2 holders may fly out of Mexico, leaving their vehicle without any time period restrictions. When leaving Mexico, and upon returning, the FM-3 or FM-2 book and a copy of the vehicle title will be needed.

The FM-2

The FM-2 "*inmigrante rentista*" visa allows the retired person to become a "semi-citizen" or "permanent resident" of Mexico in a period of five years. After completion of the five-year process, the retiree becomes an "*inmigrado*". Presently, few FM-2 visas are being issued, and *inmigrado* status is just as difficult to obtain, even after going through the five-year process.

This visa allows the retiree to leave Mexico during the five-year period with or without a vehicle. At the end of the five-year period, the vehicle must be removed from the country. As in the case of the FM-3 visa, the "*inmigrante rentista*" is given a book similar to a passport in which each border crossing in or out of Mexico is recorded.

After application approval, the holder of this visa must renew this status annually by resubmitting proof of income and paying required fees. Income requirements for the FM-2 are higher than for the FM-3, as are the renewal fees.

FM-2 status may be applied for at the Delegación de Servicios Migratorios in Guadalajara referred to above, or through the Mexican Consul General nearest one's home in the United States or Canada. Applications for FM-2 visas are forwarded to Mexico City for processing and approval.

For the FM-2 visa, the same documents as for the FM-3 are required, and additionally:

- An official birth certificate with official seal of county or state issuing agent, translated and certified.

Upon approval of the application, fingerprints are taken before the FM-2 book is issued, and twelve black and white 4cm x 4cm photographs are required (six front photographs and six profiles of the right side of the face, showing forehead and ears, without glasses, earrings, or hair covering the face or ears). Photographs may not be machine-taken.

With FM-3 and FM-2 status, the bearer has the right to leave and re-enter Mexico as many times as he wishes or remain in Mexico without leaving the country. There are some restrictions on the amount of time one may be out of Mexico and total time out of Mexico restriction.

In addition, the following benefits are enjoyed:

- Exemption, one-time only, from the General Import Tax on the following items that may be brought with the FM-2 holder or shipped into the country within the first year of residence in Mexico:

✓ All household items for an average home.

✓ An automobile, which cannot be sold in Mexico. (But may be sold outside the country, bringing another car back as often as the bearer wishes.)

✓ Clothing, jewelry and other items for the personal use of the *inmigrante rentista* and his dependents.

✓ Up to 50 books, a still and movie camera (most books are duty-free so more may be brought in during trips outside the country).

✓ Sports equipment.

✓ Used toys belonging to dependent children.

✓ The trunks, luggage and other containers that are used to bring the effects in.

✓ Exemption from the payment of Mexican Income Tax on the pension, investment income or other funds received from abroad.

✓ Exemption from Inheritance Taxes when a property owned by the inmigrante rentista is located in the Distrito Federal (Federal District, or more commonly known as Mexico City), and certain other states of the Mexican Republic. The nearest Mexican Consular office has more information about where this exemption is valid.

The *inmigrante rentista* may not work in Mexico nor engage in any renumerative activity without a special permit, which is difficult to obtain..

The above rules may be changed at any time. After the fifth year with FM-2 status, the next step is the "*declaratoria de inmigrado*" (declaration of immigration). Additional documents needed are a police letter from the nearest Mexican police Department, and two personal letters of recommendation from

Mexican nationals; all the original FM-2 requirements are re- presented to obtain this status.

An *inmigrado* is not permitted to retain a vehicle, and said vehicle must be removed from the country when the "declaratoria de inmigrado" is approved. If the vehicle is in poor condition, and not worth the expense, or risk, to take it to the border, it can be donated to the Mexican Government.

The principal advantage of obtaining *inmigrado* status is the opportunity to work in Mexico, with few restrictions. The income required is based on three variables: the Mexican minimum wage, the peso/dollar exchange rate and a day factor. The formula is:

<u>Mexican Minimum Wage x Day Factor</u>
Peso/Dollar Exchange Rate

Any of these factors may be changed by the Mexican government at any time.

Since income requirements, application, renewal and other fees are changed by the Mexican government rather frequently, it's difficult to say what tomorrow will bring. To give the reader an idea of costs, the following are the current fees charged, expressed in dollars: For a FM-3 visa, the monthly income requirement is $800 for each applicant and $400 for each dependent. The application fee is $73, and the annual renewal fee is also $73. The same costs apply for dependents. To replace a lost FM-3 book costs $28.

For the FM-2 visa, the monthly income requirement is $1,200 for each applicant and $600 for each dependent. The application fee is $157 and $157 for each annual renewal. Payment at the end of the five-year period to obtain *inmigrado* status is $180. The same costs apply for dependents. Replacement books for FM-2 *inmigrante rentista* holders cost $48. Replacement of an *inmigrado* book costs $32 U.S.

The head-of-household monthly income requirements may be reduced by fifty percent for both FM-3 and FM-2 visas if the applicant owns his home in Mexico. One must make an application with immigration officials for this reduction in income requirements and present a notarized copy of the deed to the property, and the most recent property tax receipt. The income requirement for dependents is not reduced.

Should you be out of Mexico when your FM-3 or FM-2 expires you have 30 days for renewal upon your return to Mexico. Enter the country as a tourist and report to Servicio Migratorio.

A permit to leave Mexico when your visa documents are at the immigration office for renewal now costs $15.25. You may not be out of Mexico for more than 60 days.

Upon receiving your FM-3 or FM-2 documents, you should save all receipts and papers relating to converting dollars to pesos each month. When renewing your FM-3 and FM-2 papers each year you will need to prove that you converted dollars to pesos equal to the monthly income requirements for each type visa. Usually three months proof is satisfactory.

According to Article 75, Section 1d of the Mexican Customs Law, it is not necessary to go to the "Hacienda" (Tax office) to make the payment each year when your visa is being renewed. Any bank may accept payment

A word to the wise: Always make copies of all original documents before handing them over for any sort of procedure. After going to all the trouble of notarizing, translating and certifying, these documents are very difficult to replace. Government employees are only human, as we all are; also theft, water damage or fire could destroy months and months of hard work. One step further than a simple copy is to obtain copies notarized by a Mexican Notary Public; this type of copy is, of course, more expensive, but is as good as the original in almost any situation. To take this drastic step could save many a headache and is well worth the price.

No Mexican government agency will accept copies (unless they are notarized copies as we have just mentioned). An original must always be presented - sometimes you can turn in an original and a copy, and the government agency will do a "*cotejo*" (check the original against the copy), return the originals to you and keep the copies - sometimes they keep the originals - it depends on the agency.

Does all this strike you as a bit mind-boggling? Don't think that foreigners are singled out for this "paper-chase". Many Mexican nationals also complain bitterly about the amount of documents and procedures demanded, saying that Mexico is "drowning in its own paperwork". Everybody grumbles, but do what is asked anyway. "When in Rome, do as the Romans do".

You may apply for FM-3 and FM-2 visas without using an immigration specialist, however, should you not be bilingual and familiar with the customs of the Mexican bureaucracy, this could be very frustrating and time consuming. A good immigration specialist could make things easier for you. Should you seek assistance caution is urged since some are notoriously slow and fail to return phone calls once they are paid in advance for their services. Check around carefully before you decide!

You should always carry in your car a notarized copy of (1) your car title, (2) notarized copy of your FM-3 or FM-2 visa and (3) a copy of the original permit to enter Mexico. Should both husband and wife plan to drive the car, then both husband and wife should have their names on the title of the car, even though the car is authorized on only one visa.

Once again, and being purposely repetitive, we strongly recommend that one not become engrossed in obtaining a more permanent type visa upon first arriving in Mexico. More important is to first enjoy the many pleasures and benefits of living in Mexico and to find out if you like living here. The wheels of government turn slowly and there may be many frustrations to be encountered. Why confront these immediately upon arrival? Talk to persons who have lived in Mexico for a few years and find out which type of visa they have. Find out the advantages and disadvantages of each type of visa, then determine which is best for your economic situation and lifestyle.

So You Want to Start a Business in Mexico!

by James Daniel Bowers

Having worked as an entrepreneur in a large and economically diversified midwestern city for many years and having several Mexican friends who promoted the virtues of business opportunity in Mexico, I finally decided to make the move to a large city in Central Mexico in 1989. Several months passed during which time was spent studying the Mexican economy and various business possibilities and opportunities. Finally the decision was made to start a light manufacturing operation involving importation of parts from the United States and exportation of the final product back to the United States. Most sales of the final product are now made in Mexico.

Since capital investment and start-up costs were not large, operations were expanded slowly and the business has been profitable since shortly after start-up. It was soon discovered that Mexicans like doing business with Americans. They seem to like the efficient, reliable and straight-forward way we conduct business. The business has been fortunate to establish a good base of customers and suppliers. Since the business was strongly capitalized we have been able to "ride out" some tough periods when collections were slow, however, we have lost very little on bad accounts receivable. Most business is essentially on a cash basis, with credit extended to established customers, people with which we have good rapport and mutual respect.

We must admit that starting a new business in Mexico is no easy task. Although on surface many things appear the same as in the United States, one soon realizes that cultural differences manifest themselves in many ways. It is important that to be successful in business in Mexico you must adapt to their customs. You are not going to change their ways, try as you will, so forget it! You will not understand Mexican logic, so **don't even bother to ask why!** An American who has been here for twenty-five years says that he will never understand the way Mexicans conduct business.

You will discover merits in some of the ways they do things. As with most other facets of life, what really counts are not the problems and difficult situations that arise, but how you adjust to them.

Following are some basic situations that you must adapt to:

Communications Although telephone service (Telmex) has been privatized, service has not improved appreciably. During the rainy season from June to September we have been without telephone service for up to six weeks at a time. During peak daily usage times from 10:30 a.m. to 2:00 p.m., it is often

255

impossible to reach a customer or supplier outside of your telephone exchange area. To obtain a new line may require several months time and cost up to one thousand dollars for a commercial line. Public telephones seldom work. No wonder cellular phones have sold so well in Mexico (though you're back to first base trying to hook into the traditional phone lines). To obtain repairs more promptly it is often best to locate a repair man in your area and ask him to take care of the problem. A gift of some pesos is in order for his special services.

Mail Service: Mail from the United States may take from ten days to three weeks and even longer from Mexico to the United States. Federal Express and United Parcel Service are available and, as everywhere, very expensive. Local mail may take a week. Checks are never mailed because of the uncertainty of the mail delivery service. Checks are collected by sending a messenger to the creditors place of business at an appointed day and hour, for example, Fridays from 5 p.m. to 6 p.m. Your messenger may have several places to go during this one hour period. Often checks are not available when requested.

The Land of Mañana: In Mexico the word *mañana*, in spite of what your dictionary may say, does not necessarily mean tomorrow, but means "not today" or simply sometime in the future. It is often a problem when trades people such as plumbers, electricians, computer technicians, copy machine or FAX repairmen do not show up for appointments at the agreed upon time or day. This can prove costly in time wasted by your employees as well as yourself. It takes time to develop a network of tradesmen and repair people than you can depend on.

The Decision Maker: Most Mexican businesses are family owned and operated and there may be little or no middle management personnel who are authorized to make decisions. Often the middle manager is the son or relative of the owner who may have several business interests and may be away from the office most of the time. You or your personnel may spend hours trying to develop a transaction only to find that you have not reached the "decision maker".

Prime Time: When dealing with the "decision maker" in a business you will find his hours may be very irregular. He may arrive for work by 10:30 or 11:00 a.m. and be in his office until 1:30 or 2:00 p.m. Occasionally he will return in the afternoon after a long business lunch (or a good afternoon siesta, recovering from that dinner party with clients the night before, where liquor flowed freely to "loosen up" business relations), and be in his office again from 6:30 to 7:30 p.m. He is difficult to reach by telephone since he spends a lot of time on the telephone himself (trying to collect accounts receivable, like every other businessman in Mexico), and also due to the fact that the office telephone lines are saturated during the "prime time" period (and nobody wants to invest $1,000 on another telephone line for rental office space, which cannot be moved to another location for any price). If you do manage to reach the "decision maker's" secretary and leave word for him to call chances are that he will not return your call (ever, unless you owe him money). You will learn not to wait in your office for someone to return your call. It will rarely happen!

Should you be fortunate enough to set up an appointment you may drive through busy, time-consuming traffic, walk several blocks from your parking space, only to find that the "decision maker" failed to keep your appointment. The secretary will apologize, graciously offer you coffee, and ask you to wait for just ten minutes. The person may or may not show up an hour later. As a matter of policy the writer will wait no longer than fifteen minutes. How does business get done? One often shakes his head in wonderment! (Those luncheons and dinner parties are more important than one would think!!!) In spite of these situations, you will find Mexicans wonderful people to work with once they know you, and will often go out of their way to help you. They are very intelligent and creative (just think: how on Earth do you run a profitable business if you're never there?) Usually "cold" direct sales calls are easier and more effective than going through the routine of making appointments. You must learn which is best for your business through "trial and error."

Parking and traffic: As in most large cities, parking and traffic is often a problem and much has been done in recent years to correct this. Adjusting to problems of parking near the main downtown Post Office bothered me tremendously. In the United States the Post Office is a center for commercial activity. In Mexico all day parking was allowed in front of the Main Post Office. One day I saw workmen removing the meters - an improvement, I thought! When I returned two days later signs had been erected reserving the spaces for politicians only and a new job was created by assigning a policeman to keep the "poachers" out. Many businesses use available parking for their employees rather than for customers.

Legal Services and Politicians: As in the United States, legal services are expensive and often unreliable. To initiate a Mexican corporation is a simple matter and should not be expensive for the legal work involved. There are minimum capital investment and social contribtion requirements that must be met. Finding the right attorney is no easy feat either, but an absolute necessity - who else knows how to get things done faster than a snail's pace. That is not a job for any foreigner who doesn't know the ropes. Where? when? how much? and to whom? are questions best left to the "experts". Accept these facts as a part of Mexican life and let somebody else handle the details.

Labor Laws and Unions: Even though wages are lower in Mexico, labor laws are slanted more favorably toward the worker than in the United States. Your workers must be members of a union. It will be necessary to negotiate with the union and pay the agreed upon amount. It is very expensive to fire a long-term worker with termination costs often amounting to six months' salary or more. You will need professional advice. All workers are covered by government

257

health insurance. You can anticipate problems with workers not being on time or needing time off for family problems or situations. You will find Mexicans are good workers once trained to your production methods and your expectations.

Taxes, Accountants and Government: Don't come to Mexico thinking that you will escape taxes and government interference. You will need the Mexican equivalent of a Certified Public Accountant to handle your monthly government reports. This is not inexpensive, but because of cultural differences and language problems well worth the cost. No self-respecting Mexican businessman would be caught dead without his accountant - because business would be literally dead without him. You will need a good accountant. Who stands in lines for licenses, permits, tax forms and payments? Who does all the time- consuming work? The accountant, of course. Accounting and government regulations are even more involved than in the United States.

Mexican Business Advisors: It is well to develop a network of Mexcian business advisors who can give you advice on how to handle various business problems that will arise. You will find this invaluable. Often they can guide you or help you determine potential clients and know the reputation of persons with whom you may wish to establish a business relationship.

Inflation: During the middle 1980's inflation was very serious, amounting to 150% or more annually. The current rate is less than 10% annually. Mexican businessmen have been very astute in coping with good management in an inflating economy.

How is your Spanish?: In Mexico business is, of course, conducted in Spanish, however, you will find many people who are bilingual. Should you not be bilingual you will want to have a good grasp of the Spanish language before starting business operations in Mexico. The better your Spanish the easier it will be to start your business in Mexico.

Recently an American was quoted as saying "Mexicans drag a cultural anchor that will continue to hold back their economy." Perhaps, however, things **do get done** in Mexico! Under the leadership of now President Carlos Salinas de Gortari great progress has been made and the tide of his changes will not be reversed. The population of Mexico is young and it is refreshing to see young people wanting to learn and improve their way of life. It is an attitude sometimes missing in the United States. It is a great plus factor for wanting to do business in Mexico.

You will receive great satisfaction from establishing and operating a business in Mexico. The challenges encountered because of cultural differences will be interesting and stimulating, and as you have seen, we try to take a very light-hearted view of these differences, accept them, and play along like the rest of the country does. Yes, it is a **challenge** to operate a business in Mexico, but the rewards may be worth the extra effort. **Come on down!**

Helpful Cooking/Baking Tips

- When making meringue, add one tablespoon of lukewarm water to each egg white before beating to increase volume.
- A lettuce leaf laid on the surface of hot soup will absorb grease. Remove before serving.
- To soften butter, turn a heated bowl over it.
- Heat knife when slicing cheese for thinner slices.
- One tablespoon of fresh herbs or spices is equal to one teaspoon of dried herbs.
- Add herbs during the last twenty minutes of cooking to get maximum flavor.
- A cake that sticks to the pan can be loosened by placing the cake tin over a bowl of boiling water.

High Altitude Baking Temperatures

- At all altitudes over 3,500 feet, increase baking temperature 25°.
- At 3,500 feet, add 1 tablespoon more flour per recipe, then add 1 tablespoon more for each 1,500 feet increase in elevation.

Temperature Chart

Fahrenheit	Centigrade
212°F	100°C
250°	120°
300°	150°
325°	165°
350°	180°
375°	190°
400°	205°
425°	220°
450°	230°
465°	245°
500°	260°

Equivalents

Metric	U.S.	Fluid Measure
100 grams	3 1/2 oz.	1/2 cup
250 grams	9 oz.	1 1/3 cups
400 grams	14 oz.	1 3/4 cups
600 grams	21 oz.	2 2/3 cups
700 grams	25 oz.	3 cups
900 grams	31 oz.	4 cups
1000 grams (kg)	36 oz.	4 1/2 cups

Equivalent amounts

3 teaspoons	1 tablespoon
2 tablespoons	1 fluid ounce
4 tablespoons	1/4 cup
16 tablespoons	1 cup
1 cup	250 ml
1 quart	1 liter, less 6 tablespoons
1 pound	450 grams
1 kilo	2.2 pounds
1 bar butter	1/2 cup
1 sq. baking chocolate	1 oz.
1 sq. baking chocolate	2 tablespoons
1 sq. baking chocolate	1/3 cup cocoa + 1 tablespoon fat

Some Thoughts on Costa Rica

by Nancy and Ray Christian

Being recognized more and more as a desirable tourist attraction and a possible place for retirees is Costa Rica ("Rich Coast"), a small country approximately the size of West Virginia, only seventy-five miles across at its narrowest point.

Costa Rica has a population of around 2,800,000 consisting primarily of descendants from the early Spanish settlers, with a small percentage of Indians. Natives of this tiny country are known as *Ticos*, and are friendly and helpful to foreigners.

Spanish is, of course, the country's first language, with a limited amount of English spoken, therefore one should know at least basic Spanish phrases to get around. The majority of the population is Catholic, however, other religions are respected and shown no signs of discrimination. North Americans who have lived in Costa Rica report that the country is democratic, stable and peaceful.

For the most part Costa Rica's biggest source of income depends on the large agricultural crops, such as the export of coffee, tobacco, sugar and others. The country seems to welcome foreign investments, and quite a few North Americans have resumed their private professional practice or have started new businesses employing local labor. Taxes are paid only on earned income in the country, which is a definite added incentive for many.

Visitors to Costa Rica will not be bored. There are miles of lovely beaches to explore, excellent fishing, white water rafting on the many rivers, and also hunting. There are 112 volcanoes, numerous parks and rain forests where one can admire orchids and ferns of every variety, watch the birds and butterflies galore, and for swimming there is the choice of both the Pacific Ocean and the Caribbean Sea.

San José, the capitol of Costa Rica, is located in Meseta Central Valley, and is the hub of business and cultural activity, such as the symphony, concerts, museums and library.

The weather in the Central Valley is excellent, and usually no heat or air conditioning is necessary, depending on the elevation. There is more humidity and rainfall than in the Central Mexican Highlands.

Several airlines come in and out of San José daily from all major cities in the United States. Most visitors stay in the city, where they can enjoy the various activities of the Plaza de la Cultura, and take advantage of daily tours in and around the area to other nearby points of interest.

North Americans have found living expenses to be lower in Costa Rica than in many states in the United States, although as everywhere else, they too are rising. There are very nice residential developments in and around San José, where houses and apartments can be found for a reasonable price.

As in most cities, San José also has the problem of pollution, therefore living outside the city is more desirable than in the city itself.

Other drawing points to Costa Rica include good, inexpensive medical care, low utility costs, potable drinking water in good supply (although it is wise to be alert to the possible problem of contamination due to a break in water lines, and as a precaution many residents use purified bottled water), and of course, there are year around inexpensive fresh fruits and vegetables. Imported products are very expensive, so most people content themselves, if possible, with local substitutes at much lower costs.

As delightful as Costa Rica sounds, we have also heard a few of the drawbacks which should be taken into consideration and we point these out.

First, certain areas are not considered to be very secure, especially areas favored by North Americans, and there are occasional cases of breaking and entering of homes, so that often it is necessary to have a house sitter, even for an evening's outing.

Some types of medication seem to be a problem to obtain, being either very limited or not available at all, including common over-the-counter items. This can be a big problem for many.

Driving is said to be as bad or worse as in the European countries (and Mexico!). Driving is more pleasant when going to out of the way areas where traffic is much lighter.

Some reports about Costa Rica complain about the lack of social activity and the inferior quality of cultural events. This, of course, is strictly a matter of taste and choice. For those wishing to play golf, it will be necessary to join a country club, which can be expensive. However, one will find plenty of private bridge games and a good Duplicate Bridge Club available as well as the usual interesting activities one would find in any city.

Up to date information on Tourist and Resident status is important when making plans for a trip to Costa Rica and the following regulations were in effect when this article was written.

Tourist visas are given for only a three-month period of time, after which it is necessary to leave to country for approximately 48 hours. (The immigration personnel are reportedly sometimes difficult and the lines are quite long, so patience is definitely required.)

For persons wanting Resident status, it is suggested that they obtain a lawyer's help in order to speed up what can be a lengthy procedure.

Those interested should know that the income requirement (from outside Costa Rica) is $600 a month. Another point to be considered deals with importing a car or household items. These are no longer duty free and can be expensive. On the plus side, and important to many, a person with Resident status is eligible for inexpensive health insurance, and the hospital and medical care is reported to be quite good.

Persons having Resident status and wanting to leave Costa Rica are required to have an exit visa, which costs sixty dollars and takes a week or more to get.

Costa Rica is like anywhere else, good and bad, and unless your individual "scale" tips greatly to one side, one simply accepts the good along with the bad as a part of life.

We have received several inquiries regarding Costa Rica, and although we happen to prefer Mexico as a place to retire, it sounds as though Costa Rica also has much to offer.

This article is merely a brief synopsis of pertinent information for those who have expressed an interest in Costa Rica.

(Editor's note: We greatly appreciate the contribution of up to date material offered by Nancy and Ray Christian. Although now living in Florida, they lived in Costa Rica for several years and keep well informed by friends still living there.)

Our advertising agency has chosen the following advertisers who represent some of the best businesses in the Guadalajara/Chapala area and Mexico. When you have the opportunity to visit these advertisers please let them know that you saw their advertisement in this publication.

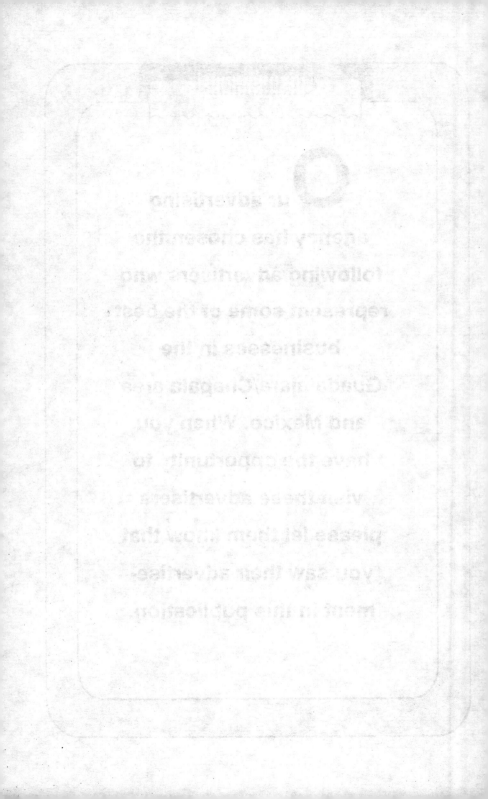

Our advertising
directory lists companies
following advertisers and
represent some of the best
businesses in the
Guadalajara/Chapala area
and Mexico. When you
have the opportunity to
visit these advertisers,
please let them know that
you saw their advertise-
ment in this publication.

MA COME NO
RISTORANTE • BAR • CAFETERIA

The flavors and aromas of Italian food are concentrated in a new restaurant on the Guadalajara scene called "MA COME NO". It is an invitation to enjoy new creations and specialty dishes for which a good appetite is a must. A look at the menu will suffice to bring out that appetite. It won't be easy to choose.

Besides the excellent food, this restaurant is beautifully decorated in the Italian style. The atmosphere is quiet and relaxed. As a suggestion, you might try the Grilled Vegetable Salad or the Toscana Salad. Can't go wrong with either one. Then, try some delicious Fiori di Zuccini with goat cheese (this is squash blossom filled with cheese).

A special plate is the Pizza de Salmon; another, Fetuccini with tomato and salmon. A main dish like Filete Grisanti merits a bottle of good wine. Pastas and other main dishes accompany the salads prepared by the customers themselves from fresh ingredients at the Salad Bar.

And, as a pleasant finish to your meal, we recommend, with your favorite cup of coffee, a "Napoleón", a dessert with its delicate layers of puff pastry and seasonal fruits in their own juice and topped with whipped cream. Or try some Ravioli with Chocolate for a new experience. This restaurant prides itself also on the hot, just-out-of-the-oven bread it serves from its wood burning oven. All the pastas are prepared fresh too, just like in Italy.

We can recommend you dine at "MA COME NO". Afterwards, we think you'll be recommending it to others.

Avenida de las Américas #302   Tel. 615-4952
Hours: daily from 2 p.m. to midnight
Valet Parking

WELCOME TO SIERRA VISTA REALTY

**Chapala,
Jalisco,
Mexico**

We are Arturo Chacon and Ricardo Marin and our combinated real estate experience encompasses many years in the Lake Chapala area. We have recently opened SIERRA VISTA REALTY and would like to let you know what you can expect from us.

SIERRA VISTA REALTY offers you prompt and efficent service in person, via telephone, fax, and e-mail whether your interest is in short or long term rentals, the purchase of a home or lot or investment property. The lakeside area, known for an excellent, pollution free, year round climate, and a short distance from Guadalajara, Mexico's second largest city, is growing and we also have some excellent sites available to investors.

We can offer you the best service at Lakeside because we are new, and frankly we want your business. We don't have a huge, fancy office; that is not our priority. We are commited to providing the best service regardless of the day of the week or hour of the day.

If you're planning a vacation, relocation of a fact-finding trip to the Lake Chapala area, we will meet your flight, make reservations for you in a local hotel, and, at your convenience, provide a tour of the area and available housing with absolutely no *pressure* and *no obligation* to you!

From the U.S./Canada: Telephone and Fax: 011-52376 -5-3072 Celular: 011-52-3-106-5911
From within Mexico: Telephone and Fax: 01-376-53072 Celular: 01-3-106-5911
Telephone after regular business hours, weekends and holidays: (011-52) 376-61624
Electronic mail: Chacon@laguna.com.mx
Mailing Address: APDO #64, 45900 Chapala, Jalisco, Mexico.
Office Hours: 9-5 Monday-Friday; 9-1 Saturday; Sundays and Holidays by Appointment.
Office Address: Ave. Hidalgo # 241 A Chapala, Jalisco, Mexico.

M.R.T.A. Newsletter

Readers of "Mexico Living and Travel" as well as others considering travelling or possibly retiring in Mexico should be aware of MRTA's quarterly publication "Mexico Living and Travel Newsletter".

This popular newsletter is for the purpose of providing current information about topics that are of interest to everyone such as: current costs, real estate, rentals, economics, popular retirement choices, places of interest to visit and many other articles.

Articles are written by contemporary retirees who are actively involved in daily living and travel in Mexico.

To suscribe:

Personal checks are accepted for the above product, drawn on U.S. banks, or Canadian Postal Money Orders in U.S. Dollars. Please allow four weeks for delivery.

Canadian orders - additional postage and handling is required! For magazine subscription for one year, please add $3.00 U.S. or for single copy of magazine add only $1.00 U.S. Write to M.R.T.A. for charges to other foreign countries.

Send order and check payable to:
M.R.T.A.
6301 SQUAW VALLEY RD. #23
PAHRUMP, NV 89048-7949

Please Allow about four weeks for delivery.
Satisfaction Guaranteed or your money refunded!

MEXICO - AN EXTRAORDINARY HERITAGE
CONTINENTAL REALTY
AN EXTRAORDINARY REAL ESTATE COMPANY

Continental
Realty, S.A.

CARR. CHAPALA-JOCOTEPEC km 4
SAN ANTONIO TLAYACAPAN, JAL
TEL. (376) 6-1994, 6-2415, 6-0406

RE/MAX®
FENIX

Each Office Independently Owned and Operated
Buen Clima Bienes Raices, SRL.

Talk to a Re/Max Fenix Professional
You will <u>notice</u> the difference

- Home Sales
- Retirement Leases
- Area Information
- Lots
- Developments
- Condo Resales
- Gated Communities
- Rental Management
- Local, National & International Multiple Listings Services.

Carr. Chapala-Ajijic #159A, San Antonio Tlayacapan, Jalisco.

Tel: (376) 6-1776   **Fax: (376) 6-1779**

e-mail: remax@laguna.com.mx

G I L

GRUPO INMOBILIARIO DEL LAGO, A. C.

WE ARE MEMBERS OF LOCAL AND NATIONAL
REAL ESTATE BOARDS AND
PROUD PROMOTERS OF THE

LA FLORESTA VILLAGE

MEMBER
Pi
A.M.P.I

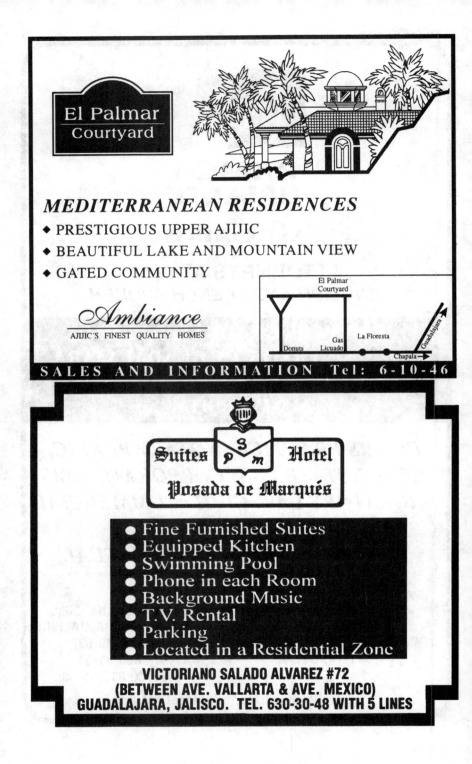

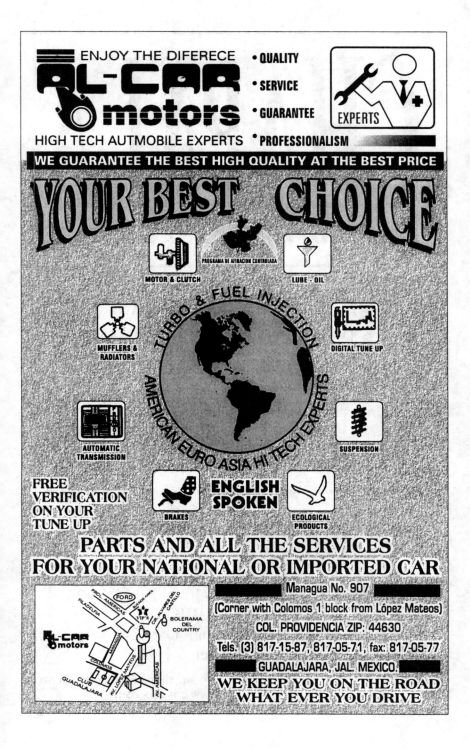

PRESIDENTE
INTER·CONTINENTAL
GUADALAJARA

Acomodations for your participants are equally imresive. There are 414 lavishly appointed guest rooms including two Presidential Suites and 24 Club Suites, 104 Inter-Continental Club Rooms, 18 Garden Suites and 272 luxury rooms. Our air-conditioned rooms feature color TV with Spectravision, purified water, direct-dial long distance service, fax, computer and voice mail connections. The hotel also provides a fully-equipped business center.

Housed in its own 128 room tower, our Club Inter-Continental, provides you with the ultimate in comfort, service and privacy. Here Club members enjoy a dedicated, controlled-access entrance with express check-in and check out, private Concierge services, complimentary continental breakfast and evening cocktails with hors d'oevures and canapés.

Every effort has been made to create an atmosphere that enhances your personal comfort. Our fully-equipped fitness facilities include a sauna, steam room, hydromasage and outdoor pool. Golf and tennis are available close to the hotel. We also offer full body masage and beauty salon, and our multilingual Concierge staff will assist with your transport needs, currency exchange and will direct you to local points of interest.

Presidente Inter-Continental Guadalajara offers an impressive choice of Mexican and international cousine. *La Moreña* offers a daily Mexican breakfast buffet, delectable Mexican specialties and snacks for lunch. At night, we also present live Mariachi music entertainment and a variety of tequilas. *Arco Iris*, open all day, serves international cuisine in a relaxed atmosphere. The *Lobby Bar*

is an ideal rendez-vous for social and business meetings.

Our biggest meeting space, the Astral, is a multifuncional ballroom, ideal for trade shows, exhibits, corporate events and banquets up to 1000 people. In addition we offer 14 ballrooms with capacities ranging from 25 to 850 people. In total, our conference and convention facilities seat 2000 people theater style or 1300 people banquet style.

Av. López Mateos Sur y Moctezuma, Cd. del Sol, CP 45050 Guadalajara, Jal. México.
Tel. 01(3) 678 1234 Fax (3) 678 1222 Lada toll free 01 500 36 330

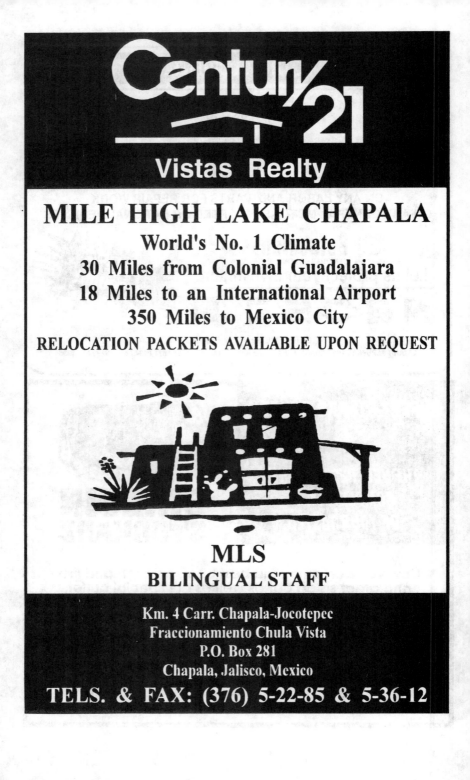

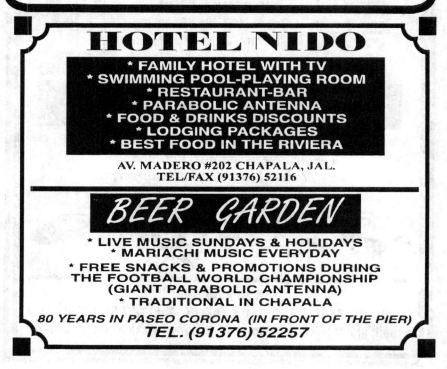

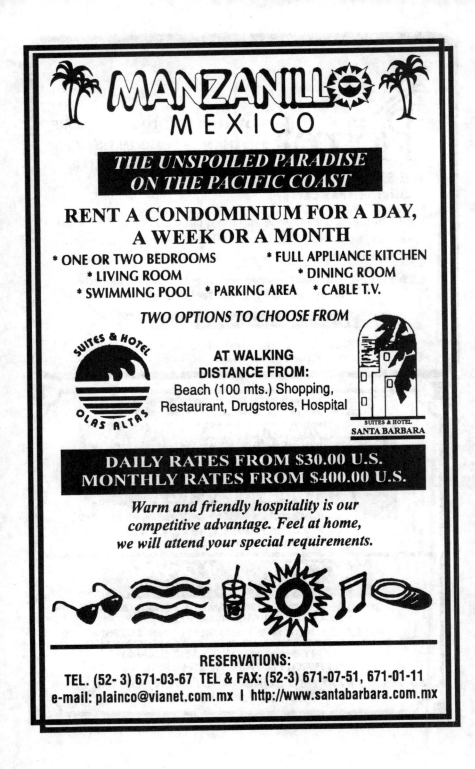

FOR ALL YOUR WATER NEEDS!

TOTAL HOUSE WATER PURIFICATION SYSTEM
- Up to 4 bathrooms 8 Gal/min.
- Sediment filter removes dirt & sediment.
- Ultraviolet sterilizer destroys bacteria, algae & dangerous viruses.
- Carbon filter removes chlorine, organic pollutants, odor & taste.
  - ☆**Price $ 399 U.S.**

WATER SOFTENER
- Removes dissolved mineral from water in your whole house.
- Makes your skin & hair feel silky smooth.
- Allows soap & detergents to get you, your clothes & your house really clean!
- Protects all of your plumbing, fixtures & washers from destructive mineral deposits.
  - ☆**From $599 U.S.**

PRESSURE SYSTEMS
- Enjoy your shower better with the highest quality in pumps & tanks.
- 2 1/2 bath house
- 3/4 H.P. centrifugal pump 20 gal. tank
  - ☆**$379 U.S.**
    - ☆ *Prices do not include IVA or installation*

WE ACCEPT CREDIT CARDS.

GUADALAJARA	*PUERTO VALLARTA*	*LAKESIDE*
PLAZA UNIVERSIDAD	PLAZA NEPTUNO	CHAPALA
Tel.-Fax. (3)642-4042, 642-4050	TEL.-FAX. (322) 12344, 12346	TEL.-FAX. (376) 5-2038
		TOLL FREE 01-800-34-376-00

YOUR NOTES

YOUR NOTES